Social Reform Movement and Women Empowerment in Dawoodi Bohras

Social Reform Movement and Women Empowerment in Dawoodi Bohras

Zenab Banu

First Published, 2020

Published by

Kalpaz Publications
C-30, Satyawati Nagar,
Delhi – 110052
Ph.: 011-47034999, 9811692060
www.kalpazpublications.com
E-mail: kalpaz@hotmail.com

Printed at: G. Print Process, Delhi

Cataloging in Publication Data—DK
Courtesy: D.K. Agencies (P) Ltd. <docinfo@dkagencies.com>

Zenab Banu, author.
Social reform movement and women empowerment in Dawoodi Bohra / Prof. Zenab Banu.
pages cm
Includes bibliographical references.
ISBN 9789353240837

1. Daudis—India—Udaipur (Rajasthan)—Politics and government. 2. Muslim women—Political activity—India—Udaipur (Rajasthan) 3. Social movements—India—Udaipur (Rajasthan) 4. Women in development—India—Udaipur (Rajasthan) I. Title.

LCC HQ1742.Z46 2019 | DDC 305.4869710544 23

Contents

Dedication

I dedicate this work to all the brave women and men of the Bohra community who initiated, nourished and continue to sustain the Reform Movement till today.

Preface

I am involved in the reform movement in the Bohra community. The Bohra reformists are fighting against highly authoritarian religious establishment headed by the High Priest. The Bohra Community is a strong petty business community and is highly submissive to any authority whether political or religious. The Syedna has exploited this fact in order to impose his rule over them. This authoritarian structure within the community militates against the democratic, political culture of the society as a whole. This is the dilemma. The educated liberal elements within the community want to democratise this structure but the Bohra priesthood has been strongly resisting this. Not only do they refuse to accept change, they are also trying to be even more rigid and unresponsive to change.

In early seventies the reform movement took a new turn in Udaipur (Rajasthan) thanks to the glorious role played by women of that city. The women of Udaipur showed extraoridinary courage in standing upto the onslaught of the priesthood. The High Priest's henchmen assaulted these women, pulled them by hair, tore off their clothes and molested them. Many of them had to take refuge in nearby jungles in Galiakot, seventy five miles from Udaipur. All this happened because these courageous women participated in the reform movement and refused to apologise and put pressure on their menfolk to do so. Not only did the women stand firmly but also urged upon their husbands, sons and brothers to carry on the fight. Since then the fight is ongoing with many ups and downs.

Scholars try to study movements when they occur. But more often than not, they are taken by surprise when another movement takes place. We have yet to make efforts in analyzing the socio-economic and political situation at the point in time when a movement is likely to take place in a particular society. Very few efforts have been made to study ongoing movements. The study of the ongoing movements provides greater insights not only into the course of the movements but also the perception of the participants.

The proposed study is an humble effort in this direction as reform movement in Dawoodi Bohra is ongoing for so many years. The achievements of the movements are like half full glass of milk. They have long way to go so that they can achieve the long term objectives. Why does a woman rebel? This question of course is central to this study.

The study covers a wide range of women activities from representation and decision making to movements' events and meetings on issues of vital situational and systematic import.

I feel indebted to Indian Council of Social science Research (ICSSR), New Delhi for awarding me Senior Fellowship and providing financial support for the study. I express my gratitude to the officials of Mohanlal Shukhadia University and friends particularly Abdul Taiyab Kherawala who embarked me to work upon this project.

I owe much to my husband Mansoor Ali RV and all other family members who have always stood by me through thick and thin. I also gratefully eacknowledge all the sources from which the study has been enriched.

Zenab Banu

Glossary

Aamil	:	An administrator, nominee of Syedna, appointed at every urban centre(where there are large Bohra population) to administer the local affairs.
Da'i/Da'i al Mutlaq	:	The leader who has been appointed by declaration of *nass* in the absence of the *Imam*, who is in seclusion; also known as Syedna
DaimUl Islam	:	A book by al-Qadi al-Nu'man, which highlights religious practices to be followed by Bohra man and women
Dargah	:	A shrine built over the grave of a revered religious figure, often a Sufi Saint.
Farz /Farizat/Farziyat	:	Mandatory
Fatwa	:	A religious order issued by the head priest
Fitra	:	Certain amount to be given to the poor and needy on Id-ul-fitr. It is mandatory
Hadiath	:	The narration of an event from the ... Collection and reported sayings, advice, and act of Prophet Muhammad.
Haqqun-nafs	:	Is levied on the relatives of the deceased
Haraam	:	An Arabic term meanings "forbidden". In Islamic jurisprudence, *haraam* is used to refer any act that is forbidden by Allah.
Hudud	:	The divine hierarchy
Iddah or Iddat	:	A customary practice imposed on women who is either widowed or divorce. For widows are expected to remain in total seclusion and dressed in white clothes for four months and ten days.
Jamaat	:	Local administrative body

Janaab : Term of respect used to address the religious priest

Khafd(pronounced at *khafz*) : The practice of circumcision of the girl child

Khafz / khatna : Women circumcision

Khums : One fifth

Kalmasum : Infallible

Kothar : Central administrative body which controls the whole community on the name of Syedna

Majalis : Literally sitting; in its technical sense, it is a meeting, a session or gathering

Maghfi : Secret

Marifah : My stical intellectual knowledge of spiritua-lity

Markaz : A smaller mosque /community hall

Misaq : Oath of unquestioning allegiance and service given by all Dawoodi Bohras to the *Da'i* at the age of puberty and renewed upon the appointment of a new *Da'i*.

Moharram : The first calendar month of the lunar calendar year which is followed by the Muslims

Mu'min : True believer who follows all the religious tenets of the community as per Islam

Na'am : Yes

Nabi : Prophet

Namaaz : Prayers that are offered by Muslims five times a day

Nass : Doctrine of declaration of successor without any ambiguity

NazarMuqam : Vow money

Nikah : The marriage ceremony in the form of contract between the husband and the wife

Purdah : The custom in some Muslim and Hindu communities of keeping women in seclusion, with clothing that conceals them completely when they go out

Quran	:	The holy book of Muslims
Ramzaan	:	Ninth month of lunar calendar when people fast the entire month
Rasikhun-filal-ilm	:	Firmly rooted in knowledge
Rasulullah	:	The name of respect given to the Prophet Mohammed
Rida	:	A kind of dress worn by women to cover themselves from other men; akin to a *burkha*
Raza	:	Permission
Sabaq	:	Lecture or discussion undertaken by the head priest or his wife
Sahifo	:	Bohra religious book prescribing the norms to be followed and prayers that are to be recited along side
Salah	:	Prayer
Saum	:	Fasting
Sharia/ Shariah	:	Orally transmitted religious laws of Islam
Sheikh	:	An honorary title amongst Dawoodi Bohra community that was historically given to those who provided great service to the community. In recent history, the title has become commercialized, meaning the title can be bestowed upon those who give enough money.
Shirk	:	Associating partners with Allah
Sila	:	Compulsory levy – an offering for the hidden Imam
Sunnat	:	Recommended / Optional
Syedna/ maula/aqamaula	:	Honourific terms for the *Da'i*, commonly used by the Dawoodi Bohras to the head priest - Syedna
Taharat	:	Ritual purification; purity; one of the seven pillars of Ismai'ili faith. This is taken to refer to hygienic and cleanliness as well as spiritual purity.
Tankhai	:	Excommunicated person in Sikh community
Tawil	:	Hidden meaning of Qura'nic verses

Thaal	:	A big plate which is used among Bohra households for the communal meals
Triple talaq	:	Instant divorce
Urs	:	Death anniversary of a Sufi saint in South Asia, usually held at the saint's shrine or tomb (*dargah*)
Waaz	:	Religious sermon
Wali	:	Guardian of bride
Wasi	:	Successor of Prophet Mohammed (PBUH) Ali Ibne Abu Talib
Wuzu	:	A kind of cleaning ritual practiced just before performing prayers
Zaban	:	Language
Zakat	:	Qura'nic tax at the rate of two and a half percent
Ziyaarat	:	Visiting the shrine of deceased saint
Ziyafat	:	A banquet, a rich party in honour of Syedna

Abbreviations

Art.	:	Article
AWDBC	:	All World Dawoodi Bohra Conference
BJP	:	Bhartiya Janta Party
BMMA	:	Bhartiya Muslim Mahila Andolan
BYA	:	Bohra Youth Association
BYANA	:	Bohra Youth Association of North America
CBDBC	:	Central Board of Dawoodi Bohra Community
CM	:	Chief Minister
CSSS	:	Centre for Study of Society and Secularism
DBWRF	:	Dawoodi Bohra Women's Association for Religious Freedom
FGC	:	Female Genital Cut
FGM	:	Female Genital Mutilation
IAS	:	Indian Administration Service
IPC	:	Indian Penal Code
LGBT	:	Lesbian, Gay, Bisexual, Transgender
MWCD	:	Ministry of Women and Child Development
NCRB	:	National Crime Report Bureau
NDA	:	National Democratic Alliance
NGO	:	Non-Government Organization
NSM	:	New Social Movement
PBUH	:	Peace Be Upon Him
PIL	:	Public Interest Litigation
POCSO	:	Protection of Children from Sexual Offences
PUCL	:	People's Union for Civil Liberties
RUWA	:	Rajasthan University Women Teachers Association

UN	:	United Nations
UPA	:	United Progressive Alliance

Chapter - 1

Introduction: The Nature of Social Movements and Dawoodi Bohra Reform Movement

Social movements are closely connected with democratic political system over the past 200 years. They have become part of a popular and global expression of dissent. The term 'social movement' was introduced in 1848 by the German sociologist Lorenz von Stein in his book Socialist and Communist Movements Since the Third French Revolution in 1848.

Today, the term "social movement" is often mistakenly applied to all forms of collective action, even those without clear political goals (D'Arcus, 2006).[1] Social movements, interest groups, or parties are frequently equated. A movement's collective action is often conflated with actions undertaken by the organizations within it; these entities are sometimes identified with the movement itself. Discussions of social movements frequently assume internal unity, overlooking their dynamic internal relationships.

The beginnings of most social movements often go unnoticed (Mansbridge and Morris, 2001).[2] They emerge within preexisting networks or homogenous communities, whose members adopt its ideology and goals. An unanticipated crisis or the deliberate, planned intervention of individuals or small groups usually crystallizes these conditions into a movement and establishes its legitimacy among constituents, other political actors, and the general public.

A social movement generally takes one of three structural forms, Segmented, Polycentric and Reticulate.

Segmented movements are constantly changing coalitions of diverse groups. *Polycentric* movements incorporate two or more competing organizations into *ad hoc* alliances around common goals.

Reticulate movements create loosely integrated networks with multiple formal and informal connections (Zald and McCarthy, 1987).[3]

Many social movements focus on the pursuit of social justice, although their definitions of social justice have varied depending on the historical context in which they emerged and the demographic composition of their members. Social movements have influenced public policy by addressing its substance and goals, the structures through which it is developed, and the processes that determine and implement social priorities. Often, the "window of opportunity" for movements to shape policy is limited, although some movements have maintained long-term involvement in the policymaking process by building institutions which are compatible with existing political structures.

Different authors have attempted to provide a definition of what constitute social movements. Diani defines social movements as informed network of individuals and/or organizations, sharing a collective identity and the same side in political and/or cultural conflict.[4] Social movements have also been viewed as collectively aligned with some degree of organization and continuity outside institutional channels for the purpose of promoting and resisting change in the group, society or world order of which it is a part.[5]

However the definition of what constitutes a social movement has been contentious largely because of the diversity of collectivities that may be termed social movements.[6] In the same light, Charles Tilly states that for many years he had avoided the term 'social movement' because it sponged up so many different meanings and therefore obscured more than it clarified.[7]

Indeed in the early stages of the development of social movement theory, social movements were viewed negatively. Early studies of social movements in the 18th and 19th centuries perceived Social movements as "madding crowds" and associated them with extremism, deprivation and violence. Up until the 1960s, social movements were to a large extent perceived as dangerous mobs who acted irrationally, blindly following demagogues who sprang up in their midst.[8]

The 21st century was however the hallmarks of the interpretation of social movement. It is also a period when the perception of social movement was redefined from a negative perspective to a recognized institution of social change. As a result of this new view of the positive contribution of social movements "in the last fifty years alone, the American Civil Rights Movements, the peace, environmental and feminist movements, revolt against authoritarianism in both Europe and the third world and the rise of new Islamic movements have brought masses of people into the streets demanding change. They often succeeded but even when they failed their actions set in motion important political, cultural and international changes."[9]

In short, social movement is an effort by a group; its aim is to bring a change in the society; it may be organized or unorganized; it may be peaceful or violent and its life is not certain. It may continue for long period or it may die out soon. It is not mobs or crowd but is concerted organized action group that is much more integrated.[10]

Life Cycle of Social Movement

Although social movements around the world differ from each other in many ways but they generally go through a life cycle marked by the progressive stages of emergence, coalescence, bureaucratization and decline. Hence social movements are not eternal.

Emergence

Social movements start when people realize that there is a specific problem in their society which they want to address. This realization can come from the dissatisfaction people feel or information and knowledge they get about a specific issue. At the first stage, the social movement defines the problem it is going to address.

The first stage of the social movement is known as emergence. Within this stage, social movements are very preliminary, and there is little to no organization. Potential movement participants may be unhappy with some policy or some social condition, but they have not yet taken any action in order to redress their grievances, or if they have, it is most likely individual action rather than collective action. For example, a person may comment to family that he or she is dissatisfied with a particular issue.

An example of this stage would be the Civil Rights Movement in the early 1950s. There was, of course, a general and long standing sense of discontent among the African-American population in South. However, they were not yet organizing the mass and continued actions that came later, characterized by the Civil Rights Movement. It was not until after the Brown v. Board of Education Supreme Court decision in 1954, which outlawed segregation in public schools, and the 1955 arrest of Rosa Parks in Montgomery, Alabama for refusing to comply with segregation laws on city buses by giving up her seat to a white man that Civil Rights Movement would proceed to the next stage. The emergence of Bohra social reform movement may have seen in the unrest among the individuals on the issue of *raza* (permission) and *baraat*(social boycott), they were in turmoil which lead them unimaginably distressing position.

Coalescence

The second stage of the social movement life cycle is known as coalescence. Stage two is characterized by a more clearly defined sense of discontent. It is no longer just a general sense of unease, but now a sense of what the unease is about and who or what is responsible. This is the stage when the social movement and the issues is focuses on become known to the public. At this stage, a social movement develops its plan of action, recruits members, holds protest marches, forms networks, and gets resources. Most importantly, this is the stage at which the movement becomes more than just random, discontented individuals; at this point, they are now organized and strategic in their outlook.

The American Civil Rights Movement again provides a good example. After the initial emergence, the movement began a series of high profile campaigns that sought to highlight the plight of African-Americans in the segregated South. These campaigns included the Montgomery Bus Boycott and the lunch counter sit-ins in which African-American students would sit down at segregated counters and wait to either be served or to be dragged out by the police. These events galvanized support for the movement, and prominent leaders, such as Dr. Martin Luther King, Jr., began to emerge. After many years of successful but hard fought campaigns and strong leadership, the movement became a more prominent political force. Bohra reformists organize themselves under the banner of Central Board of The Dawoodi Bohra Community. The mission and strategies of the movement were set up to explain that it is a movement for the protection of human rights, civil liberties and other secular matters. It has nothing to do with religion.

Bureaucratization

In Bohra reform movement all the functionaries were honorary. The zeal of volunteerism made them loyal to work day and night. A corpus of 16 lakhs under a trust namely Ikhwanus Safa Trust was grown up to meet out the expenditures.

The third stage of the social movement life cycle is known as bureaucratization. As a movement grows, it often tends to become bureaucratized and paid leaders and paid staff replaces the volunteers that began the movement. It also means that clear lines of authority develop. More attention is also devoted to fundraising.

Decline

Different theoretical models proffer varying explanations for the failure of social movements. The classical model attributes their decline to tendencies toward oligarchy and conservatism, or the institutionalization of the movement's values and goals into dominant culture. Resource mobilization theorists emphasize the loss of critical assets particularly from key external supporters. Theorists who focus on political processes stress changes in "opportunity structures" and in the way in which allies, neutrals, and opponents respond to the challenges movements present. Their studies conclude that the environmental "set" is often as significant as the strategic choices of movements in determining their success of failure. Finally, some theorists analyze the internal dynamics of movement organizations and attribute their decline to inflexible structures, failure to accommodate new members, gaps between members' and leaders' goals, and a misdirection of energy and resources toward internal disputes, rather than external enemies. Bohra reform movement is ongoing movement.

Causes of Social Movements

Social movements do not just happen. It is social unrest which gives rise to a social movement. The following factors may be caused to social unrest:

(i) Cultural drifts

The society is undergoing constant changes. The values and behaviour are changing in all civilized societies. In the course of cultural drift most of the people develop new ideas. To get these ideas operative in society they organize movement. The development of a democratic society, the emancipation of women, the spread of mass education, the removal of un touchability, equality of opportunities for both the sexes, growth of secularism are the examples of cultural drift.

(ii) Social disorganization

A changing society is to some extent disorganized because changes in different parts of society do not take place simultaneously. One part changes more rapidly than the other producing thereby numerous lags. Industrialization has brought urbanization which has in its turn caused numerous social problems.

Social disorganization brings confusion and uncertainty because the old traditions no longer form a dependable guide to behaviour. The individuals become rootless. They feel isolated from the society. A feeling develops that the community leaders are indifferent to their needs. The individuals feel insecure, confused and frustrated. Confusion and frustration produce social movements.

(iii) Social injustice

When a group of people feel that injustice has been done to it they become frustrated and alienated. Such feeling of injustice is not fertile soil for social movements. The feeling of social injustice is not limited to the miserable poor. Any group, at any status level may come to feel itself the victim of social injustice. A wealthy class may feel a sense of injustice when faced with urban property ceiling Act or high taxes intended to benefit the poor. Social injustice is a subjective value judgment. A social system is unjust when it is so perceived by its members.

Thus, social movements arise wherever social conditions are favourable. It may be noted that in a stable, well integrated society there are few social movements. In such a society there are very few social tensions or alienated groups. The people are contented. But in a changing and continuously disorganized society the people suffer from tensions. They are not fully contented. In such a society they perceive social injustice and become dissatisfied. It is the dissatisfied who build social movements. The modern society is more afflicted by social movements.

The people who are more susceptible to social movements are those who are: Mobile and have little chance to become integrated into the life of the community; not fully accepted and integrated into the group and are termed marginal; isolated from the community; threatened by economic insecurity and loss of social status; free from family responsibilities or are estranged from their families; and maladjusted.

Classification of Social Movements

Cultural anthropologist David F. Aberle described four types of social movements based upon two fundamental questions (1) who is the movement attempting to change? (2) How much change is being advocated? Social movements can be aimed at change on an individual level *e.g.* Alcoholics Anonymous, which is a support group for recovering alcoholics or change on a broader group or even societal level *e.g.* anti-globalization. Social movements can also advocate for minor changes such as tougher restrictions on drunk driving (see MADD) or radical changes like prohibition. The diagram below illustrates how a social movement may either be alternative, redemptive, reformative or revolutionary based on whom the movement strive to change and how much changes the movement desires to bring about.

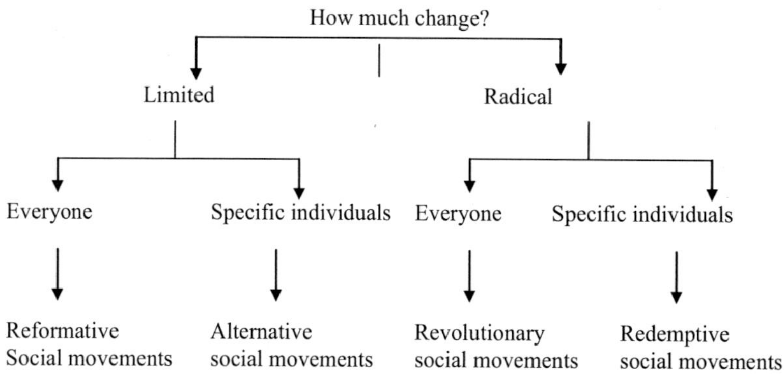

Generally it is not easy to give a classification of social movements because sometimes a movement is of mixed nature or is of a different type at different stages of its duration. However, social movements have been classified as follows:

(i) Migratory movements

Migratory movements take place when a large number of people leave one country and settle at some other place. The reason for mass migration may be discontent with present circumstances or the allurement of a bright future. Mere migration of people does not mean migratory movement.

There is a migratory social movement only when there is a common focus of discontent, a shared purpose or hope for the future and a widely shared decision to more to a new location. The Zionist movement, the movement of Jews to Israel was a migratory movement. Similarly, the movement of people from East Germany to West Germany can be called migratory social movement.

(ii) Expressive Movements

When people are faced with a social system from which they cannot flee and which they feel powerless to change, the result is an expressive social movement. In an expressive social movement the individual comes to terms with an unpleasant external reality by modifying his reactions to that reality. He somehow makes life bearable. He tries to ignore the miserable present and fixes his gaze upon a glorious future. The Hippie movement is an expressive social movement.

(iii) Utopian Movements

A Utopian movement is one which seeks to create an ideal social system or a perfect society which can be found only in man's imagination and not in reality. There have been a number of Utopian socialist in the nineteenth century such as Robert Owen and Charles Fourier. Such movements are based on a conception of man as basically good, cooperative and altruistic. The Sarvodaya movement can be called a Utopian movement.

(iv) Reform Movements

The reform movement is an attempt to modify some parts of the society without completely transforming it. Reform movements can operate only in a democratic society where people have freedom to criticize the existing institutions and may secure changes. The movements to abolish untouchability, dowry system, preserve wild life, control population growth and women's entry in Sabrimala temple.

(v) Revolutionary Movements

The revolutionary movement seeks to overthrow the existing social system and replace it with a greatly different one. The reform movement wants to correct some imperfection in the existing social system but a revolutionary movement wants to root out the system itself. Revolutionary movement's flourish where reform is blocked as that revolution remains the people's only alternative to their present misery. The communist movements in Soviet Russia and China were revolutionary movements.

(vi) Resistance Movements

The resistance movement is an effort to block a proposed change or to uproot a change already achieved. The revolutionary movement arises because people are dissatisfied with the slow rate of social change whereas resistance movement arises because people consider social change too fast. The D.M.K. movement against Hindi can be termed resistance movement.

(vii) Gender and Social Movements

The feminist movement refers to a series of campaigns for reforms on issues such as reproductive rights, domestic violence, maternity leave, equal pay, women's suffrage, sexual harassment and sexual violence. The movement's priorities vary among nations and communities and range from opposition to female genital mutilation in one country or to the glass ceiling (the barrier that prevents minorities and women from advancing in corporate hierarchies) in another.

First-wave feminism refers to a period of feminist activity during the 19th and early twentieth century in the United Kingdom, Canada, the Netherlands and the United States. It focused on de jure (officially mandated) inequalities, primarily on gaining women's suffrage (the right to vote).

Second-wave feminism refers to a period of feminism activity beginning in the early 1960s and through the late 1980s. Second Wave Feminism has existed continuously since then, and continues to coexist with what some people call Third Wave Feminism. Second Wave Feminism saw cultural and political inequalities as inextricably linked. The movement encouraged women to understand aspects of their personal lives as deeply politicized, and reflective of a sexist structure of power. If first-wavers focused on absolute rights such as suffrage, second-wavers were largely concerned with other issues of equality, such as the end to discrimination.

Finally, the third-wave of feminism began in the early 1990s. The movement arose as responses to what young women thought of as perceived failures of the second-wave. It was also a response to the backlash against initiatives and movements created by the second-wave. Third-wave feminism seeks to challenge or avoid what it deems the second wave's "essentialist" definitions of femininity, which (according to them) over-emphasized the experiences of upper middle class white women. A post-structuralist interpretation of gender and sexuality is central too much of the third wave's ideology. Third wave feminists often focus on "micro politics", and challenged the second wave's paradigm as to what is, or is not, good for females.

Global Feminism

Immediately after WWII, a new global dimension was added to the feminist cause through the formation of the United Nations (UN). In 1946 the UN established a Commission on the Status of Women. In 1948 the UN issued its Universal Declaration of Human Rights which protects "the equal rights of men and women", and addressed both equality and equity issues. Since 1975 the UN has held a series of world conferences on women's issues, starting with the World Conference of the International Women's Year in Mexico City, heralding the United Nations Decade for Women

(1975-1985). These have brought women together from all over the world and provided considerable opportunities for advancing women's rights, but also illustrated the deep divisions in attempting to apply principles universally, in successive conferences in Copenhagen (1980) and Nairobi (1985).However by 1985 some convergence was appearing. These divisions among feminists included: First World v/s Third World; the relationship between gender oppression and oppression based on class, race and nationality; defining core common elements of feminism v/s specific political elements; defining feminism, homosexuality, female circumcision, birth and population control; the gulf between researchers and the grass roots; and the extent to which political issues were women's issues. Emerging from Nairobi was a realization that a feminist is not monolithic but "constitutes the political expressions on the concerns and interests of women from different regions, classes, nationalities, and ethnic backgrounds. There is and must be a diversity feminisms, responsive to the different needs and concerns of women, and defined by them for themselves. This diversity builds on a common opposition to gender oppression and hierarchy which, however, is only the first step in articulating and acting upon a political agenda". The fourth conference was held in Beijing in 1995. At this conference the Beijing Platform for Action was signed. This included a commitment to achieve "gender equality and the empowerment of women". The most important strategy to achieve this was considered to be "gender mainstreaming" which incorporates both equity and equality, this is that both women and men should "experience equal conditions for realizing their full human rights and have the opportunity to contribute and benefit from national, political, economic, social and cultural development".

Theories of Social Movement

Social movement theory is an interdisciplinary study with the social sciences that generally seeks to explain why social mobilization occurs the forms under which it manifest, as well as potential social, cultural and political consequences.

Deprivation Theory

According to proponents of the deprivation theory, some social movements are born when certain groups of people in a society feel that they are deprived of a specific good, service or resource (McAdam, McCarthy and Zald, 1988)[10]. Within the deprivation theory camp, there are two branches: absolute deprivation and relative deprivation. The proponents of absolute deprivation treated these grievances of the affected group in isolation from that group's position in society. Proponents of relative deprivation, on the other hand, regarded a group to be in a disadvantageous position vis-à-vis some other group in that society.

The deprivation theory, seemingly, provides a powerful reason as to why some social movements may be born. However, it does have one major disadvantage that is difficult to explain away. It feels to explain why in some cases deprivation fails to ignite the birth of a social movement. This gives rise to the suspicion that while the existence of a deprivation may be necessary condition for the birth of a social movement, it may not be a sufficient condition for the social movement to be born. In other words, for a social movement to be born, deprivation needs to be present along with other factors (that the deprivation theory overlooks) in order for a social movement to be born.

In spite of the above difficulty, it seems that the deprivation theory may provide a partial explanation as to why a social movement is born. For example, one can argue that the feminist movement was born in the 1960s because prior to that time women were "deprived" by society of rights and opportunities (especially in terms of a career) that were only accorded to men.

In a similar manner, one can argue that the civil rights movement in the U.S. was born because before that movement non-white people were "deprived" of basic rights and privileges that their white counterparts enjoyed. Again, we must keep in mind that in the two above-mentioned situations, deprivation of basic rights and opportunities was one of the causes as to why those two movements were born – we have to also look for other factors that acted in conjunctions with deprivation to give birth to those two movements.

Resource Mobilization Theory

The resource mobilization theory invokes the importance of the availability of suitable resources in the birth of a social movement. This theory thus says that when some individuals in a society have certain grievances, that they may be able to mobilize necessary resources to do something to alleviate those grievances. The term "resources" in this context refer to things like money, labour, social status, knowledge, support of the media and political elites, etc. (Dobson, 2001[11]; Foweraker, 1995;[12] McAdam, McCarthy and Zald, 1988; Phongpaichit, 1999[13]). One of the great advantages of this theory is that it offers a convincing explanation as to why in some situations some grievances may give birth to anything similar.

One of the major criticisms of this theory is that it has an extremely strong "materialist" orientation in that it gives primacy to the presence of appropriate resources (especially money) in explaining the birth of social movements. There are social movements that have been born even when resources (especially financial ones) were scarce.

This theory does provide a good explanation of why some social movements have been able to grow at an exponential rate, even in the presence of seemingly insurmountable obstacles. The civil rights movement in the U.S. is a classic example of this type. The leaders of that movement – primarily Martin Luther King, Jr. and his colleagues in the Southern Christian Leadership Conference – were able to successfully elicit the support of thousands of supporters (including many sympathetic whites) in launching and propagating the movement. They were able to do that in spite of the fact that a majority of the white population at that time were strongly opposed to some of the fundamental objectives of the movement (ex. the ending of separate public facilities for whites and non-whites and the awarding of voting rights to blacks).

Starr (2000) discusses in detail how many "new" social movements (that are categorized by many under the umbrella term "anti globalization movement") try to mobilize resources, primarily human resources, by appealing to grassroots organizers. These grassroots organizers first try to gather "manpower" in their local areas and then bring them together in mid-level regional gatherings, and finally organize protests (and even boycotts) at the national and international levels.

True to their name, such "new" social movements frequently utilize the Internet (email, bulletin boards, chat rooms, listservs etc.) to carry out their mobilizing activities. Starr (2000)[14] draws particular attention to the relative successes and international appeal of the environmental and the anti-WTO movements to the use of modern telecommunications technologies to bring people together (or mobilize them) across international boundaries and geographic barriers (like seas and oceans). All future work on resource mobilization theory and how it applies to the "new" social movements of recent years will have to take into account the overwhelming presence and influence of modern technologies (the Internet, cell phones, etc.) on the process of "resource mobilization".

Political Process Theory

Political process theory treats social movements as a type of political movements in that the origins of a social movement are traced to the availability of political opportunities. More precisely, this theory looks at the social movement in question for that of the state – or the power of the government in charge. If the government's position is strongly entrenched and it also is prone to repressive behaviour, then the chances are high that a social movement might fail. If, on the other hand, the government is week or more tolerant of dissenting behaving, then the chances are high that any social movement that is born might have the opportunity to grow and flourish.

Few social movement theorists would have any problems with the political process theory emphasizing the importance of political conditions and attendant political opportunities (or lack thereof) in determining the chances of success for a nascent social movement. The primary criticism of this theory is that it focuses too much on political circumstances and ignores cultural factors that might be strong enough to mitigate the effect of the political factors.

Foweraker (1995) looks at several examples of social movements in Latin American countries and how the power of the State (or government) has affected the outcomes of these movements. One of the poignant examples is the case of Chile where pro-democracy movements were brutally dealt with by the oppressive U.S. backed government of General Augusto Pinochet (who died in 2006). Foweraker(1995) contrasts the fortunes of the pro-democracy movement in Chile with that of the Green (environmental) movement in many West European countries. Whereas in the Chile case, the ruthlessness of the State crushed the pro-democracy movements repeatedly, in West European countries the presence of friendly and cooperative national governments fuelled the growth of the Green movement to what it is today. These two contrasting cases are vivid examples of how the outcome of social movements is intimately tied to the nature of the governments (or political systems) that these movements have to contend with.

Structural Strain Theory

The structural strain theory was proposed by Smelser (1965)[15]. The theory advocates that any nascent social movement needs six factors to grow. These six factors are: people in a society experience some type of problem (deprivation); recognition by people of that society that this problem exists; an ideology purporting to be a solution for the problem develops and spreads its influence; an event or events transpire that convert this nascent movement into a bona fide social movement, the society (and its government) is open to change for the movement to be effective (if not, then the movement might die out); and mobilization of resources takes place as the movement develops further.

The structural strain theory can be used to understand the births and growth of the U.S. civil rights movement. During the 1960s, there was increasing recognition amongst both blacks and some whites in the country that the then current state of discriminatory racial affairs could not go on (especially in light of the fact that at that very moment the U.S. was portraying itself in the Cold War as the global champion liberty and equality). Discontent, in the form of sporadic protests and boycotts, was spreading slowly. However, what truly ignited the civil rights movement was the unforgettable bus incident involving Rosa Parks. The incident was the catalyst that converted the incipient civil rights movement into a truly national phenomenon – and it paved the way for the judicial-legal revolution that was to change the face of American Society forever. It must be noted that the Kennedy and Johnson Administrations were both receptive to these changes and they did not try to repress the nascent movement as it was slowly growing.

Thus, the structural strain theory does provide an appropriate analytical framework that can help us understand the origins and subsequent growth of the U.S. civil rights movement.

New Social Movement Theory

The term new social movement (NSMs) is a theory of social movements that attempts to explain the plethora of new movements that have come up in various societies roughly since the mid 1960s (i.e. in a post-industrial economy), which are claimed to depart significantly from the conventional social movement paradigm. There are two central claims of the NSM theory. Firstly, the rise of the post-industrial economy is responsible for a new wave of social movement. Secondly, these movements are significantly different from previous social movements of the industrial economy. The primary difference is in their goals, as the new movements focus not on issues of materialistic qualities such economic well-being but on issues related to human rights (such as gay rights or pacifism).

The most noticeable feature of new social movements is that they are primarily social and cultural and only secondarily, if at all, political. Departing from the worker's movement, which was central to the political aim of gaining access to citizenship and representation for the working class, new social movements concentrate on bringing about social mobilization for the cultural innovations, the development of new lifestyles, and the transformation of identities. It is clearly elaborated by Habermas[16] that new social movements are the "new politics" which is about quality of life, individual self-realization, and human rights; whereas the "old politics" focused on economic, political and military security. The concept of new politics can be exemplified in gay liberation, the focus of which transcends the political issue of gay rights to address the need for a social and cultural acceptance of homosexuality. Hence, new social movements are understood as "new", because they are first and foremost social, unlike older movements which mostly have an economic basis.

New social movements also emphasize the role of post-material values in contemporary and post-industrial society, as opposed to conflicts over material resources. According to Melucci[17], one of the leading new social movement theorists, these movements arise not from relations of production and distribution of resources, but within the sphere of reproduction and the life world. Consequently, the concern has shifted from the production of economic resources as a means of survival or for reproduction of social relations, symbols and identities. In other words, the contemporary social movements reject the materialistic orientation of consumerism in capitalist societies by questioning the modern idea that links the pursuit of happiness and success closely to growth, progress and increased productivity and by instead promoting alternative values and understandings in relation to the social world. As an example, the environmental movement that has appeared the late 1960s throughout the world, with its strong points in the United States and Northern Europe, has significantly brought about a "dramatic reversal" in the ways we consider the relationship between economy, society and nature.

Further, new social movements are located in civil society or the cultural sphere as a major arena for collective action rather than instructional action in the state, which Claus Offe[18] characterizes as "bypass[ing] the state". Moreover, since now social movements are not normally concerned with directly challenging the state, they are regarded as anti-authoritarian and as resisting incorporation at the institutional level. They tend to focus on a single, or a limited range of issues connected to a single broad theme, such as peace or the environment. New social movements concentrate on the grassroots level with the aim to represent the interests of marginal or excluded groups. Therefore, new collective actions are locally based, centered on small social groups and loosely held together by personal or informational networks such as radios, newspapers, and posters. This "local- and issue-centered" characteristic implies that new movements do not necessarily require a strong ideology or agreement to meet their objectives.

Additionally, if old social movements, namely the worker's movement, presupposed a working class base and ideology, the new social movements are presumed to draw from a different social class base, i.e., "the new class". This is a complex contemporary class structure that Claus Offe identifies as "threefold" in its composition; the new middle class, element of the old middle class, and peripheral groups outside the labour market. As stated by Offe, the new middle class has evolved in association with the old one in the new social movements because of its high levels of education and its access to information and resources. The groups of people that are marginal in the labour market, such as students, housewives, and the unemployed participate in the collective actions as a consequence of their higher levels of free time, their position of being all the receiving end of bureaucratic control, and their inability to be fully engaged in society specifically in terms of employment and consumption.

One of the principal criticisms of the theory is that it tends to downplay the conflicts between various socio-economic classes of society, however, even in a postmodern society, different socio-economic classes do exist and they do exist and they do experience conflicts with one another. Another criticism is that it tends to treat movements, like the women's rights movement, the environmental movement and the anti-globalization movement as belonging to the same type, even though these movements clearly are quite diverse types of social movements. The pigeon-holing these diverse movements into one category may be an exercise in intellectual futility.

Social movements influence policy by changing in government and public's policy preferences and its intensity of concern about particular issues. Therefore, social movements have important consequences as part of the political and policy process. Many scholars study social movements because they indeed believe that they are an important source of policy change. As a source of policy change, social movements do not only influence promulgation of new policies but also ensure that the policy is transformed into collective benefits for the larger group. Therefore, social movements can have deep and long lasting consequences for public policy. They emerge because there is problem or matter of concern in society.

Dawoodi Bohra Reform Movement

The Bohras Shia Ismaili, Mustali Fatimi faith - strongly attached to its closely knit and hierarchical organisation have been in ferment on the question of certain vital reforms which are being vehemently opposed by the priesthood. The reform movement started in the early twentieth century and the pivotal question was, at that time, dissemination of Western education within the community. The priesthood sought to impede the efforts of the advocates of Western education by imposing various sanctions against them. This in turned raised the issue of democratic freedom and individual rights. The priesthood claimed and enforced this claim in the most ruthless manner- that its actions were unquestionable and that individuals did not enjoy any rights such as far as the Dawoodi Bohra religion was concerned (AsgharAli, 1980).

There is yet another factor which impedes the growth of reformist movement among the Bohras. It is the religiously accepted role of the ordained priest on occasions like marriage and death. There is no concept of priesthood in Islam as any layman can perform a *nikha* or burial ceremony. However, it is among the Ismailies that concept priesthood comparable in its hierarchical structure, to that of Christians has developed. The occasion of marriage and death are fully exploited by the priesthood to force even the most recalcitrant to give in. The community is still not prepared for understandable reasons, to breakout, this unislamic practice.

The economic factor also plays its part in perpetuating the dominance of the priesthood. In India as yet due to backwardness, even modern professionals like doctors, lawyers, architects, engineers etc. depend on the members of their own caste or community for their clientele. A non-confirming member would, in the event of social boycott, lose his clients who are his follow religionists. The priesthood has in this manner brought many professionals to their knees. There are numerous such instances. Hardly anyone stand by his or her convictions in such circumstances. Even business partnership suffers on this basis. A reformist Bohra loses his job if he was working with other Bohra firm and or a reformist employer would lose his Bohra employees. Even a product from a factory of a reformist Bohra is not allowed by the priesthood to be consumed by other member of the community.

The media has also played a role in widening the base of reform movement. Previously, a large number of people were not aware of the real issues involved, but now, thanks to electronic and print media a large number of people have come to know the truth about Bohra reform movement. The vehemence with which the priesthood opposed the *Nathwani Commission* (a fact finding commission about the atrocities committed by priesthood on the name of social boycott) and the repressive measures which was used to force the Bohras to oppose the commission had exposed its (priesthood's) vulnerability.

Frantz Fanon, in his well known book *The Wretched of the Earth,* has described how the Western colonisers humiliated, insulted and tortured - both physically and mentally- the people of colonial world, permanently affecting their psyche. In a preface of the above book Jean Paul Sartre, addressing the Western audience says: "Our victims know us by their scars and by their chains, and it is this that makes their evidence irrefutable. It is enough that they show us what we had made of them for us to realise that we have made of ourselves. But it is of any use? Yes, for Europe is at deaths door".

Metaphorically speaking the Bohra priesthood is coloniser and the Bohras a colonised people. The priesthood humiliates, insults, tortures and treated them as slaves, like the Western coloniser treated their Asian and African people. The Bohras bear permanent scars like the ones Sartre refers in his preface. These Bohra victims know their priesthood by their scars and by their chains. This evidence of psychological injury is irrefutable of their estrangement from the tyrannical priesthood.

Of course, for the colonised people it was a political fight. With the proper leadership and strategy they overthrew the political hegemony of the West, but such a direct struggle against religious authorities is not possible, and even if waged, has very limited chances of success. So also it is with the process of social change. It is extremely difficult to break age-old traditions which have been elevated to a religious status. These struggles assume a very tortuous course and call for intense suffering and heroic sacrifices.

The status of Bohra women is almost similar like other Muslim women. They hardly have intercourse with women of another community; neither have they kept in touch with NGOs working for the development of women nor try to contact other social welfare agencies. In short their house, community, *jammat khana,* mosque, and *durgha* are the limit of their world. In this situation the weapon of social boycott becomes very effective. Whenever a boycott is declared against any person, his wife, sister or mother cannot stay with him or maintain any contact with him, if they do, they face the same fate. Her co-religionists will not invite her to feasts or any social functions. She will not be able to marry her children with her brother-in- faith. Thus Bohra women, even they choose to stay with the boycotted man feel terribly isolated and ultimately compel him to fall in line and apologise to the high priest. The reformists have, because of this peculiar problem, lost many of the veteran fighters. Very few women show such extraordinary courage to stand by their husbands or brothers or sons when they are socially boycotted by the priesthood. The high priest has fully exploited this situation to his advantage in order to disrupt the reformist movement.

Conclusion

The Bohra reform movement in Udaipur (Rajasthan) could be sustained because the priesthood committed blunder of assaulting their womenfolk publicly and thus antagonising them against itself for good. The support of the women for the movement thus proved very valuable in Udaipur. It is also important to note that the percentage of education is quite high both among women and men in this city. The enthusiastic women members, young and old alike, fought with unflinching courage. They did all the Bohras proud. The sacrifice and heroic fight constitute a saga of bravery and courage in the history of Bohra reformist movements. The reform movement is on going till today only because women support is there and social transformation is visible as *raza (*permission of priesthood) has almost vanished in matters like *nikha, Namaze Imamat, dafan-kafa*n in reformist Bohra Youth group.

The Dawoodi Bhoras are also the only community in India known to practice *Khatna or female circumcision* (FGM), and for the past several months many Bohra women have been actively agitating to end this practice. Both electronic and print media have covered it.

Women empowerment raises the status of women from equal participation in Jamaat affairs to equal decision maker. A woman elevated to the post of president in Mumbai Jamaat. Udaipur Bohra youth Girls' Wing emerged as strong women pressure group to protect and safeguard women rights. Girls' Wing has also been striving hard to educate Bohra women in secular and worldly affairs related to women development.

Therefore, an academic analysis is inevitable in order to understand and evaluate the Dawoodi Bohra reform movements and its impact on women empowerment.

Notes and References

1. D'Arcus, *Boundaries of Dissent: Protest and State Power in the Middle Age,* New York, Rutledge, 2006.
2. Mansbridge and Morris, In John Idriss Lahai, Khanyisela Moyo (Eds), *Gender in Human Rights and Transitional Justice,* Springer.
3. Zald and McCarthy. *Social Movements in an Organizational Society: Collected Essays.* Transaction Books, 1987, pp.188-190.
4. Diani, Mario 'The Concept of Social Movement'. *The Sociologica Review,* 40:1, (1992), pp.1-25.

5. McAdam, Doug and Snow David, 'Social Movements: Conceptual and Theoretical Issues', in McAdam, D. & Snow, D. (Eds.), *Social Movements: Reading in their Emergence, Mobilization and Dynamics,* Ruxbury, Los Angels, 1977.

6. Charles Tilly, *Social Movements,* 1768-2004, Paradigm Publishers, Boulder, 2014.

7. Charles, Tilly, 'From interactions to outcomes in social movements', in Marcogivgni, Dong, McAdam and Charles Tilly (Eds.), *How Social Movement Matters,* University of Minnesota Press, Minneapolis, 1999, P.257.

8. Jeff Goodwin and James Jasper, *The Social Movement Reader - Cases and Concepts,* (2nd Ed.), Wiley Blackwell, Oxford, 2004.

9. Sydney Tarrow, (3rd Ed.), *Power in Movement: Social Movements and Contentious Politics,* Cambridge University Press, Cambridge, 2011.

10. McAdam, D., McCarthy, J.D. and Zald, M.N. (1988). Op. Cit., 695-737.

11. Dobson, C. 'Social movements: A summary of what works'. *The Citizen's Handbook: A Guide to Building Community in Vancouver.*,2001, Retrieved Dec 2, 2006, from http://www.ven.bc.ca/citizens-hanbdook/movements.pdf.

12. Fowarekar, J. *Theorizing Social Movements.* London: Pluto Press, 1995.

13. Phongpaichit, P. 'Theories of social movements and their relevance for Thailand'. *Social Movements in Thailand*, 1999. Retrieved Dec 5, 2006 from http://pioneer.netserv.chula.ac.th/~ppasuk/theorysocmovt.doc.

14. Starr, A. *Naming the enemy: Anti-corporate movement confronts globalization.* London: Zed Books, 2000.

15. Smelser, N.J. *Theory of Collective Behaviour,* New York: Free Press, 1965.

16. Habermas, J.1987, 'New Social Movements', in Telos 49, pp.33-37.

17. Melucci Alberto. *Nomads of the Present: Social Movements and Individual Needs in Contemporary Society,* Philadelphia, Temple University Press, 1989.

18. C. Offe, 'New Social Movements: Challenging the Boundaries of Institutional Politics', *Social Research,* 1985: Winter, 52 (4), 817.

Chapter - 2

Reform Movements in Indian Muslims

Islam is misunderstood religion. It is widely criticized by those, who have little or no knowledge about Islam, the faith, its teachings and its philosophy. People may wonder to hear that Islam is a progressive religion which was first to confer fundamental rights to all the human beings and which advocated for the equality of men and women. It opposed all discrimination, be that of caste, creed or faith. The concept of human rights is relatively newer and a modern one. Several hundred years ago, nobody in the West knew about this. But, Islam had bestowed all rights-based on humanity – fifteen centuries ago, on Muslims and Non-Muslims alike, at the time of its advent. Ironically, people in today's world and even some of the scholars are not aware of the hard facts in this regard.

The first forty years after the *hijra* of the Prophet could be described as the early formative period of Islam. The Prophet's central vision was, during ten years after his migration to Madina, concretised through his own exemplary behviour, supplemented of course, by the exigencies of the situation. Islam due to historical circumstance of its origin, always emphasized concrete over the abstract. It was, and still remains, a historical project and more of a praxis than abstract philosophical doctrines. Its concreteness is assimilated best of the Arab traditions which did not conflict with its central vision. The Islamic Shari'a can be said to be rooted in this sense in the Arabian collective tradition although the central vision of Islam, in a way has been summed up in the Quranic verse.

"Righteousness is not that you turn your faces (in prayer) towards the east or the west; but righteousness is this, that one believeth in God, in the last day, in the angles, in the Books and in the Prophets, and for the God, giveth of his wealth to his kindred and to the orphans and to the needy and to the wayfarers, and to those who ask and to affect the freedom of the slave, and observeth prayer and payeth the poor one and is of those who are faithful to their engagements when they have engaged in them, and endureth with fortitude poverty, distress and moments of peril-these are they who are true in their faith and these are they who are truly righteous." (Q: 2:177)

It would be seen that it is inspired by equality, social justice and brotherhood. This vision found expression though Arabian traditions and institutions and thus can be called the Hinyan period of Islam.[1]

The later conquests which began after the death of the Prophet brought the Muslim Arabs face to face with Heinic and Sassanid traditions which through cultural and intellectual interaction left deep imprint both on Islamic thought and practice. Speculative elements over the concrete now began to assert themselves. Thus, according to Iqbal, inductive and concrete spirit of the Koran was superseded, during this period, by speculative and deductive thought. During the Ummayad and the Abbasid period the frontiers of Islamic society went to expanding assimilating alien traditions in one form or the other. These accretions enriched and deepened the Islamic thought and thus this period should be described as the Mahayan[2] period of Islam.

When Islam spread to India, it did so through latitudinarian and assimilative practice of Sufi saints rather than rigid and exclusivist practices of Ulama or the jurists. Wahadat-Al-Wujud of Ibn Arabi which inspired these Sufi saints was assimilative rather than rejectionists. Thus, many of Vedantic tradition, representing different vision of life, tended to become part of Indian Islam. Thus, Atindranath Bose says, the Islam knocked on the Western gates of India; and the Sufis, inspired by the Islamic idea of equality, came as the torch bearer of a liberal folk philosophy… Their spirit was free from those superstitions and rigidities which caused stagnation among the classical Indian and Islamic schools. Against the sterility of the orthodox system, the new popular appeals awakened a fresh spiritual fervor and let loose great creative power which so long lay dormant. A new philosophy grew up based on the material of human value. It trusted in the latent divinity of the human soul in the universality of love and in the dynamic power of emotion. It released powerful spiritual energy hitherto pent up by social barriers among the dumb millions of the soil Sindh and Bengal were the last nurseries of this syncretizing popular philosophy.[3]

The Sufi saints found close parallel in Hindu philosophy and did not hesitate to acknowledge this fact, as against Ulamas who remained reconciled to any attempt to 'syncretization'. The Sufis recognized the essence of (I am truth) in 'aham Brahmasami 'and that of Wahadat-al-Wajud in adavita Vedantian. Significantly, this was the vigorous period of social and cultural synthesis of the two peoples, nourished by the teachings of Sufis like Khwaja Moinuddin Chisti of Ajmer, Ali Qalandar of Panipat, Syed Jalaluddin Bukhari and Qulabul Alam of Bengal, Fariduddin of Pak-Potan, Syed Giyasu Daraz of the Deccan, Pir Sadaruddin, Imam Shah and Damal Shah of Sindh and Gujarat, Mohammed Sadiq of Nasik and Mir Shamsuddin of Kashmir, Niazmuddin of Delhi, Salim Chisti of Agra and Saints like Ramananda, Chaitanya and Eknath of the Hindu faith.

Rational Thinking of Indian Muslims

In the early 19th century, the first signs of Muslim awakening appeared under the leadership of Sharialullah of Bengal. This was happening due to the Christian missionaries' influence of Western ideas and modern education. Hence, they set themselves to the task of purifying and strengthening Islam and promoting Islamic learning. The ideas of self-reliance, self-respect and national pride were propagated.

Shariatullah started the *'Faraizi Movement of Bengal'* in 1804 which took up initiative to the cause of the peasants. He also expressed strong disapproval to the caste system among Muslims. During the first half of the 19th century only a handful of Muslims of Delhi and Calcutta had taken to English education. Most of them kept themselves away from it because of the attitude of the *Ulema* or *Muslim* priest, and the unwillingness of the upper class Muslims to reconcile themselves to the British rule. The Revolt of 1857 created discontentment among British about Muslim due to their active participation. Hence, being part of the few enlightened, educated Muslims, Shariatullah felt the need for adopting a cooperative policy towards the rulers and improving their social condition with the help of the British.

A few movements were also launched aiming at the spread of modern education and removing social abuses like Purdah and Polygamy. The *Mohammedan Literacy Society* of Calcutta, founded in 1863 by *Nawab Abdul Latif* (1928-1893) was one of the earliest organizations to take steps in this direction. It played an important role in the spread of education, particularly among the Muslims of Bengal as well as promoting Hindu-Muslim unity.

Wahabi Movement

It was also known as *Walliullah Movement*[4] which started in response to the western influences and was inspired by the teachings of *Shah Walliullah* who was regarded as the first Indian Muslim leader. The entire movement was moving around the legacy of Islam – *'Quran and Hadis'*.

Shah Walliullah felt that time has come when every injunction of the *Sharia* and every law of Islam should be presented in rational way.[5] He also believed that in the social as well as religious matters the Prophet was guided by the cultural milieu, mental attitude and the social usage of his contemporary society in which he was born.[6] Shah Walliullah appreciated Sufi spirituality. He built a bridge between Sufis and Ulama (Islamic scholar).

Ahmadiya Movement

This movement was started by *Mirza Gulam Ahmed* in 1889 in order to spread western education among Indian Muslims. The movement was based on liberal principles, just like Brahma Samaj.

Aligarh Movement

Sir Syed may be regarded as the greatest liberal among the Muslim thinkers in India. He was the spokesman of the inchoate aspirations of the Muslims, ruined and uprooted by the rebellion. He wanted to make all Muslims realize the significance of age and take up the challenge of the times. This constituted the basis of his efforts at Muslim awakening known as the Aligarh movement. Such movement was necessary because the Muslims suffered from the depressing feeling that they had lost political power forever and were in danger of losing their culture and civilization. They were frustrated and lacked a sense of direction and aspiration.

Sir Syed, however, refused to follow the footprints of the religious philosophers of the past; his interpretation of religion was rational and free from dogma. He believed that there was no antagonism between Islam on one hand and reason and science on the other. It may be mentioned that there had so far been no movement of social reform and renaissance among the Muslims of India. The *Wahabi* leaders were preoccupied with political action and gave little attention to social reform.

Sir Syed was inspired by the liberalism of the West by Burke, Bentham, Lord Macaulay and J.S. Mill. He largely anticipated the basic tenets of liberalism as advocated later by Dadabhoy Naoroji, Surendranath Banerji and others. This impact of liberalism led him to resolve the conflict between the new values of the West and the conservation and dogmatism of the Indian Muslims.[7]

Launching a series of reforms within Muslim society, Sir Syed started a periodical entitled "*Tahzib-ul-Akhlaq*' to popularize his reformist views. In fact the *Tahzib-ul-Akhlaq* was launched on the pattern of "Tatler and the Spectator" containing thought provoking essays, discussions on general issues concerning morality. Sir Syed thoroughly condemned the social evils like slavery, polygamy, pretentious behaviour and other such outdated and corrupt practices. But on some issues called outdated by others, Sir Syed favoured them believing that they were right. When the Christians criticized the practice of Hijab (veil) among the Muslims women and even frowned at it, Sir Syed was in favour. Even some renowned Muslim intellectuals like Nazir Ahmad and Mohammad Abdul Halim Sharar strived hard to redeem Muslims from this practice but Sir Syed deemed it a good traditional practice and good for them because it was part of Islamic civilization.[8]

He was a champion of Women's rights. He pointed out evils of widowhood. He said, "the women is in need of gentle treatment at the hands of man because of her delicate nature and especially the widow deserves all human sympathies." At that time widow remarriage was a taboo in Indian society. He appealed to the Muslims, "to encourage widow-remarriage and earn the blessings both in this world and the next for their virtuous deeds."[9] He pleaded for organized charity to fight the cause of widows. Often it is claimed that he was against female education but the reality is otherwise. He was fully in favour of educating girls. But he was of the opinion that first the task of educating boys should be taken on priority basis.

Sir Syed established a chain of educational institutions on his journey to transform Muslim society. Graham states, "Syed Ahmad's first venture in the field of education can be traced to a Persian Madarsa he established in Moradabad in 1859. Though the Madarsa was founded on old classical lines but it had some important features which distinguished it from other Persian schools. Study of modern history was part of curriculum in Madarsa. The emphasis on history was so much high that people believed that it was opened especially for the study of modern history.[10]

Here we must keep in mind that the first and foremost mission of Sir Syed was to recover lost glory of Muslims and his educational movement was the vehicle to achieve it. Under the circumstances prevailing at that time of history he made many compromises and had given much importance to communal harmony. When he founded school at Ghazipur, he switched over from modern history to English language as far as emphasis is concerned. He gave importance to English language much though in the school other languages like Urdu, Persian, Arabic and even Sanskrit were being taught. The first patron of Ghazipur School was Raja Hardev Narain Singh. Under his policy of communal harmony[11] Sir Syed has included Hindus also in his initiatives of educational revolution because he was aware that without cooperation of the majority community he will not be able to walk few miles. According to Begum Naz, 'for the Ghazipur School Sir Syed raised funds from Hindus also. In fact the first patron was Raja Hardev Narain Singh. It is not commonly known that Sir Syed had wanted to open a university at Banaras for which he had sent a manifesto to British government. His attitude changed only when Banaras Hindus started an agitation against Persian and Urdu script in favour of Devnagri and Hindi.[12]

Sir Syed was quite brave and highly positive. He firmly believed that he will succeed in his mission. He fought a tireless battle against those practices which he deemed were outdated and wrong and took extreme pains to reinstate what he deemed as right and futuristic. In every possible way his efforts were directed towards defending Muslims and Islam and he strove hard to see that Muslims do not remain object of mockery and cynicism. He was a hardcore rationalist. His religious, social, political and educational views were intertwined. It can be said that Sir Syed was forerunner in modernizing Muslims and even Islam. W.C. Smith observes, "He (Sir Syed) was genuinely tolerant, deeming a man's religion as his private affair which should not be obtruded and hardly even discussed between these of different faiths lest friendship he weakened. The slightest religious bigotry distressed him.[13]

When he established Mohammedan Anglo-Oriental College, he kept its doors open for every community. He never discriminated on the grounds of religion while appointing the faculties and staff. Thus, he appointed Theodore Beck as Principal of the College despite the fact that he was a Christian. His secularism was perfect, practical and in motion. In fact, today's politician should learn a lesson from him in this regard.

He wrote on college boarders a short pamphlet "College Life or New Life" for the resident students. Therein he says, "first and foremost of all, mutual love and amicable conduct towards one and another is the fountainhead of all bliss and blessings here. All the students, lying as they are on the lap of this Alama Mater, no matter whether they hail from Hindustan or the Punjab, East or West or South, are your brothers first and last. If you did not treat and love them like brothers it would mean that you infringed the first principle of being the sons of one and the same "wise mother". This was the concept of Sir Syed in respect of brotherhood on the campus and certainly it was the base of what today we call "Aligarianship".[14]

Sir Syed was joined by some other eminent people in this crusade to reform Muslim society in India like Maulvi Chiragh Ali, Maulana Shibli Naumani, Nawab Mohsin-ul-Mulk, Nawab Viqar-ul-Mulk, Maulvi

Zafarullah and Khwaja Maulvi Zainul-Abidin. Among them Shibli Naumani was a multifarious personality combining in him a historic, patriotic and cortical skills and temperament. Nawab Mohsin-ul-Mulk was also a highly renowned writer and had intimate relations with Sir Syed. Though Nawab Mohin-ul-Mulk was not convinced by religious views of Sir Syed but later on he began subscribing them. Sir Syed was of the opinion that a progression in the social and political status for the Muslims was not possible without winning the goodwill of the British rulers. The whole group stated above with Sir Syed worked together in unison towards reforming and uplifting Muslim society in India.

Syed Ameer Ali

Ameer Ali due to the influence of Sir Syed asserted that "To suppose, therefore, that every Islamic percept is necessarily of human intellect.[15] He also argued that certain injunctions of the Quran were historically relevant only to the Prophet's day. It means that Islam as preached by the Prophet is not wholly applicable to all the spheres of life.

According to Ameer Ali, no law is immutable. It becomes out of date after a radical change in the society. Therefore, law should be in consonance with the exigencies and the requirements of the time.[16]

It is significant that Ameer Ali supported the abolition of polygamy. He regarded it "as much opposed to the teachings of Mohammed as it is to be general progress of civilized society and true culture."[17] Ameer Ali held that polygamy is abhorrent to the laws of Islam.[18] He also opposed the existing practice of Divorce. "The Prophet looked upon the custom of divorce with extreme disapproval and regarded the practice as calculated to undermine the foundations of society. He repeatedly declared that'... Nothing more displeases God than divorce,[19] said Ameer Ali. These ideas regarding to Muslim personal law impel a change which permits polygamy as well as divorce. The change perhaps will be more in keeping with the spirit of Islam than the maintenance of the status quo.

Chiragh Ali

Chiragh Ali's view of Islam was also strikingly secular and liberal. To him, "Islam as a religion is quite apart from inculcating a social system. The Mohammedan polity and social system have nothing to do with religion". Islam is so sufficiently elastic that it can adopt itself to the social and political revolutions going on around.[20] It is not a barrier to the political, social or moral innovations.[21] Chiragh Ali regarded the Prophet primarily as a reformer who supplanted ancient Arabian superstitions by monotheism, elevated the moral standard of Arabs and other people and improved the lot of women by restricting polygamy, discouraging slavery, and abolishing infanticide.[22] To Chiragh Ali, the Mohammedan common law or Shariat is by no means unchangeable or unalterable.[23] The Prophet did not compile any code, but permitted the Muslims to frame any code of Civil or Common law and to found systems which would harmonize with the times and suit the political and social changes going around them.[24]The Prophet, Chiragh Ali believed, never combined the Church and the State into one[25]. These ideas supplement Sir Syed's views on Islam.

Khuda Baksh

Khuda Baksh also forcefully advocated the separation of religion from social and political life. He attempted to free Islam from the "fetters of Authority and the Dead Hand of the Past.[26] He held that "it would be a merest affront to contend that religious and social systems, bequeathed to us thirteen hundred years ago, should now be adapted in their entirety without the slightest change or alteration.[27] He did not consider Quran as *Corpus juris civils* to be accepted for all time.[28] His view was that the subordination of religion to the State is a step forward in the direction of reform and progress.[29]

Khuda Baksh was a supporter of secular politics. He did not consider the institution of Khilafat a basis of the unity of the Muslim world.

Aga Khan

Another important representative of this liberal school is Aga Khan (49th Imam of Ismaili- Nizari) who never deviated from the liberal track. He believed that "Islam…within it…has the capacity to be moral and spiritual force of enormous significance, both stabilizing and energizing the communities among whom it is preached and practiced. To ignore Islam's political influence for good, Islam's healing and creative power for societies as also for individuals, is to ignore one of the most genuinely hopeful factors that exist in the world of today.[30] He always tried to prove that "Islam is essentially a progressive and tolerant faith."[31] In the true spirit of Sir Syed's religious thought Aga Khan attempted to battle again orthodoxy and reactionary ideas prevailing among Indian Muslims. In this approach, one finds on the whole realistic and secular appraisal and assessment of the forces at work. He does not deny the importance of religion but attempts to offer a non-religious solution to the Muslim problem. But Sir Syed could not fully succeed in making Aligarh, the rendezvous of intellectual renaissance. The Aligarh students received education and training only for government jobs. They remained ignorant of their religion and religious traditions. They were enamoured of Western culture and civilization. With this sorry state of affairs, and anti-Aligarh movement inevitably started. It embodied the germs of religious revivalisms, reaction against the west, going back to original Islam.[32]

Maulana Abul Kalam Azad

Maulana Azad was an outstanding Muslim intellectual of modern India. By training religious and by conviction rational and modern, he tried to reconcile religion with reason without injuring either. He had great regard for Sir Syed's efforts which aimed at an intellectual revolution in the Muslim mind. Under the influence of Sir Syed, he realized that a person has no claims to be called educated in modern world unless he studied modern science, philosophy and literature.[33] He also displayed distrust in the anachronistic institution of the ulema.[34] According to him, many old concepts and values became outmoded and unnecessary.

Azad endeavoured to follow and employ Sir Syed's rational technique. This phase, however, lasted for a very short period. In the meantime he came into contact with the writings of Rashid Raza of Egypt. Thereafter he began to deviate from Sir Syed. He found that the application of rationalism results firstly in skepticism and then leads to the negation of religion. Azad could not reconcile himself to such possibilities. He began to think that Sir Syed's approach to religion was faulty and unconvincing.[35] It was inadequate and illogical. He believed that Sir Syed had no answer to questions like existence of God, attributes of God, eternity of soul, inspiration of prophethood etc.[36] These theological deviations became the basis of differences in political approach as well. But it will be unfair to Azad to infer that he rejected the views of Sir Syed in Toto Rejection of some recession to orthodoxy either.[37] Under Sir Syed's influence he strongly felt that there is no conflict between the Quran and science. Moreover, Azad never denied that what is of lasting value in Sir Syed's thought was an attempt to do away with imitation (Taqleed) and vigorous support to ijtihad.[38]

Azad's monumental work Tarjuman-ul-Quran[39] presets the best exposition of Azad's religious thought. He was intent on discovering the unity of all the religions rather than maintaining that Islam was one true faith. He applied this approach for the study of the realities of the present day.[40] Three major elements can be seen in Azad's philosophy of religion. The first is unity of God. Azad's concept of God lays emphasis on the inherent universal urges of human nature. The quest for God is one's own personal quest. If a man is introspective he will notice that "his life, every moment of his existence disclose, a world of activity propelled by the *Rububiyat* of God".[41] In the context of this fundamental agreement, other differences, according to him, were of no consequence. Shariat or "the path" of rules of conduct do vary from religion to religion. Azad says that "they differ not in the roots but in leaves and branches, not in the spirit but in the outward form or body".[42]

The second element in Azad's philosophy is the emphasis on right action. It implies actions based upon the eternal truths laid down by all scriptures. This is also the teaching of the Islam.

The third element in the Azad's thought is life after death. Death is not the end of life. It opens out a new life where one has to account for one's past action which would in turn, determine the character of future existence.[43] The idea of life after death is always an impulse and intensive for righteous living in this world.

Azad arrived in the concept of the unity of man from his principle of the unity of God and from the second element of righteous action and conduct. Azad developed a further element of his doctrine, the necessity and importance of tolerance. The principle of toleration is the core of his religious philosophy. Tolerance is a condition precedent for the realization of the unity of all the religions. "But even as your way is excellent in your own eye, even so in other people's eyes their way is excellent. Toleration therefore is the only way."[43] Azad laid great emphasis on Hindu-Muslim unity which he regarded as a legacy of our long history. According to him nationalism in India was impossible of realization without Hindi-Muslim unity. Azad stressed unity as much he considered it clearer than the freedom of country itself.[44] He was always optimistic and felt that the differences between the Hindus and the Muslims would never become so grave as to lead to mutual warfare and bloodshed. They are to be resolved in a spirit of compromise and toleration. In India "every kind of faith, every kind of culture, every mode of living was allowed to flourish and find its own salvation."[45] The question of Indian first or Muslim first was irrelevant for him. I am proud of being an Indian. I am part of the indivisible unity that is Indian nationality. I am indispensable to this noble edifice and without me this splendid structure of India is incomplete" he observed in 1940.[46]

Azad criticized by fanatic Muslim like Maulana Maudoodi on one hand and by the leader of the Muslim League on the other. Maduoodi is critical because he believed Muslim themselves should form a party guided by the Quran. He therefore described Azad's advice to the people to join the Congress as suicidal.[47]

But what Maduoodi really resents is Azad's abandonment of revivalism and romanticism. Azad however, would never have taken such a retrograde step. The League whose approach was fanatical and unreal criticized Azad as enemy of the Muslim interest in India. Despite the criticism unlike Sir Syed he was completely successful in erecting the edifice of progressive and modern religion and political philosophy.

In short, we see that there have been two predominant reformists trend so far. The first trend was to purge Islam of all later accretions and restore its pristine purity. The emphasis in this was of course, in rigorously enforcing Islamic Shariat. The masses of course, were steeped in local traditions and could hardly appreciate this puritan zeal. It was more so as the reformists of this variety never stressed the Central Islamic vision of a just and egalitarian society. On the contrary, they tended to support the statuesque. The masses were, thus more attracted by the Sufi saints who not only respected local traditions making them integral part of Islam but also remained aloof from the ruling classes who exploited the masses. Their monasteries also provided an escape from the harsh realities of life.

Secondly, the trend from modern reform is of recent origin. It was led by those who had reaped the benefits of modern education and for who bread was no longer a problem. Their liberal reinterpretation of religion served their own class interests and had hardly any appeal of the masses. Without through economic transformation it is not possible to overcome social backwardness and for them a mutant religious orthodoxy of native variety would continue to have great appeal. Modernism for them is a symbol of western licentiousness leading to corruption of morals and hence unacceptable.

Indian Muslims are extremely poor and backward. Any reform of reinterpretation of Islam would have to keep this face in mind. In other words social justice (*adl*) will have reemphasized as constituting the central vision of Islam. The concept of private property as developed during the medieval ages will have to be redefined in keeping with the earliest phase of Islam preferably the Meccan phase. Islam did not throw the gauntlet to the powerful vested interests and fought against them. Khalifa Umar in his later phase and Khalifa Ali throughout his life fought intensely for bringing about just distribution of wealth in the society and laid down their lives at the altar of social justice. For them Islam did not mean prayer and fasting only; above all it was a serious project to establish social justice. Umar refused to allow private property in land and Ali so rigorously enforced equal distribution of *baitul-mal* (state treasury) that his own close comrades deserted him on this issue as they expected special favours.

It is very clear from the early history of Islam that revelation was not meant for sanctifying the existing conditions but for changing them for the better, for realizing social justice and establishing equality. Thus continuous improvement of social conditions with the availability of technology, just relations of product which would result in equitable distribution of social wealth and progress become integral part of revelation.[48] A new revolutionary theology must be developed on these lines if Islam is not to be confined to a set of ritual and hair-splitting and barren exercises on the lives of the medieval Muslim jurists. Moral health and social justice, and not the personal law were goal of the Islam.

Indian Muslims and Reform Movement in Post-independence India

Partition was great tragedy for Indian Muslims for several reasons. It not only divided their families but it also caused migration of cream of their society to Pakistan, especially from U.P. (Uttar Pradesh). Thus the Muslims almost lost their middle class intelligentsia to Pakistan leaving behind poor and illiterate Muslims completely under the influence of conservative theologies. The Muslims of India have still not recovered from this tragedy. To create new intelligentsia and a strong middle class will take quite some time.

India opted to be a secular country and this decision had several repercussions. Right at the stage of constitution making there were debates about uniform civil code. There were heated discussions. Muslim members opposed adoption of uniform civil code. Ultimately, a compromised was accepted. It was decided to put it under Directive Principles of the Constitution and in the mean while the personal laws of all communities will apply. This was done at the intervention of Jawahar Lal Nehru and other leaders. They had assured the Muslims and the leader of Jamiat-ul-Ulama-i-Hind that they need have no apprehensions about freedom of religion in India. They will be free to follow their religion and its laws.

In mid-sixties a Lohiaite socialist[49] from Maharashtra Hamid Dalvai launched a campaign for enforcement of uniform civil code.[50] He also declared himself to be a non-believer and also maintained that Muslims are basically fanatics and rigid and would never change. Such extreme positions on the part of Hamid Dalvai did great disservice for the cause of reforms. His campaign was totally misconceived and helped the conservatives to adopt more rigid position. They launched a counter-campaign and convinced Muslims that there was a 'conspiracy' to destroy Islam. It was in response to Mr. Dalvai's campaign for uniform civil code that the Muslim Law Board was formed in the mid-sixties which became a bulwark against any change or reform in Muslim personal law.

It is important to note here that any movement for reforms, if it has to succeed, should be firstly within the frame-work of religious scripture, and secondly, the reformer should be persuasive and use proper strategies to convince his fellow-religionists. Raja Ram Mohan Roy, for example was great scholar of Hindu religion and quoted from Vedas to prove that there was no concept of Sati[51] in it and that is should be discontinued in order to uphold original teachings of Hinduism. Sir Syed, Maulvi Mumtaz Ali Khan, Maulvi Khuda Baksh and others to their ilk, also adopted similar strategies. They wanted to bring reforms within the framework of Islam. However, Hamid Dalvai, being a non-believer, completely disregarded religious sensibilities of Muslims and mounted an attack on Islamic laws. It became totally counterproductive and rigidified positions. Any movement for genuine reform in Muslim Personal Law became more problematic. In such an atmosphere even a scholar of Islam and a legalist like A.A.A. Fyzee found it difficult to argue for reforms.

Pakistan went ahead with the necessary reforms in Muslim personal law. (President) Ayub Khan appointed a committee to recommend reforms which consisted both of modernists and the 'Ulama'. The committee recommended necessary reforms after taking opinion of people through questionnaire and Ayub Khan implemented them through a presidential ordinance in 1962 ignoring a dissenting note by one of the 'Ulamas'. Even (President) Zia-ul-Haq could not dispel this ordinance during his hey days of fundamentalism.

This became possible in Pakistan as it had a strong middle class to advocate reforms and also Muslims were in overwhelming majority and there the theory of conspiracy against Islam could not work. In all Muslim countries from Indonesia to Algeria reforms have been affected. The Qur'anic laws are quite favourable and empowering for women but since medieval ages theses Qur'anic injunctions have been interpreted in a way to perpetuate male domination. For this purpose even some controversial *hadith*(Sayings of the Prophet) were used superseding the Qur'an. Thus proper interpretation of these Qur'anic provisions can greatly help in giving women their much needed rights. And this is precisely what has been done in most of the Muslim countries.

In India increasing communalization of politics made it even more difficult to usher in reforms in Muslim society. The communalization reached its peak during the eighties when series of major communal riots took place making Muslims more and more insecure. It was during this period that the controversial Supreme Court judgment on maintenance was delivered popularly known as the Shah Bano Judgment.

The members of Muslim personal law board and other Muslim leaders reacted sharply against this judgment and launched a massive movement against it. Unfortunately, one of the more otherwise sober Muslim leader and president of Muslim Personal Law Board even likened this movement to the Khilafat Movement[52] during early twenties. The Shah Bano movement was a great mistake. Such an aggressive attitude towards a reformative measure was not called for. It only hardened the majority communalism and cause greater harm to Muslim.

The Shah Bano movement dashed all hopes for reform in Muslim personal law. Perhaps the Supreme Court judgment came at a wrong time. By mid-eighties the Muslims were feeling intensely insecure due to major communal riots at Moradabad (1980), Biha rsharif (1981), Baroda and Meerut (1982), Neili, Assam (1983), Bhivandi-Mumbai (1984) and Ahmedabad (1985). The opportunist leaders exploited this intense feeling of insecurity among Muslims to oppose the Supreme Court judgment. It was certainly not against the Qur'anic spirit though delivered under the provision of a secular law.

Supreme Court of India again banned triple *talaq*(divorce) and delivered a huge verdict on triple, calling the practice unconstitutional and in violation of Art14 of the Indian Constitution which provides the equity before law. Three out of five judges on the panel concurred that the practice of triple talaq unconstitutional. The remaining two declared it to be constitutional while simultaneously asking the government to ban the practice by enacting a law.

Metamorphose into a convenient stick in the hands of majoritarian force to beat the Muslims with. It was politicized to the extent that it became a topic of heated debate during the UP elections in September 2018 as a huge step towards "empowering Muslim Women". A sentence of three years be can be awarded to those who indulge in instant triple talaq – the offence last problem facing Muslim women. Prime Minister Narendra Modi expressed his concern about the plight of Muslim women who needed emancipation. He said it is his government's responsibility to give Muslim women justice by enacting a law. Hence his government formulated Bill- 'The Muslim Women (Protection of Rights of Marriage Bill 2017) to criminalize the practice of *intant talaq.* But that could not be passed in Parliament in August 2018. After that the government approved an ordinance making triple talaq a punishable offence is non –bail able i.e.only a magistrate and not the police can grant bail. Bail can be granted only after hearing the wife. Maintenance and allowance to the wife is decided by the magistrate.

To replace the ordinance again the Muslim Women (Protection of Rights on Marriage) Bill 2018 was introduced in Lok Sabha during winter session and passed but could not get approval of Rajya Sabha till the end of 9th February, 2019.

Again Jamat-e-Islami-Hind and other Muslim orthodox organization called it an Interference in the personal laws of the community and had declared to oppose it while Bharti Muslim Mahila Andolan(BMMA)and other Muslim women organizations had welcomed it but they demanded that discriminatory practices like '*halala'*, '*muta marriage* 'underage marriage and polygamy must had also be addressed in the Bill. All these issues are linked to triple talaq. The Jammate Islami too has its women's wing. The Jammat women came out on the street to oppose the Bill. The fundamentalists set women against women. It is heartening that more and more women's group are coming over those women who are immersed in traditions and thus have internalized and willingly accepted coercive measures imposed on them by male dominated society. The women activists while working among them, should not ingnore their religious sensibilities, if they want to win them to their side rather than alienate them.

Conclusion

Reforms cannot be postponed for long. The provision for triple divorce must go and polygamy should be either abolished or severely restricted. It should also be noted that in every society contradictory trends of orthodoxy and religious reforms exist. Which trend will have upper hand will depend on balance of social forces. The balance of forces can be tilted in favour of reforms if there is will. Islam never emphasized individual salvation, it is serious project for social change for the better and that is what the prophet did and earned the wrath of powerful vested interest.

References

1. Asghar Ali Engineer, Reform movements in Indian Islam – A dissenting perspective, *Bohra Chronicle,* June 2017.
2. Ibid.
3. Atindranath Bose, *The Cultural Heritage of India,* Vol. I, pp.460-462.
4. The Wahabis in India were directly inspired and guided more by the teachings of Shah Waliullah than by those of Mohammed bin Abdul Wahab of Najaf. The

Wahabi movement was a call for restoration of the condition of life as obtained during the time of the prophet. They were 'anabaptist in faith' and 'republicans' in politics.

5. Shah Waliullah, *Hujjat-ullah-il-Baligha* (The Profound Evidence of Allah), Vol.1, P.130, Sheikh Gulam Ali & Sons, Lahore.
6. Mojn Shakir, 'Secular Trends in Contemporary Muslim Thought', in B.N. Pande (Ed.), *National Integration,* Secular Democratic Forum, Allahabad, 1970, P.75.
7. Moin Shakir, *Khilafat to Partition,* Kalamkar Prakashan, New Delhi, 1970, P.18.
8. Begum Naz, *Sir Syed Ahmad Khan,* National Book Foundation, 1922, P.24.
9. Ibid, P.25.
10. Supara Note 5; P.70.
11. Supara Note 6; P.26.
12. Ibid, P.28.
13. W.C. Smith, *Modern Islam in India,* 1943, pp.8-9.
14. Sir Syed, *Muqalaate-e-Sir Syed,* Vol.1, edited by Sheikh Mohammed Ismile, pp.75-81.
15. Ameer Ali, *Spirit of Islam,* P.172.
16. Ibid, P.476.
17. Ibid, P.230.
18. Ibid, P.233.
19. Ibid, P.243.
20. Chiragh Ali, *The Proposed Reforms,* P.XXXVI.
21. Ibid, P.ii.
22. Ibid, P.XXXV.
23. Aziz Ahmed, *Islamic Modernism in India and Pakistanm,* pp.59-60.
24. Chirag Ali, Op. Cit, P.11.
25. Ibid, pp.10-11.
26. Khuda Baksh, *Islamic Civilization,* Vol.11, P.75.
27. Ibid, P.220.
28. Ibid, P.284.
29. Ibid, Vol.11, P.105.
30. Aga Khan, *The Memories of Aga Khan,* P.332.
31. M. Dumasia, *The Aga Khan and his Ancestors,* P.94.
32. S.M. Haram, *Aab-i-Kausar,* P.75.
33. Azad, *India Wins Freedom,* Asia Publishing House, Bombay, 1960, P.3.
34. A.R. Malihabadi, *Azad ki kahani khud unki zabani*, P.30.
35. Ibid, P.383.
36. Ibid, P.405.
37. Moin Shabir, Op. Cit., P.140.
38. Azad, *Al Balagh,* 14, 21, 28 January, 1916, Vol.1, P.125.
39. Abu Salman Al Hindi, *Imanul Hind (Tameere-e-Afkar)*, P.213.

40. Azad, *Nigarishat-e-Azad*, P.10.
41. Azad, *Tarjumanul Quran* (Ed.) by S.A. Latif, Vol.1, P.4.
42. Mahadeo Desai, *Maulana Azad,* pp.70-71.
43. Ibid, P.73.
44. Qazi Abdul Ghaffar, *Asar-e-Abul Kalam Azad,* P.282.
45. Speeches of Maulana Azad, 21st Dec., 1947, P.21.
46. Quoted by Abdullah Butt, *Abul Kalam Azad,* P.34.
47. Abul Ata Maudoodi: *Musalman Aur Maujuda Siyasi Kashmakash,* Vol.1, P.40.
48. Asghar Ali Engineer, Op. Cit., P.11.
49. Refers to socialist ideas associated with the Indian nationalist Ram Manohar Lohia.
50. In this context, he refers to a uniform code of laws that would be applicable to all Indian citizens irrespective of their religious application.
51. *Sati*, a practice associated with the self-immolation of a widow of her husband's funeral pyre, was campaigned against by social reformers in the 19th century and banned by the British. Hindu fundamentalist groups are now trying to reinstate the practice in India in the name of tradition.
52. The Khilafat movement was a mass social movement launched by Indian nationalists to contest the removal by the British of Caliph in Turkey. This local movement, directed against the British was conducted in the name of international solidarity.

Chapter - 3

Dawoodi Bohras: Religion, Spirituality, Literature, Social Customs and Traditions

The Bohras[1] are converted from Hinduism to the *Shi'ahIsma'ili* sect of Islam. The Conversion took place mainly in the twelfth century A.D. in Gujarat in India. The converted were mainly from the Hindu middle and upper castes and mainly from the castes engaged in trade and commerce. The conversion was mainly result of the work of some Arab missionaries from Egypt and Yemen.[2] Also later on the indigenous converts undertook the missionary activities in other contiguous regions like the areas that today constitute Rajasthan, Madhya Pradesh and Maharashtra. Thus today the Bohras in India mainly live in these areas and number around 10 lakhs. They are mainly engaged in small trade though now a newly educated professional class is also coming into existence.

Religion and Religious Beliefs

The Bohras who later split into number of sub sects like the Jafariyas, Dawoodis, Sulemanis, Alavis, etc. are mainly Isma'ili branch of the Shi'ah Muslims. Like all other Muslims they believe in *tawhid*(i.e. oneness or unity of God), *risalah* (i.e. the prophethood) and accept Muhammad (PBUH) as the last Prophet of God. They accept the holy Qur'an as the revealed word of Allah and all their beliefs, like those of other Muslims, is based primarily on it. Thus far, they have everything in common with other Muslims.

However, like other Shi'ah Muslims, they believe that the Prophet's son-in-law 'Ali was both spiritual as well as temporal successor of the holy Prophet and that the Prophet himself nominated him, under direct injunction from Allah, as his spiritual successor. That it was an ordinance from Allah to appoint 'Ali as his successor, the Isma'ilis invoke the Qur'anic verse 5:67. The verse says, "O Messenger, deliver that which has been revealed to thee from thy Lord; and if thou do (it) not, thou hast not delivered His message. And Allah will protect thee from people. Surely, Allah guides not the disbelieving people."

The other Muslims popularly known as Sunni Muslims interpret this verse very differently. For example, Imam Raghib, the noted lexicographer of the Qur'an, says referring to the meaning of *ismah* (i.e. protection). "The *ismat or protection,* of the prophets is God's protection of them, in the first place, by characterizing them with purity of essence (i.e. creating them pure from every sin in their very nature), then by granting them bodily as well as spiritual excellence, then by granting them help and keeping them firm (in trials), thereby sending down tranquility upon them and by protection of their hearts (against evil)". In *Ruhulma'ani* by Saiyyid Mahmud al-Alusi, also we find similar explanation that their protection means their *protection from sins* from among all people.[3]

However, the Isma'ilis insists on the hidden meaning of this verse and maintains that through this verseAllah required His Messenger to convey to the believers the message that Allah desires 'Ali to be appointed as the heir and successor to the Prophet and that on conveying this message if a section of the people (*nass*) oppose you out of their jealousy or ambition, then Allah will protect you against them. The Shi'ahs and the Isma'ilis maintain that the holy Prophet was worried that if he nominates 'Ali as his successor, some of his close companions who aspire to become his political successor, would vigorously oppose him and he, for this reason, was hesitating to declare 'Ali as his *wasi* (i.e. legatee). After his verse was revealed, the Shi'ahs maintain the holy Prophet gathered all Muslims while returning from the last pilgrimage (*Hajjah al-wada*) at a place called Ghadir al-Khum and raised 'Ali until his armpit was revealed, and he said "Ali is the *mawlah* (master) of those whose *mawlah* I am" and then he prayed to Allah that Thou love those who love 'Ali and Thou consider Thine enemy those who consider 'Ali their enemy.

The Sunni Muslims also vouch for the authenticity of this hadith but conclude that the Messenger of Allah (PBUH) appointed 'Ali as his spiritual successor, not a temporal one. These differences between the followers of the Prophet led to the first major schism in Islam. Muslims now split on this question of successor ships to the Prophet into two sects *i.e.,* the Sunnis and the Shi'ahs. The Sunni Muslims adopted the concept of *Khilafah*(i.e. elected temporal successor ship to the Prophet) and the Shi'ah Muslims evolved the doctrine of *Imamah* i.e. spiritual and temporal leadership after the Prophet. The Isma'ilis, who branched off from the Shi'iah Islam, stressed the concept of *wasayah* (i.e.legatee) of 'Ali in addition to the doctrine of *Imamah*. The Shi'ahs though accept the concept of *was ayah* consider the institution of *Imamah* as primary. The Isma'ilis, on the other hand, considers *was ayah* and *Imamah*as two separate categories. 'Ali according to the Shi'ah Muslims is the first Imam in the chain of twelve imams (hence they are called twelvershi'aha) and according to the Isma'ilis 'Ali was *wasi* and not imam. According to them Hasan, the elder son of 'Ali, wasthe first imam in the chain of Imams.

The major split between the Shi'ahs and Isma'ilis took place in the second century of Islam on the question of successor ship to Imam Jafar-al-Sadiq (who was 6th Imam according to the Shi'ahs and 5th according to the Isma'ilis). The Twelver Shi'ahs (known as Ithna 'AshariShi'ahs) accepted Jafar-al-Sadiq's younger son Musa Kazim as the next Imam while the Isma'ilis accepted his elder son Isma'il (IthnaAsharis believe that Ismail died in the life time of Imam Jafar-al-Sadiq. However, Ismailis believe that to protect him from persecution, his father Jafar-al-Sadiq sent into hiding and people assumed him dead. He was reportedly seen by eyewitnesses after his alleged death) as the next i.e. sixth Imam. In both cases i.e. succession to the Prophet Muhammad (PBUH) and to Imam Jafar-al-Sadiq, though the dispute was of succession, it resulted in development of very different theologies. Though there is much common between the twelver Shi'ahs and the Isma'ilis, their theological differences are no less significant. Both the IthnaAshari and the Isma'ilis, their theologies developed along very different lines. However, as both were the persecuted minority sects in the world of Islam, their mutual relationship, unlike between the Sunnis and the Shi'ahs, never became conflictual and antagonistic. The common bond with the family of the Prophet *ahl-al-bayt* was so strong that the differences on the question of successor ship to Imam Jafar-al-Sadiq remained secondary.

Despite these differences on the question of succession either the holy Prophet or to that of Imam Sadiq, the fundamental beliefs in a *tawhid, risalah*, finality of prophet hood etc. remained common. There never was any compromise on these beliefs. Not only this, the ritual system i.e. prayer (salah), fasting (saum), charity (zakah), pilgrimage (hajj) and Jihad also is common. However, the Ithna'Asharis add *walayah* (love of 'Ali and family of Prophet) to these five pillars (*da'a'im*) of Islam and the Isma'ilis further add *taharah* (which implies both bodily and spiritual cleanliness). Thus according to the Sunni Islam there are five pillars of Islam while according to the Isma'ilis (of whose the Bohras are an Indian offshoot), there are seven pillars of Islam. It is after these pillars that the principal book of

Isma'ilis jurisprudence is known as *Da'imal-Islam.*[4] This book is the most fundamental to the Bohras as far their religion, their beliefs and their spiritual practices are concerned. This book is also the principal source of Isma'ili hadith literature. By their ritual practices or spiritual practices of the Isma'ilis in general, and the Bohras, in particular, this book has great significance. The importance of this book can be gauged from the fact that Iran has incorporated Daim-ul-Islam into their constitution. This book was written by a great Isma'ili *Da'i* (a missionary, a summoner to the faith) Saiyyidna Qadi-al-Nu'man(This book took 30 years to complete and was checked and approved by 14thIsmaili Imam Al-Mu'iz li-Din Allah).We will speak more about the office of *Da'i* little later. However, it is important to note here that the Qadi was one of the intellectual giants of the Isma'ili stream of Islam. He was a jurist, a theoretician, a theologian, a historian and a judge. He was the chief Qadi of the Fatimid rulers (the Isma'ilis Imams who ruled over Egypt from 3rd to 6th century. Hijrajh belongs to the progeny of Fatimah, the daughter of the Prophet and hence were known as Fatimids). He also wrote a book on the hidden meaning of the pillars of Islam, which is known as *Ta'wil al-Da'a'-im-al-Islam* in which he explains away the hidden meaning or the real meaning of various Islamic rituals like the walayah(love), taharah (cleanliness), prayer, fasting, hajj, zakah and jihad. It is very important to study this book to understand the real significance of the spiritual practices of the Bohra Muslims.

Before we throw light on the Bohra spiritualism it is important to note that the Bohras, particularly the Dawoodi Bohras, are a very closely-knit community tightly controlled by the high priest (*Da'i*) and are both highly Islamised in their religious practices and highly Indianised in their cultural practices and ethos. The ordinary Bohra is highly conscious of his separate priesthood. The priesthood makes every effort, not only to keep tight spiritual and secular control over the community but also keep it separate from the Islamic mainstream. Syedna Burhanuddin has gone to another extreme in cutting the Bohras off from not only Sunni but also from the Shi'ah Muslims. Any contact with other Muslims, the high priest thinks, will loosen his control over the community.Such isolation helps in keeping Bohras blind followers and makes them ignorant about the real religious concepts of Islam.

The Bohra Religion and Spiritualism

We have briefly discussed above the main features of the Isma'ili religion. We would now discuss the sources of its spirituality. The Dawoodi Bohras are highly religious people. They adhere to their religious practices and are highly pious. However, there are some peculiar characteristics of Bohra faith which mark them out from other mainstream Muslims. It is necessary to understand these characteristics in order to understand the sources of spiritualism of the Isma'ili Shi'ahs. All Shi'ah Muslims in general believe in *Tawil* (i.e. hidden meaning of the Qur'anic verses). That the Qur'anic verses have hidden/original meaning the Shi'ahs deduce from the Qur'anic verse 3:7 which is as under: "He it is who revealed the Book to thee; some of its verses are decisive – they are the basis of the book – and others are allegorical. Then those in whose hearts is perversity follow the part of it which is allegorical, seeking to mislead, and seeking to give it (their own) interpretation. *And none known its interpretation save Allah, and those firmly rooted in knowledge...*"

The words *al-rasikhun fi al-ilm* (those firmly rooted in knowledge) who knows *t'awil* besides Allah is, according to the Shi'ahs, the imams in the progeny of 'Ali and Fatimah. The Isma'ilis, a sect to which the Bohras belong, particularly attach great importance to the doctrine of *t'awil* and they see hidden meaning to each and every verse of the Qur'an. This original or hidden meaning is known only to 'Ali and Imams in his progeny. They are *al-Rasikhun fi al-ilm*. They can teach this knowledge to a selected few from amongst the believers. True spiritualism, as far as the Bohras are concerned, lie in the initiation into this hidden knowledge *m'arifah* coupled without m'arifah is a futile exercise, devoid of meaning and spirit. The Isma'ilis lay great stress on t'awil and m'arifah. It is the core, the gourd, while Shi'ahs by itself is a mere shell, a manifestation. They also distinguish between a Muslim and a m'umin" the former is one who outwardly professes Islam without being aware of its real significance while the latter is one who is true believer, who is aware of real meaning and spirit of religion and also has m'arifah (knowledge) of the significance of various *hudud* (i.e. the right place of every religious office in the divine hierarchy).

The concept of *hudud* – the divine hierarchy is the core concept of the Isma'ilis. It is maintained that one who dies without the *m'arifah* of *hudud* (the hierarchy) lives in vain. Allah will not accept from him/her whatever he/she did in practicing the injunctions of shari'ah.

It is interesting to throw some light on the concept of hudud as evolved by the Isma'ilis. According to the Isma'ilis the first who was created by Allah was *uqul* (i.e. intellects). Then the first one to accept *uluhiyyah* (Divine Existence) was designated as *aql-i-awwal* (i.e. the first intellect), then second one to accept as 'aql-i-thani' (second intellect) and then *sab'ah-al-'uqul* (seven intellects). The last intellect to accept Divinity was designated as *aql-i-ashir* (tenth intellect), also known as *ashir-e-mudabbir* i.e. the tenth intellect who manages this universe.

It is very important in the Isma'ili theology to assign every authority *hudud* its rightful place in the hierarchy. One who exceeds ones limit, is a rebel and it is a cardinal sin. Real *shirk* (in the Qur'anic terminology associating partners with Allah and it is cardinal sin) is associating one had with another thus transgressing is rightful place. It is the duty of a *mu'min*(i.e. true believer) to have proper *ma'rifah* of these *hudud* and not to transgress their respective position in the hierarchy. It is this *ma'rifah* which is real source of spiritual life in this world.[5]

The Isma'ilis have also evolved a doctrine of what is called *mathal* and *mamthul* i.e. theresemble and one who is its counterpart in this world. For the intellects in the other world i.e. hierarchy in the spiritual world is replicated in our own physical world. The holy Prophet is at the apex of this hierarchy, followed by his *wasi* (legatee) 'Ali who is succeeded by Imam. As the Prophet is the seal of all Prophets after him, and hence no *wasi* after 'Ali, the hierarchy after 'Ali is headed by an Imam from his progeny. Thus the hierarchy (*darajat*) of *hudud* in this physical world is as under: The Prophet-*Wasi*-Imam and in the absence of the Prophet and *Wasi*Imam will be the *mamthul* (representative) of *'ashir-e-mudabbir'* or the Tenth Intellect on this earth.

The Isma'ilis evolved another hierarchy after the holy Prophet and *Wasi* were no more among the people. As pointed out the Imam will head this hierarchy and will have *Da'i* (a summoner to the faith), *Ma'dhun* (one who is permitted to run the mission under the supervision of *Da'i*) and *Mukathir* (one who assists the *Ma'dhun* by entering into religious polemics with non-Isma'ilis and convinces them of the truth of the Isma'ili doctrines). The Mukathir is in turn assisted by number of *masha'ikh*(religious preachers). And, during the period of seclusion of Imam (called daur al-satr) it is *Da'i* who heads the hierarchy. The current period is a period of seclusion for Ismaili – Musta'ali-Taiyab Bohras (but not for the followers of Aga Khan who is a living Imam).The present hierarchy of Da'wah-al-Hadiyah (i.e. rightly guiding mission) is headed by *Da'i*. The Bohras believe that the twenty first Imam, Imam Taiyyib, went into seclusion after his father and twentieth Imam was assassinated and that Imamah continues in his progeny and one day the Imam on earth will appear when suitable conditions prevail. But until then the D'awah al-Hadiyah or also known as the Fatimi Da'wah will be headed by *Da'i*. The present *Da'i* is the fifty third[6] in succession and this chain of *Da'i* will continue until Imam himself appears to set things right on this earth.

The last Imam will be known as Qa'im al-Qiyamah i.e. one who will set up the Day of Judgment and with him the daur-al-kashf (i.e. the period of revelation) will begin. In this period all believers will be truly appear spiritual persons and would be perfect in spiritual practices (*murtad*). These spirituality perfect persons will need not outward control of Shari'ah and hence shari'ah for them will no more be obligatory. In the Isma'ili theology, shari'ah is called *siyasat al-nasf* i.e. a device to control one's self and one's desire and once one achieves self-control through spiritual practices, one does not need such outward control and in daur al-kashf everyone will achieve this much desired control through spiritual perfection, this outward control *takalif-e-shari'ah* will be no more obligatory. But until the onset of daur al-kashf, the shari'ah practices will remain obligatory.

Another important aspect of the Isma'ili or Bohra spirituality is absolute obedience to the *hudud* (religious hierarchy). Thus a Bohra can perfect his/her spirituality only if the totally submits himself/herself to the authority of the Prophet, *Wasi*, Imam and *Da'i*. Any transgression is strongly disapproved of the seriously interferes with spiritual perfection. Sayyadi Sadiq Ali[7] a nineteenth century Dawoodi Bohra poet, has laid great emphasis on m'arifah i.e. knowledge of, and obedience to, the *hudud* in his poetry called *nasihat* (i.e. Advice). No spiritual perfection is possible, according to him, without inculcating, these qualities in oneself. Mere observance of Shari'ah practices will not lead to true spiritual perfection, according to him.

Bohra doctrine requires an oath to be sworn, promising fealty and obedience to the Imam and *Da'i*, and an undertaking to conform to the belief and practice outlined in it, by anyone who would be a *mumin* – each Bohra child upon attaining puberty, any non-Bohra adult wishing to convert and any dissident wishing to be received back into the fold. This is the *mithaq* (covenant), also known by its synonyms *bay'at* (pledge of allegiance), and *'ahd'* or *'ahd-al-awliya'* (commitment or pledge of (God's) elect). The Bohra believe this practice dates back through the ages to the first Imam who took the *mithaq* to those who accepted his *daw'at*, and that the *mithaq* was administered by all the earlier prophets, by Muhammad, 'Ali', the Imams and the *Da'is* to their adherent. The text of the *mithaq* forms the blueprint for Bohra belief, delineating the key elements of Bohra ideology and practice.[8] The introductory section of the text emphasizes that the oath can only be administered if the initiate accepts the covenant willingly and without coercion; if doubts exist, commitment should be postponed until such time as certainly is achieved. In the *mithaq* ceremony, the *Da'i* or his representative reads the text, outlining the conditions for becoming a Bohra, and the initiate responds by saying *na'am* (Arabic 'yes',

I swear an oath to the effect than I accept these conditions). Engagement in the *mithaq* constitutes formal acceptance of the doctrines[9] of the *da'wat* and the authority of the Imam and *Da'i*.

The present *Da'i* and his predecessor have used *mithaq* to claim absolute authority over their followers. It was for this reason that the plaintiffs in the Burhanpur Dargah case challenged the very text of the *mithaq* being used by the *Da'i*. They claimed that the extent text had been tampered with by the fifty-first *Da'i* and to prove their contention they produced the original text of *mithaq* from the *Tufat al-Qulub*, compiled by the third *Da'i*mutlaq Syedna Hatim around A.H. 560. The book is accepted as the most authentic by all the Bohras. The text of *mithaq* recorded in *Tuhfat al-Qulub*and whose translation was produced in the court is as follows:

1. Then he (the Dai) should begin with praising and adoring God, with praying God for blessinghis Prophet and the pure Imams in taking from him the vow of allegiance to God, to his angles, to his Prophets, to the Wasis and Imams and that of the Imam of his own time. May God bless all of them, and the oath of faithfulness to him (i.e. Imam) according to what is prescribed for him in the book of covenant and (he should take vow) that he will believe in God, his angles, his apostles and their Imams, from *Wasi* to the present Imam that he will perform the devotion outwardly and inwardly, that he will assist the Imam of his time, and will not turn disloyal to him and that he will not divulge anything of the secrets of the Deep to him who does not deserve and also to him who has not taken the covenant, that he will not be dishonest to anyone of the Momin (faithful) who are with him in the covenant that he will love him who loves the Imam, and will be hostile to him who is hostile to the Imams, that he will sever his connection from their enemies, that he will show sincerity to God and his favourites (i.e. Imam), and that if he will break the covenant then the same thing will be imposed upon the breakers of the oath. *He* (*the Dai*) should call them towards the Imam of their time, ascribe the knowledge to him (i.e. Imam)and should not attribute a single letter of that to himself (i.e. Dai), (vide the book of exhibits in the Privy Council on Appeal from the High Court of Judgment at Nagpur pp.833, part I)
2. The whole emphasis in this text of *mithaq* given in *Tuhfat al-Qulub* is on the authority of the Imam. It is very clearly stated that the end of this text that, "He (the Dai) should call them towards the Imam of their time, ascribe the knowledge to him (*i.e.* Imam),

and should not attribute a single letter of that to himself (*i.e.* Dai)". But the text which is used by the *Da'i* or his authorized agents does not conform to Syedna Hatim b. Ibrahim's text and gives more credit and authority to the *Da'i*. In this text *Da'i* is mentioned alongside the Imam. Thus it is stated:

(1) And if the Imam of the time or his *Dai* calls upon you to war against the enemy then you should make war. You should help with your life and property. And you should obey the *Imam* of the time or his *Dai* sincerely. Say yes.

(2) And whatever the *Imam* of the time or his *Dai* orders you to obey you should obey the *Dai* and you shall not become a sinner (by disobedience); and you shall not become hostile to the *Dai*. You shall not lay claim to the *Daiship*. You shall back up the *Dai* as true and you shall not falsify the *Daee*.

(3) And you shall accept the order of the *Dai* of *Imam* in all things. And you shall not use those things which the *Dai* shall forbid you, and you shall not take steps (towards it). *You shall love him whom the Dai loves. You shall be enemy to him whom the Dai is hostile. You shall war against him against whom the Dai makes war. Any person transgressing those engagements to the Dai he is outside the pale of religion, whether he be great or small, whether he is a close relation or a distant one. You shall not have any intercourse with him. You shall not correspond with him openly or secretly. You shall not do any act calculated to be friendly to him. And by no manner or means or pretence you shall see the enemy of the Dai. The enemy of the Dai is your enemy. Say yes.'*[10]

Thus we see that the whole text as it was compiled by the third *da'imutlaq* Syedna Hatim bin Ibrahim has been tampered with and his clear instruction that the *Da'i* should not ascribe anything to himself fragrantly violated. The fifty-first *Da'I* Syedna Tahir Saifuddin had to admit it in the court of law in the above case. It appears that due to the challenge of the reformists *mithaq* has been transformed into something which it really not intended to be. This change in its character, however, cannot be supported by the earlier religious tradition as it has operated for the past several centuries. In the new *mithaq* the *Da'i* has been given the pre-eminence which he did not earlier enjoy. The *mithaq* in its present form is worse than charter of slavery. Bohras are made to believe that the Dai is the owner of their mind, body, soul and properties (including mosques). All this has an important bearing on the reformist movement as we shall see later.

The Taxes and the Tithes

A Dawoodi Bohra today has to pay a number of compulsory levies. These levies are collected with regularity. They include (1) *Zakat,* (2) *Sila*(3) *Fitra* (4) *Nazarmuqam* (5)*Haqqun-nafs* (6) *Khums* and (7) *Salam* i.e. personal offering to Syedna. Of these the first, third and sixth have Islamic sanction. Zakat has been prescribed at the rate of two and a half per cent by the Muslim *ulama* (The holy Qur'an prescribes *zakat* but not its rate). The grand jurist of the Fatimids Syedna Qadi an-N'uman has also prescribed the same rate in his *Daim-al-Islam. Fitra* is also according to the Islamic *Shari'as* and is to be given to the poor and needy on Id-al-Fitr (the Ramadan Id). It is to be given on behalf of all the members of one's family. *Silat-al-Imam* or simply *sila* is a much later invention and neither it is obligatory according to the Islamic *Sharia'as* nor has it been mentioned even in the *Da'im-al-Islam.* But *sila* is also being collected as a compulsory levy ostensibly as an offering for the hidden *Imam.*

Nazar Muqam is actually vow-money. Usually intimes of trouble the Bohras take a vow to spare a particular amount as vow money if their difficulty is solved. This amount is collected by the priesthood from such families. Usually every Bohra family spares some amount by way of *Nazar Muqam* ever year. *Khums* literally means one-fifth and is levied, according to the Islamic *shari'as* on war-booty, mined ores to other metals, unexpected gains like hidden treasures, etc. However, the Bohra priesthood levies *khums* arbitrarily, especially on businessmen. Lastly *Hqqun-nafs* is a later invention and is levied on the relatives of the deceased. It could be anything from 119 four anna coins to 119 guineas depending on the status of the deceased. Haqqun-nafs has not been prescribed by *shari'a.* In 1920 the author of Gulzare-Dawoodi had estimated the income of the fifty-first *da'i* from all these sources as around Rs. 11 lacs. He writes: "Thus the average annual income of the Head Priest is not less than Rupees 11 lacs a year (In a footnote the author has given the details of income under different heads). During the last 4 years of war, when the Bohra merchants earned exceptionally big sums in profiteering business, Syedna had also an increased share in his income.[11] Currently it is very difficult to estimate the income of Syedna and his family as no accounts are declared (in fact,the question of accountability is one of the important points in the reformist agitation as we shall see later). The collection of these levies and tithes has been centralized and no one has access to these registers except perhaps, the members of Syedna's own family. However, a reformist leader Late Noman L. Contractor had prepared a rough estimate of Syedna's income at that time (much before his own death) through various sources. According to this estimate the priestly family gets the following amounts *Sila -Fitra* from India and abroad Rs.630,00,00, *NazarMuqam* Rs.80,00,000 from India and the same amount from abroad, personal *salaam* to Syedna about Rs.41,20,000 from India as well as abroad, *Zakat* Rs.448,00,000 from India and abroad. *Haqqun-Nafs* figures not given, *Salaam* offered to Syedna at the time of meeting him in person Rs.20, 77,000 and Rs.3, 00,000 as *salaam* on the occasion of Diwali while writing Bismillah on the account book. In addition to this is *NazarMuqam* from the poorer families, amounting to about Rs.8, 00,000. This entire works out to about Rs.743, 93,000 per year. Also, there are cash boxes kept at various mausoleums in India which yield around Rs.1.80 crores and similarly about Rs.1.30 crores from abroad. All this works out to around Rs.11,43,93,000 per annum.[12] However, these figures seem to be little exaggerated as the population base assumed is around 1,60,000 families in India and 40,000 families aboard. But the Dawoodi Bohra population is not as high as that. Though the actual figure is anybody's guess, it can be safely assumed that it runs into several crores both from India as well as abroad.

In addition to these fundamental concepts and practices, Bohra piety had some unique features, such as distinctive supererogatory rites of worship. On nights of special sanctity, they perform the *washshiq* and *wasila.* The *washshiq* is a ritual prayer after the mandatory *isha* prayer, usually consisting of 24 *rak'ats*(prayer cycles). The *wasila* follows the *washshiq*. It is a ritualized but spontaneous entreaty of God in Lisan al-Da'wat(Gujarati spoken by the Bohra priests, Dai and his family) by the prayer-leader, appended to a liturgical recitation in Arabic.

Majalis

Bohra religious assemblies for everything other than ritual prayer are called *majalis* (singular, *majlis,* literally 'sitting'). The individual presiding over a *majalis* is termed the *sadr.* He sits in a central space surrounded by male members of the congregation. Women usually sit in concealed enclaves or in the main space with a divider between them and the men, from where they can view the proceedings without being seen themselves. In women only *majalis*, a female *sadr* presides. In every *majalis,* the congregation chants religious poems, elegies, *marsiya, madeh* (inpraise of Dai) and the *sadr* frequently delivers a sermon of varying length (ranging from half an hour to two hours called *bayan,* literally 'clear exposition'.

The *Da'i* personally presides on a regular basis at religious gatherings, leading worship, delivering *waaz* (sermons) and officiating in *majalis*. In Ramadan, he leads the Bohra in ritual prayer. His Muharram *waaz* are organised in a very grand scale every year in different cities throughout the world. Up to 100,000 to 200,000 Bohra men, women and children gather to hear him speak. Some of his *wa'z* are relayed in audio and video format via internet or satellite, often live, to Bohra congregation worldwide.

The anniversaries of the births and deaths figures prominent in the *da'wat* spiritual hierarchy are days of *barakat* (divine grace), which the Bohra celebrate or commemorate with a *majalis.* Birth anniversaries are called *milad* or *salgirah*, and celebrated with a *'khushini majalis'* (*majlis* of celebration). Death anniversaries are called *'urs'*, or, in the case of martyr, *shahadat*, commemorated with a *majalis* of Qur'an recitation, where all attendees simultaneously and inaudibly recite separate chapters of the Qur'an for the benefit of the soul of the deceased. The Qur'an recitation is followed by the *'sadaqallah'* ('God Spoke Truth'), a prayer in Arabic beginning with those words for the deceased, recited aloud by the *sadr*. Next comes a recitation of elegies for the deceased, followed by elegies for Imam Husain.

Ziyarat

Visiting the shrines of deceased saints, called *ziyarat,* is a meritorious act.[13] The shrine visitor kisses the tomb of the saint, places petals or sweet basil leaves on the grave and recites the Qur'an *surats* of *al-Fatiha* and *Yasin* for the benefit of the soul of the deceased. On the eve of *'urs'* a particularly propitious time for *ziyarat* – visitors ceremonially spread upon the tomb a fragrant paste of sandalwood and rosewater called *sandal.*

Fixed Lunar Calendar

In keeping with Fatimid tradition, the Bohras follow the fixed astronomical version of the Islamic Hijri lunar calendar; at times their feast days occur before or after those of other Muslim denominations. For example, they always fast full 30 days during Ramadan each year, rather than varying it according to the sighting of the moon. Many Bohra religious events are identical to those followed by Sunnis and the Twelver Shi'a. A celebration shared with other Shi'a is 'Id-i-Ghadir', which according to all Shi'a marks the day the Prophet Muhammad publicly appointed 'Ali' as his successor at the spring of Ghadir ul Khumm, this celebration is an affirmation of the fundamental Bohra doctrine of *walayat.*

Religious learning is available to the general Bohra community in several formats. One of these is the 'Jami'a Sayfiyya', important academy of Bohra religious studies, founded by the 34th Dai Syedna Ismail Badr-al-Din in the 17th century. It was an institution that provided free board and lodging to students who came to study with the *Da'i* in Jamnagar. It remained a peripatetic kind of *madrasa,* moving with the *Da'i* until in the early 19th century, the 43rd *Da'I* Syedna 'Abd-I Ali Sayf-al-Din expanded it along more formal lines in Surat. In the early 20th century the 51st *Da'i* Syedna Tahir Saifuddin further developed it along the lines of a modern seminary. The *Da'i* added a branch in Karachi, Pakistan in 1983. In 1998 he founded the Surat Jami'a aegis a new institute named Ma'had al-Zahra for the memorization and study of the Qur'an. The *da'wat* funds the Jami'a and provides free tuition and board to students. The number of applicants has increased steadily over the years, and many more applications are received than there are spaces. In 2006, the Surat Jami'a had 149 professors and 717 students (440 male, 277 female). The Karachi Jami'a had 60 professors and 452 students (231 male, 221 female). In most towns with a Bohra population, there is religious schools.[14]

The *da'wat* administering body for schools, *madrasas* and all religious education structures is the Da'irat al-Tarbiyyat wa al-Talim (popularly called Attalim) which supervises religious study curricula used in Bohra *madrasas* worldwide and publishes and distributes elementary religious study manuals and prayer books. According to recent studies, the Bohra have significantly higher educational levels than the Indian norms, for the *da'wat* leadership encourages women as well as men to pursue both religious and secular education. In addition to institutions of religious leaning, the *da'wat* also owns and runs several secular educational institutions. Bohra schools and colleges exist today in most cities with a Bohra population, and are most numerous in India; in Greater Mumbai itself there are 30 Bohra secular schools. *Worldwide*, there are 470 Bohra schools.[15] These are open to non-Bohra as well, but require the Bohra children to take religious classes in addition to the regular secular curriculum.

Language

Although influenced in a limited fashion by Arab and Persian social norms, Bohra social practice is above all a blend of Islamic 'orthopraxy' and Mughal-Rajput Indian culture. An example of this amalgamation is the Bohra language named *Lisanal-Da'wat* or '*Da'watnizaban'* (literally, the language of the *Da'wat*). Its substructure is the Indo-Aryan language Gujarati, a derivative of Sanskrit, spoken mostly in the Indian province of Gujarat. The grammar and sentence structure of *Lisan al-Da'wat* appear to have remained in accord with Gujarati without any perceptible change (A close parallel to the evolution of *Lisan al-Da'wat* might be that of Urdu, currently the national language of Pakistan, which is blend of the Sanskrit-based Hindustani with Arabic and Persian).

The vocabulary and script of *Lisan al-Da'wat* have become progressively more Islamized. Arabic and Persian vocabulary are gradually displacing the Gujarati and Sanskrit-based lexicon; this is especially true of vocabulary related to religious matters, such as the use of Arabic *din* (religion) rather than the Gujarati *dharam,* and the use of the Persian *ruza* (fast) rather than the Gujarati *vrat.* The Bohra *nasihats* provide a clear illustration of this gradual absorption: *nasihats* composed by Sayyidi LuqmanJi bin Sheikh Da'ud in the 12th/18th century have a much smaller Arabic Persian lexical content and a much larger Sanskrit-derived Gujarati one than *nasihats* composed by Sayyidi Sadiq Ali Sahib in the 19th century; these latter, in turn, are less Arabicized than *nasihats* composed by Sayyidna Tahir Saifuddin in the 20th century. The script in which Lisan al-Da'wat is currently written is Arabic Persian *naskh* rather than Gujarati Devanagari. But some Bohra publications even today are written in the Devanagari script (e.g. the weekly magazine *Nasim-i-sahar*, The Bohra Chronicle) and significant numbers of lay Bohra use the Devanagari rather than the Arabic script. The shift in script, too, has gradual and remains in ongoing one.

Dress

The Bohra mode of attire is similarly a mélange of the Islamic and the Indian. The wearing of traditional community dress (called *quwmi libas* or *Libase-i-Anwar*). Women wear *rida* outside the home, comprised of a full-length skirt (*lehenga* or *ghaghra*) and a triangular garment (*parr* or *pardi*) covering the head and bosom down of the hips; the *parr* has a flap that is sometimes used to cover the face. The *rida* has evolved into its present form in the last 30 years of so; earlier. Bohra women wore different version of the *burka*. Bohra men wear plain white calf-length robes (*kurta-saya*), with loose cotton trousers (also called *idhar*), and a while crocheted cap (*topi*) with some gold and black, Business attire is often Western-style trousers and shirt, with many choosing to include the *topi* as head covering. One ceremonial occasion the clergy wears a more elaborate costume, a full-length white muslin robe with a gathered waist (*jama*), folds of while muslin arranged over the shoulder (*dupatta*), and a white turban (*paghri*). Many of these garments – the *jama,* for example – are similar to those worn earlier in the Mughal court. Others, such as *kurta*, are commonly worn in a shorter version by a large number of Indians today.

The wearing of traditional community dress (called *qawmilibas* or *libas-i-anwar*) is *de rigueur* at Bohra religious and social gatherings and is encouraged at all times. This emphasis is of a dual nature; observation of Islamic law and preservation of Bohra cultural identity. According to the legal or cultural nature of the directive, there are gradations in the required dress code. The veil, as mentioned earlier, is required for women since it is considered mandated by Islamic law. The wearing of the Bohra cap by men, on the other hand, is encouraged rather than required, since it is a religio-cultural stipulation rather than a legal prescription.

Niyaz

Large communal *iftar* meals are also common during the fast of Ramadan. Like the *niyaz,* banquets for specific celebrations are given specific names. A meal to which all the Bohra living in a particular city are invited is called a *jama'at*. A banquet to which the *Da'i* or a high-ranking *da'wat* personage is invited is termed as *żiyafat.*

Administration by Al-Wazarat-al-Sayffiya

A central administration headed by the *Da'i* oversees the administration of all Bohra affairs. All personnel are answerable to the *Da'i*, who lays out the broad parameters for their performance and inspects specific matters from time to time. The central offices of all the administrative departments are in the Badri Mahal complex in Mumbai, which the brothers and sons of the *Da'i*have offices. One of the important departments is al-Wazarat al-Saiffiya, which appoints and supervises local representatives (called *amil,* plural *ummal*) in cities, towns and villages. In 2006 there were 340 *amils*[16] worldwide. Each *amil*is the head of the Bohra council in his city (called the *jama'at* committee), which is made up of people from the local community. Most *amils* are graduates of Jami'a Saifiyya, and combine religious knowledge with administrative skills. Under the *amil* is a local man – called the *walimulla* - who is appointed to lead the ritual prayer in the former's absence. Additionally, each jama'at is divided into sectors named *muhalla*, and each of these is locally administered by a governing body (called a *tanzim* committee). *Jama'ats* from the same district are grouped together for administrative purposes and are collectively called a *jam'iyyat*. In towns where the number of Bohra is small, an *amil* is generally not appointed, and instead a *wali mulla*[17] leads the ritual prayer.

Social Organization

There are numerous Bohra social organization that undertake a range of activities including the maintenance of *masjids* and communal areas, charity schemes and the organization of trips of pilgrimage sites, social gatherings and athletic events. Bohra charity organizations are numerous and include giving free medical facilities, scholarships, interest free loan schemes, orphanages, free food and clothing and subsidized or free housing. The larger charities are funded and overseen by the *da'wat*, under whose auspices many are administered by local Bohra communities. Community members often contribute funds to these charities, especially at the initial set-up stage. Branches of many of these organizations exist in most cities of the world which have a substantial Bohra population.

Conclusion

Dawoodi Bohra, are a very closely-knit community tightly controlled by the high priest (*Da'i*) and are both highly Islamised in their religious practices and highly Indianised in their cultural practices and ethos. The ordinary Bohra is highly conscious of his separate identity and is made to jealously guard it by the priesthood. The priesthood makes every effort, not only to keep tight spiritual control over the community but also keep it separate from the Islamic mainstream. The previous High Priest, 52nd Dai Syedna Muhammad Burhanuddin had gone to another extreme in cutting the Bohras off from not only Sunni but also from the Shi'ah Muslims. Any contact with other Muslims, the high priest thinks will loosen his control over the community. His absolute control over the lives of Bohras is made possible by keeping them ignorant about fundamental principles of Islam and by not allowing them to independently read any translation of the Holy Qur'an.

The present *Da'i* Syedna Mufaddal Saifuddin and his religious assistants, are wrongly exploiting the doctrine of knowledge of, and obedience to, the *hudud*. This doctrine relates only to the spiritual sphere. It was devised by the Isma'ili authorities for spiritual perfection of their followers. It was close to the concept of *bhakti* in India wherein not only complete obedience to God but absorption in Him is the goal of the bhakta. The sufis also had evolved this doctrine in their own way and called it *fana fi'Allah* i.e. ones destruction in God.

Be it the bhakti or the Sufi practice, the ultimate aim was spiritual perfection for ultimate salvation, perfection to the extent that the *bhakt* or '*abd*' (servant) becomes part of the Ultimate Being. The Isma'ilis or the Bohras in India also evolved similar doctrine in their own way. The ultimate aim of a m'umin (spiritually perfect being) is to be absorbed in the being of '*ashir-e-mudabbir*' (i.e. tenth intellect) as one cannot go higher than that and it is the ultimate spiritual salvation. The complete absorption can come only through complete identification and hence the need for complete obedience.

Thus it will be seen that this concept has nothing to do with the obedience in non-spiritual matters. Such obedience will interfere with spiritual perfection. The present *Da'i* and his entire establishment unfortunately has totally given up the spiritual pursuit and have been after this worldly gain and are exploiting the Isma'ili doctrines devised for spiritual perfection and ultimate elevation to the status of 'ashir-e-mudabbir, for personal and this worldly interests. It is for this reason that a serious cleavage has appeared in the Dawoodi Bohra community and the reformists are challenging the wrong practices imposed on the Bohras by the present *Da'i*. A *Da'i* in the Isma'ili religious hierarchy holds the highest position the absence of Imam who is mamthul (representative) of 'ashir-e-mudabbir in this world. Such a being should strive to achieve spiritual perfection so as to elevate him to the highest and the august office and guide his followers in spiritual matters. However, as the Sufi movement degenerated at the hands of those *sajjada nashins* who gave preference to the worldly pursuits to the spiritual pursuits of their great masters, the Bohra *Da'i* and his establishment also degenerated into such material pursuit sacrificing their spiritual goal. Such a leader cannot demand total obedience as stressed in the Isma'ili spiritual literature.

Like in other religious groups the ordinary Bohras have no proper knowledge of their religion and they are often exploited out of their ignorance. It is also to be emphasized that blind faith can never lead to spiritualism, let alone to spiritual perfection. Blind faith is the product of ignorance and ignorance leads to darkness, not to light. Thus spiritual perfection is possible only with enlightened faith and enlightened faith is borne out of deep knowledge. It is for this reason that the Isma'ilis tried to achieve balance between m'arifah (knowledge) and spiritual devotion. Spiritual devotion loosen its very purpose if it gets bogged down in the worldly mire.

Bohras were once considered highly spiritually devoted people. However, their religious leadership has totally led them astray. They can now neither achieve material success (as the high priest intensely exploits them) not can they achieve spiritual perfection.

Notes and References

1. Bohras from the Gujarati word *vehhar* meanings 'dealing' or 'honest dealings'. See the Gujarati lexicon by I.R. Gala and P.L. Soda, *Gala Vishal Shabdkosh* (Mumbai, 2000), p.167,*vahevaru*. This etymology seems the most plausible one, as the majorities of the early Bohra were, in fact, traders, and as the Bohra are also called '*vohra*' ('b' and 'v' being interchangeable at the beginning of words

in Gujarati). Another etymology of many sects or paths derived from the Hindi phrase *bahu rah* is proposed by S.T. Lokhandwalla, "The Bohras, A Muslim Community of Gujarat', *StudiaIslamica,* 3 (1955), p.120 n.1. This etymology seems less convincing since converts to all religions are usually form different sects and paths that is not a feature novel enough to effect nomenclature. The *Da'udi* (popularly transcribed 'Dawoodi') in 'Da'udiBohra' refers to their recognition of the *da'i*-ship of SyednaDa'ud b. Qutub Shah who reigned from 999/1591 to 1021/1612 and was opposed by Sulayman bin Hasan, the first *da'i* of the Sulaymani Bohra. A third group is the 'AlaviBohra'. Doctrine differences among all groups appear to be minimal.

2. It was during al Mustansir's reign (AD 1035-1095) two eminent dais (missionaries) Ahmed and Abdullah were sent via Yemen to India. They landed at the part of Combay. The activities of these missionaries were quite peaceful. They learn the local language and established contact with the priest of a nearby temple. After defeating him in religious polemics they converted him to Islamic faith. Through the priest they converted the minister Bharmal and after that they interested in converting the Raja himself to win general support. The priest told them that Raja could be converted only, if the elephant-God of this temple, for which the Raja has great regard, is made to fall from its hanging position in mid-air. On close examination Abdullah found that the elephant was hanging in mid-air without any support as there were four powerful magnets of equal pull hidden in the four walls of the temple. The magnets were removed one by one thus bringing the elephant-God tumbling down on the floor of the temple. The Raja shook with terror. On being shown more miracles by the missionary and he embraced the new faith. See Sheikh Muhammad Ali ibn Mulla Jiwabhai, *Mausame-i-bahar,* Vol.III, Safdari, Bombay n.d. pp.328-329. Also see Satish C. Mishra, *Muslim Communities in Gujarat,* Asia Publishing House, Bombay, 1963.
3. Maulana Muhammad Ali, *Holy Qu'ran,* Lahore, 1973, pp.262.
4. Daaim-al-Islam written by the 10th century Fatimid jurist al-Qadi al-N'uman and authroised by the Fatimi Imam-Caliph al Mu'izz.
5. Sec. Asghar Ali Engineer, *The Bohras*. Vikas Publishing House, Ghaziabad, 1980, P.343.
6. Who is 53rddai, yet not cleared as the matter is subjudicial in Mumbai High Court. There are two claimants – one Syedna Mufaddal Safuddin and other is Syedna Tahir Fakhruddin. He will be 54th in sequence as his father Syedna Khuzema Qutubuddin had already died before the settlement of the case of claimant. Now court accepted Syedna Tahir Fakhruddin as the successor of Syedna Khuzema Qutubuddin and plaintiff of the case.
7. For Saiyyidi Sadiq Ali Sahib, worldly needs were so insignificant, as his life was totally devoted, in trying to impart knowledge to the generations to come. He has done it, in simple words, written in poetry form. But people are so busy in the worldly life so the wisdom in truth, instilled in these *nasihats*is simply lost on them.
8. For details of Bohra shrines with brief historical notes on the saints buried there, see. *Tuhfatla'aliakhbar al-hudat,* ed. HudhayfaMuhyi al-Din (Mumbai, 1414/ 1993). See also www.mazaraat.com.

9. Asghar Ali Engineer, Op. Cit., pp.158-159.
10. Vide Para 988 of the judgment of in suit no.941 of 1971 in the High Court of Judicature of Bombay.
11. Mian Bhai Mullah Abdul Hussain, 'A Short Note on DawoodiBohras', *Gulzare-Dawoodi,* Progressive Publications, Surat, 1920, P.2.
12. See the cyclostyled note prepared by Noman L. Contractor and circulated to the press in India from Delhi, 1972.
13. TahiraQutubuddin, 'The DaudiBohraTayyabis: Ideology, Literature, Learning and Social Practice' In: Farhad Daftary, *A Modern History of the Ismailis: Continuity and Change in a Muslim Community* (ed.) I.B. Taurus, 2010, p.344.
14. Ibid, P.344.
15. Ibid.
16. *Amil* (literary governor). These clergymen are trend in Bohra seminary in Surat, Gujarat, and appointed through centrally controlled system. A whole religious beaurocracy has developed in the office, Mumbai which controls religious and social life of Bohra throughout the world.
17. *WaliMulla. WaliMulla* is a subordinate position who generally follows the *farman* of the *amil*of that region. At village or small *taluka* level, they lead to *namaz.*

Chapter - 4

Main Issues of the Bohra Reform Movement

There was no known dissidence in the Dawoodi Bohra community until the appointment of 47th Dai Syedna Abdul Qadir Najmuddin. Some believe that 46th Dai passed away without appointing his successor and the elders appointed Syedna Abdul Qadir Najmuddin as a caretaker Dai only and not Dai-ul-Mutalq. The reform movement is not concerned about the succession issue at all. Reformists recognize the Dai but the Dai does not recognize the reformists.

Succession issue is very much different from the issues involved in a reform movement. The reform movement is all about human rights, fundamental rights guaranteed in the Indian Constitution, freedom of association, freedom to start a bank, freedom in secular affairs of the community, secular education, transparency, accountability, administration of waqf properties etc.

Considering this social perspective we can trace the beginning of the reform movement to certain issues raised in Udaipur towards the end of the nineteenth century and in Burhanpur in the beginning of the twentieth century. In both these places the issues raised were pertaining to social and secular matters.

The priesthood in the Bohra community maintains that the religious and secular can harmoniously blend while the reformists believe that the two cannot be continued in the present democratic set-up. May be the two authorities blended together during the feudal era which had authoritarian ethos but it is no longer possible in our own times wherein democratic values prevail. In Udaipur, in late nineteenth century; the reformists asserted their secular rights vis-à-vis the Syedna without challenging his religious authority.

Litigation followed in Udaipur and Burhanpur and interestingly in both the cases, the contention of the reformists that the high priest cannot exercise coercive authority in secular sphere was upheld by the court. In subsequent litigations – like Chandabhai Gulla case – Syedna's claim to authority in the secular affairs of the community was rejected outright. It is also interesting to note that before consolidation of the British rule in India, most of the dissensions in the Bohra community were regarding successions to the office of the Da'i but after the consolidation of the British rule, there was no dissension about succession but mostly about legitimacy of exercising secular authority. Those who dissented on the succession issue should be referred to as dissenters as it involved religious issues of *nass* (doctrine of rightful appointment) and those who challenged the legitimacy of Dai's secular authority should be referred to as reformists because in this case no religion doctrine or dogma was involved.

Aims of the Bohra Reform Movement

1. To prevent religious leaders from interfering in the secular and personal affairs of the followers:

   The root cause of of the reformists' grievances can be attributed to the fact that instead of acting as a spiritual head, the Syedna is acting as an oppressive materialistic despot-extorting money and forcing bhoras in his strange hold. Syedna runs after power and pelf.

   The reformists are not challenging either religious dogmas or religious authority of Dai. They only challenge the high priest's right to exercise secular authority and also they oppose coercive imposition of religious authority. The Holy Qur'an also maintains that there can be no coercion in religious matters. It proclaims this doctrine in the ringing words "*la ikrah fi al-din*" (there is no compulsion in religion). The Quran also proclaims "....the right way is indeed clearly distinct from error. So whoever disbelieves in the devil and believes in Allah and he indeed lays hold in the firmest handle which shall never break."

Thus it will be seen that to accept the right way or the path of error is left to human person after it is made distinctly clear. There is no coercion involved at all. Thus when the reformists oppose coercive imposition of religious authority, they base it on the holy Qur'an. The Qur'an also requires the Prophet to "Call to the way of thy Lord with wisdom and goodly exhortation, and argue with them in the best manner." (16:125). It would thus be seen that coercive imposition of religious authority is opposed to the spirit of the Holy Qur'an.

As for the secular authority the Syedna has no religious sanction. It may be argued that the Da'i in the past did exercise secular authority also and there is some truth in his assertion. But it should also be understood that exercise of secular authority by the Dais in the past was part of their social contract with the community. In other words it was done with the unspoken consent of the community, not against its will. Secondly, it was protective exercise of secular authority rather than coercive exercise. Let me elaborate this a little.

In the past the community faced external threats. There were no democratic channels available then to fight these threats. The high priest, with his high status and prestige in the society, took the community in his protective cover and enabled it, through his prestige and authority, to successfully face the external threats. Also, it is our experience that when external threats are grave, centralization of power proves more beneficial. The external threat in the case of the Bohra community persisted for many centuries and centralization of power remained a felt need for a long time. In fact, over a period of time, there evolved an unspoken, unwritten contract between the high priest and the Bohra community which legitimized this exercise of centralized authority.

However, with the advent of the British, and later, with the acceptance of political and social democracy, things changed drastically. Now there is no external threat and there is no need for the high priest to exercise any secular authority. When the 51st and 52ndDa'is not only refused to leave the secular domain to the community but intensified exercise of secular authority and that too increasingly coercively, there began a protest movement against it. The Reformists desired changes in the social conditions of the community and attempted to define social and religious domain separately. It can be rightfully described as reform movement. The reformists strongly feel that there should be not only complete stop to the coercive exercise of secular authority by the Da'i but also he should restrict his religious authority to "wise and good words" as described by the Holy Qur'an.

2. To uphold freedom of conscience

The reformists also believe that there is no place for blind and slavish submission to any authority, religious or otherwise. Even the Holy Qur'an lays repeated emphasis on reason and exhorts humankind to think, to brood and to use faculty of reason. The reformists thus refuse to submit blindly to any authority. They call upon their fellow community members and others to exercise faculty of reason which is the highest gift of God. Thus it is very important aspect of the Bohra reform movement. Blind submission is uncalled for not only in secular matters but even in religious matters. The Syedna and his orthodox followers construe this as defiance of religion, this is untrue.

In fact true religiosity can never be equated with blind submission. True religiosity is a creative synthesis between reason and faith and intellect and intuition. Thus the reformists justly claim that far from disowning religion, they represent true religious spirit. The reformists represent intellectual and philosophical traditions of Isma'ilis as embodied in the epistles of Ikhwanus Safa (Rasa'il Ikhwanus Safa). The Rasa'il Ikhwanus Safa embraced with unique openness of mind all that is best in; the available knowledge in the world. The Imam and the Du'at (The High Priests) who compiled the Rasa'il were the most eminent intellectuals of their time. They enriched, through their intellectual contribution, knowledge and encouraged faculty of reason. They never demanded blind submission. The reformist Bohras are true inheritors of Ikhwanus Safa tradition.

The faculty of reason harmonically blends with freedom of conscience. The reformist Bohras thus upholds freedom of conscience. The Bohra high priest on the other hand ruthlessly suppresses freedom of conscience. Naturally blind submission cannot go hand in hand with freedom of conscience. Freedom of conscience is noblest and highest achievement of human development. It cannot be sacrificed at the altar of any authority. The reformists consider it as cardinal doctrine of their movement.

3. To uphold human rights and human dignity

The reformists also uphold the human rights and human dignity. In fact there can be no freedom of conscience without concept of human dignity and human rights. Violations of human rights are an integral part of authoritarian cultures. The reformists are, therefore, totally opposed to any form of authoritarianism and mental regimentation. Their whole fight is against authoritarianism. The revolt by the Bohra Youth in Udaipur in 1973 was a challenge to this authoritarianism. They fought to uphold their rights and freedom of conscience. Subsequently in Bombay, Godhra, Surat, Ahmedabad, Lathi, Bhavnagar, Aurangabad, Hyderabad, Malegaon and several other places conscientious persons took up the fight. The Bohra high priest adopted, like any authoritarian ruler, highly coercive measures to suppress the fast spreading movement. However, he failed to suppress the voice of human conscience. Bohra from several other countries such as the UK, Pakistan, Thailand, USA, East Africa, Canada, Sweden, Mauritius, etc. joined us to strengthen the reform movement.

4. To enforce accountability:

The doctrine of accountability is as fundamental to the Bohra reform movement as freedom of conscience. In fact one cannot go without the other. it is authoritarianism which rejects accountability to the people. The reformists take the doctrine of accountability in its widest sense. It is social, religious, politics as well as financial accountability. The Syedna imposes worst kind of socio-religious authoritarianism and hence there is no question to accepting doctrine of accountability. What is worse, he refuses to accept even financial accountability. He and his family members collect millions of dollars every year from the community in a most coercive manner. The money so collected is never accounted for.

The reformists maintain that the money so collected does not belong to the Syedna or his family and cannot be appropriated by them. The money should be accounted for and spent on the welfare projects and uplift of the poor and needy. The Syedna and his family cannot take away even a paisa from it. In fact the Syedna's family has collected huge fortunes over several decades and use repression against the community to stifle any criticism, for such blatant misappropriation of community funds. Audited accounts must be published for all to see.

The reformists maintain that even the Prophet of Allah (PUBH) never refused to give account whenever anyone asked. Hazrat 'Ali too readily revealed accounts whenever anyone raised any doubt. How can then a Da'i, an humble servant of the Prophet maintain that he is not accountable to the community. Ever paisa collected from the community must be accounted for by the Syedna or any other member of his family and staff. The zakat money should be spent on the poor and needy, widows and orphans, for discharge of debts of indebted and travelers and in other manners in the way of Allah as laid down by the Holy Qur'an.

5. To abolish *Baraat* and Raza

The high priest used to declare excommunication against anyone who questioned the functioning of the priestly establishment and other community institution. But when the Supreme Court in its judgment delivered in 1962 made excommunication justifiable in the court, Syedna found it almost impossible to resort to it. He then devised another way – *baraat* – social boycott which is declared orally without any written record to escape rigors of law. *Baraat* disallows other community members from speaking to reformists, happily married couples are forced to divorce, reformists are prevented from attending marriages or funerals of relatives, and bans them from masjids and all other community premises, making them practically untouchables. The High Priest and his establishments have been using the weapon of *baraat* most ruthlessly. His minions of course resort to it even more arbitrarily. It is being done to terrorize the community into submission. The reformists say that it is un-Islamic and strongly violative of human rights. The reformists have raised this issue from various public fora and also have drawn attention of the Central Government and have submitted memoranda to various prime ministers and presidents of India demanding law against it. Though the government has not enacted any law so far the reformist campaign against *baraat* has created strong public opinion against it and has generated sympathy for its victims.

Similarly, the reformist Bohras are against the compulsory requirement of Raza (permission) from the priesthood before carrying out any religious ritual or secular activity. The priesthood declares *Baraat* against any person who does anything without the Kothar's permission and this includes even daily prayers, Haj, marriage, divorce, funeral rites, publishing a newspaper, translating or teaching Quran, contesting an election, establishing a school, establishing a bank, forming an association or any other activity. Neither in Islam nor in modern democratic society there is any place for such enslavement of human beings by other human beings. Freedom of conscience at stated above, is most fundamental and anything violative of it would be totally opposed. Thus the reformists oppose the concept and practice of raza. Raza thus has no place and must be thrown out. Every person who is sufficiently knowledgeable should be free to perform all religious rites like daily prayers, nikah (marriage oaths), namaz-e-janazaa (funeral prayer) and similar other things without any prior permission from any authority.

6. To form *Jamaat* by elections

Jamaat is a committee of local Bohras for managing the community affairs of that town. Previously each *Jamaat* was formed by local people by consensus. However, Amil (the priest) in each town was appointed by the High Priest for religious duties only.

Syedna Taher Saifuddin, 51st Dai, in order to get greater grip on every Bohra affair, started nominating his henchmen in every *Jamaat* all over the world.

The reformists oppose nominated *Jamaat*, because the nominated members often do not represent the local Bohras. They want to establish elected *Jamaat* and insist that election should be through universal franchise and both men and women should have right to vote. Nominated bodies are like the puppet in the hand of local Amil. The nominated members always try to please their master and over look the interests of the common people of the community. This struggle for reform has not been confined to the Bohras of India. Other countries where the Bohras are in sizeable number have also witnessed it. Quite a good number of Bohras of Indian origins have settled in East Africa. After great deal of efforts on the part of the Bohras of East Africa, the high priest had to ultimately yield to their demand of granting a democratic constitution for managing the affairs of the community. The *Jamaat* constitution called the "Constitution of Dawoodi Bohra *Jamaat* Corporation" was approved by 51stDai and was adopted in 1955.[1]The reformists in India were unaware of this important development in Africa. They were planning to hold a conference in Bagasara to chalk out a programmed of action for realizing their long-standing demand for democratization of the *Jamaat*'s management.

Udaipur revolt began with the abolition of Najmi Committee (which was nominated by Dai) in 1973. Presently reformists in Udaipur, Malegaon, Aurangabad, Mumbai, and Birmingham, Leisters, UK and other places have *Jamaats* which are elected through universal franchise. All these Reformists Jamaats are affiliated to the Central Board of Dawoodi Bohra Community (CBDBC).The Central Executive Committee and other office bearers of CBDBC are also elected every two years.

7. Freedom to establish secular educational institutions

Raja Ram Mohan Roy was one of the earliest propagators of modern western education. Similarly in the early 19th century the first sign of Muslim awakening appeared under the leadership of Sir Syed Ahmed Khan. In Dawoodi Bohra with the turn of the 20th century some Bohras were under the influence of British rulers determined to establish educational institutions for the community. For this at first a primary modern school was established around 1901 known as Madrass-a-Hakimia. This madrasa was sought to be converted to a middle school in 1910. The reformists had been trying to balance the orthodox Islamic view with that of the modern value. The 50th da'i Syedna Abdullah Badruddin did not like this and therefore in April 1910 he imposed certain terms on the managing committee, one of which was that the local Amil was to supervise the tuition given in the school and to close it at his discretion. Thus strong differences arose between the committee and the high priest. The school committee then decided to get the Hakimia School Society registered and accepted a government grant despite strong objections from the Syedna. The staunch followers of the Syedna withdraw from the committee and strong communal feelings were aroused. Syedna in order to downgrade that school established another in the same town called the Qadariya School. The Bohra high priest started harassing even those who studied in Hakimiya School. They were under constant threat of excommunication. The trustees the students of Hakimiya School were even prevented from entering into the mausoleum of Sayyidi Hakimuddin at Burhanpur which led to the filing of Civil Suit no.32 of 1925 which was known as the 'Burhanpur Dargah Case'. It involved the very important question of discrimination within the community.[2]

They tried to ban Saifee Imdadia committee, Udaipur by denying *raza* for helping needy students with scholarship and free books. They even threatened dire consequences against the volunteers if they continued their welfare activities. Syedna discouraged rational –critical thinking and a scientific temper of mind. Syedna Tahir Saifuddin and his successor have even forbidden reading translation and tafseer(explanations)of the Quran (which is in Arabic), and other religious books!

Progress of Dawoodi Bohra Reform Movement

Social boycott in the court of law

If anyone disobeys Syedna's dictates or fails to pay the dues demanded, he/she is put under complete boycott. A boycotted person is shunned by all Bohras including his/her parents, children, brothers and sisters. No one can maintain relations with such verbally excommunicated person. If one does, he/she will also be boycotted. Such a boycotted person cannot attend funeral of his/her near and dear ones, participate in their marriage functions or any family occasions. Only a Bohra can know what kind of curse it is to live under the boycott period.

One Asghar Ali a crusader of western education was to marry in April 1917. His marriage dinner was attended by Hasan Ali, editor of the 'Gulzar' magazine. Hasan Ali had been excommunicated earlier by the Syedna and inviting him to a community dinner was nothing short of 'sacrilege'. The local Amil fined father of Asghar Ali for extending an invitation to an excommunicated person. Aggrieved by this, he filed an extortion case against the Amil. The Amil retorted by excommunicating the plaintiff the brother Asghar Ali, his father K.B. Fakhruddin, Habibullah, pleader and ImranAli pleader (the latter three being the members of the managing committee and the life and soul of the Hakimia School) in August 1917. From then onwards the Bohra high priest started to confront even those who studied at the

Hakimia School. They were under constant threat of excommunication. The trustees and the students of Hakimia School were even prevented from entering into the mausoleum of Sayyidi Hakimuddin at Burhanpur which led to the filing of the Civil Suit no.32 of 1925 which was known as the Burhanpur Dargah Case.[3]

The reformists after independence contacted the Congress leaders of the then Bombay State and persuaded them to legislate against the practice of excommunication so often resorted to by the Bohra high priest. Therefore a Bill was introduced in the Bombay Assembly when B.G. Kher was Chief Minister and Morarji Desai Home Minister. B G Kher and Morarji Desai while piloting the bill against excommunication are reported to have said that "Bohra high priest runs a government within the government and that he enjoys monstrous powers."[4] The bill was passed by the then Bombay Legislative Assembly and was called the "Prevention of Excommunication Act, 1949". The high priest challenged it in Bombay High Court and prayed for declaring it Ultra virus of Constitution. The Bombay High Court upholding the legislation passed by the Legislative Assembly. But the high priest challenged it in the Supreme Court. A constitutional bench consisting of four judges of the Supreme Court heard the petition and it was upheld by the majority of three judges. Recently Maharashtra has become the first State in the country to enact law against social boycott from caste Panchayats. In 1997 the reformist filed the review petition to review the Supreme Court's order of 1962. The matter is likely to be heard soon.

Educational conferences

The reformists strove against all the odds to run a school. Though the Bohras were instructed by the priesthood not to contribute funds, the members of the Hakimia School Committee did not lose heart. They decided to organize a conference with a view to discuss the problems of education in the community.

The first idea of organizing an educational conference was conceived on 4 December 1919 at the time of the inauguration of Hakimia Hospital. After the inauguration ceremony a meeting was held under the chairmanship of Hafiz Khanbai Mulla Abdul Ali in the afternoon. It was decided to hold a "Dawoodi Bohra Educational Conference" in order to spread education among the Bohras in a big way. To organize the conference a committee of 27 members was formed. The committee included some prominent Bohras like Hafiz Khanbhai Mulla Abdul Ali, Seth A.M. Jiwanjee of Mombasa, Seth Ibrahimbhai Sir Adamjee Peerbhoy, Sheikh Faizullabhai Hamdani,

Seth Muhammadali Mamuji, etc. The committee was of a representative character as it included members from various parts of India and abroad.

It took more than one and a half years to finally issue a circular for holding the conference at Burhanpur. The conference began on 4 December 1921. It took place in the hall of Hakimia School, Burhanpur. It was presided over by Khan Bahadur Muhammadali Abdulqadar Kanga (J.P.) the day was considered auspicious, it being the birthday of Imam Az-Zaman. On that day a grand procession was taken out which was joined by even the supporters of the Syedna. In the afternoon that day the session was attended by the government officers, municipal members and other public figures. The chairman said in his address that when the notice of this conference was published in *Gulzar-i-Hakimi* it was ridiculed and many thought that it was impossible to hold any such conference. However, it had become a reality. "The Prophet has said that everything takes place at the appropriate time…I hope that this conference will be a boon to the coming generations. The fruits of the seeds we have sown will be tested by the coming generations and I hope that this conference will integrate the scattered efforts of various individuals and institutions to spread the cause of education among the Bohra community."[5]

After this inaugural address, a constitution drafted by the committee was discussed and approved by delegates. It was then decided to raise the necessary funds for the Dawoodi Bohra Education Conference. Many well-to-do Bohras present contributed generously. But what was a moving gesture was the donation of the gold bangles of their daughters by two poor and afflicted Bohras. Two more such conferences were arranged in 1923 and 1926 as a result of which more Bohras realized the importance of education and created such an atmosphere that gradually even the priesthood was forced to surrender and reluctantly allowed more and more educational institutions to be opened.

The conference of 1944

Another important event of the Bohra Reform Movement was the conference of 1944. In 1943 there was marriage in the family of Hatim Alvi at Karachi. Many prominent reformist Bohras got together on this occasion. There it was decided to convene a conference in Bombay at the Sunderbhai Hall in January 1944 to give a new direction to the reformist movement.

There was great deal of opposition to it by the Bohra high priest and his followers. The high priest mobilized an armed mob to prevent people from going to the hall. The venue, therefore, had to be abandoned. Thereupon Abdul Tayyib Sharafali Mamuji offered the terrace of his building Asma Manzil in Nagpada as an alternate venue. There was difficulty in persuading the authorities to grant permission to hold the conference there. Sir Yusuf Ali who was to preside over the conference being indisposed, Hatim Alvi was requested to take his place. Having realized his failure to stop the conference, the high priest now initiated moves for mutual negotiations. At the instance of Muhammad Ali Allahbaksh the conference was postponed for three days.

However, the high priest adopted delaying tactics and was more interested in postponing the conference indefinitely than in arriving at mutually agreed plan of action. The negotiations, therefore, broke down and the conference was resumed after three days. The sessions of the conference were arranged in the evenings on the terrace of Asma Manzil at Nagpada, Central Bombay, in order to avoid trouble by the orthodox followers of the Bohra high priest. The whole emphasis of the conference was on the dissemination of education among the Bohras. With this view a resolution was adopted. The resolution proposed by Dr. Tahir Ali Kajiji was as follows: "This conference emphasizes the need for modern education for the community and considers it a fundamental task for its progress. This conference, therefore, resolves to take suitable steps for providing facilities for education to the Bohra youth. It will be necessary to establish a central organization for this purpose in Bombay.[6]

The above resolution was supported by the advocate Imranali of Hakimiya Education Society. Hatimbhai Shaikh Faizullah Bhai Hamdani, Education Inspector, Miss Zulekha Vasi, Solicitor Dadla and many others. The Chairman of the conference Hatim Alvi made it clear in his concluding speech that the reformist movement was not against the *D'awat*(i.e. the religious mission) or the *Da'i*. Its main aim was to spread education, reduce unemployment and create opportunities for the technical and industrial progress in the Bohra community. On the last day of the conference it was decided to create a fund in order to give concrete shape to the above resolution. Sir Yusufali Alibhai Karimji announced a donation of one lakh for this purpose. Other donations totaling to Rs.99,000 were also announced and thus a corpus of about two lakhs was created. A committee comprising many prominent persons was constituted to implement the programme chalked out in the conference. From the corpus fund a building was brought and its income was utilized for giving the scholarships to Bohra students.

As a result of this conference the high priest also felt compelled to announce certain schemes which benefited the community a girls' high school was established at Muhammadi Bagh, Khokha Bazar, Bombay; a scholarship society was established to provide facilities for higher studies and fund was also raised to establish a hospital – a facility the community so far did not enjoy. The high priest also made personal donations to some of these funds. In fact, he had to do all this in order to counter the effect of the conference.

Bagasara Conference 1957

Bagasara conference was held in Dec 1957 in a town in Kathiawad region. This conference had deeper implications for the high priest as one of his close associates and advisor Mohammed Ali Allah Baksh, feeling neglected, joined the reformists and attended this conference. Tayyebbhai Zarif of Calcutta and Fazle Abbas Zamindar, a former Muslim Leaguer of Gujarat – turned congressman also attended this conference.

However, there was an important addition to the rank of reformists, in this conference. Noman Contractor, a self-made industrialist, took part in the conference and proved to be much more consistent and steadfast in his standing than other leaders who at one or the other time apologized and left the reformist fold due mostly to the pressure brought on them by other family members or business and other considerations. Contractor, though he too dithered once in 1968, faced all odds but stuck to his position and played a leading role in directing the movement for reforms till his death. In fact after the sons of Adamjee Peerbhoy his contribution was most significant in sustaining this movement against very heavy odds. Thus the Bagasra conference became symbolic of a new phase which was more vigorous and dynamic.

The conveners of the conference, perhaps for first time, carefully avoided any religious controversy. They were not interested in the question of *nass* (proper appointment of the successor, next Dai). Their avowed aim was to bring about improvement in the socio-economic status of the community. The resolutions passed called only for welfare measures similar to those carried on by other castes and communities. It was resolved to provide facilities for scholarship, hostels and technical education, a cooperative credit society to relieve unemployment, and cooperative housing and social reforms like curbs on costly community dinners. Therefore Wright Jr. says in this regard: "Several of these measures were already supposed to have been undertaken by the sect's official organizations, but the reformists charge that funds promised or even announced as given by the Syedna for their support are not, in fact, forthcoming(I have heard such complaints from several non-Bohra organizations too). Without a detailed audit of the community's accounts it is impossible to evaluate these accusations of diversion of the funds. A reading of a sample of letters to the editor in the Gujarati newspaper, Bombay Samachar would indicate at least that there is considerable discontent among Daudis with the operations of their service organizations."[7]

The Bagasra Conference once again perturbed the high priest and his establishment and the pontiff began his counter offensive. Letters were sent to the Amils (Priests or agents of the High Priest in each town) to hold *Jamat* meetings to condemn the Bagasra Conference and those who participated in it. Well-planned attempts were made to isolate the supporters of the Bagasra Conference. The priesthood, as we shall see later, whenever faced with a challenge from the reformists, tries to create hysteria in the community by false and misleading propaganda against the reformists through its splendidly well-organized and tightly controlled propaganda machinery. Punitive action is taken by the High Priest if a Bohra is found in mere possession of the Reformist's literature. The reformists, on the other hand, just cannot match this resourcefulness of the priestly establishment. This has been one of their main failures. We will analyse later, in detail, the various other causes of their failure to register satisfactory, if not brilliant success.

Alarmed by the reformists' efforts to regroup themselves the high priest revived his old strategy of wooing the politicians mainly belonging to the ruling party in order to frustrate their attempts at reform in the community. The high priest was in a much better position to do so as his resources had now multiplied. The Bohras had, due to a booming market during the Second World War, and later, due to expanding business and industrial enterprises in the post-independence period, made a lot of money. These rich businessmen, many of them not even adequately literate – made or were rather made to offer huge amounts to the high priest to win recognition in the community. The high priest ingeniously devised various titles like N.K.D. (*An-Nashit fi Khidmatit D'awa*). M.K.D. (*al-Muayyid fi Khidmatit D'awa*) etc. in addition to the traditional titles of Mulla and *Shaikh*. These titles had modern glamour too since they are designed to look like qualifying degree titles. As an inducement to offer large sums of money ranging from a few thousands to a few lakhs these titles were bestowed to rich businessmen. The high priest multiplied his fortunes by these ingenious devices and utilized a part of it to win political support from the ruling party.

Bombay Conference 1959 and creation of' Pragati Mandal'

The reformists decided to convene another conference in May 1959 in Bombay itself. The high priest has always dreaded such conferences perhaps because he knows that the statements for change are very strong and little success on the part of the reformists would soon snowball into movement of serious proportions. Whatever the reason, both the high priests, fifty-first as well as the fifty-second, have always overreacted to any such meetings or conferences. The high priest normally uses his storm troopers to break such conferences and tries to galvanize his supporters into action by a relentless campaign of hatred using words with religious overtones like *kafir, munafiq* etc. against the reformists. However, this time the high priest adopted different tactics to sabotage the conference. These tactics, for that matter, were adopted during the 1944 conference also but with different effect.

The high priest called Fazal Abbas Zamindar and Noman L. Contractor and persuaded them to postpone the conference so as to call a joint conference later. The reformist leaders agreed and a document was prepared to that effect and was signed by two reformist leaders and the five members of Shiat-e-Ali including two past mayors Ishaqbhai Bandukwala and Salehbhai Abdulqadar, on behalf of the High Priest, who was more interested in getting the conference postponed than in a joint conference, started raising technical issues as to who was a Dawoodi Bohra and who was not. Consequently only the reformists met in December and founded the Madhyastha (central) Pragati Mandal in order to give new direction to the movement and to coordinate activities of various local committees. Noman L. Contractor who had made his debut at the Bagasra Conference was elected president thus signaling a new and dynamic leadership. The reformists could not have had a better choice.

More conferences followed at Ahmedabad in February 1961, Dhar in May 1963 and Godhra in November 1963. The conference at Godhra triggered off new events. Godhra became the hotbed of reformists' activities. Noman L. Contractor also hailed from this place and it is said that more than 50 per cent Bohrasof this town in Gujarat have reformist sympathies. At one stage during this period, the reformists even planned black flag demonstrations against the high priest in Godhra. The high priest, as usual, retaliated by declaring *baraat* (social boycott) against all the reformists and instructed his *Amil* at Godhra not to perform their marriages or funeral rites. Thus the reformists were compelled to get their marriages solemnized by Muslim Qazis and bury their dead by themselves. However, the Godhra reformists, though sincere to their cause, could not resist social pressures for long and many of them re-entered the orthodox fold by tendering apologies to the high priest. Only a few were left in the field, they too saw no other way but to follow suit.

Due to defections of Allabux and Fazal Abbas Zamindar, the two leaders of the new trio (the third leader was Noman Contractor), the reform movement received another setback. However, even in these trying circumstances, Noman Contractor, Husainibhai Sanchawala (the then editor of *Bohra Bulletin,* the official mouthpiece of the reformists now renamed *'The Bohra Chronicle*) Mohsin Nagree and some others kept the banner aloft. Turning to the Gandhian method of Satyagrah, these reformist leaders took out *prabhat-pheris* (early morning processions) from the Bohra *muhalla* of Bhendi Bazar in Bombay on four consecutive Sundays including the holy month of Ramzan in 1965. The Bombay dailies, including the English ones which normally do not show much interest in the dispute among the Daudis, reported these events. At considerable risk to their lives Huseni Sanchawala and Zaitun Kapasi (an ex-M.L.A. from Gujarat) went on *satyagraha* outside the Saifee Masjid (the main Bohra mosque in Bombay) in protest against auctioning of places inside the mosque for making money, as it was highly repugnant to the principles of Islam. According to the principles of Islam a mosque is a house of God where anyone can pray at any place. It does not allow any auctioning or charging money for the places for prayer in the mosques, as the high priest does. The *satyagraha* had to face the fury of the high priest's blind followers.

Noman Contractor and others from the reformist group took out a 'shroud procession' also to protest the recurrent violent assaults on the reformists by the high priest's followers. Noman Contractor, Huseni Sanchawala and other wrapped themselves in shrouds to march through the *muhalla*, an act symbolic of their preparedness to sacrifice their lives for the cause "Kill us once for all" was the message of this unique protest march. Of course, there was heavy police bandobust which had cordoned off that area. The crowd of fanatics would have otherwise really tried to kill the reformist leaders. Noman Contractor and his colleagues were taken into safe custody by the police and driven off in a jeep. Nothing much happened in India after the mid-sixties as under threat of social boycott many a person left the reformist fold.

The fifty-first high priest SyednaTahir Saifuddin died in November 1965 after celebrating the golden jubilee of his succession to the 'throne' of *D'awa.* He was succeeded by his eldest son Muhammad Burhanuddin who, it was generally believed to be pious and lenient. Thus after the death of the fifty-first pontiff, the reformists had to adopt the policy of wait and watch. Reform movement remained stagnant after the Indo-Pak war of 1965.However, in the meanwhile, certain developments took place in East Africa and then the revolt in Udaipur began. After the formation of CBDBC since 1977 all World Dawoodi Bohra Conferences have been organised within the interval of two years.

The first conference was organised in Udaipur on 17-19 February, 1977. Syedna had started his machination to sabotage the conference at any cost. He himself came down to Galiakot with 15000 fanatics to oppose this conference. The Conference was being held under the shadow of guns. The Conference building was completely surrounded by the police and no one was allowed to enter. Kamalelshwar, the noted Hindi writer who was to inaugurate the conference, too was refused entry. He telephoned the district collector who fortunately knew him and with his permission he could enter the hall. The conference was presided over by Hatim Durbar from Canada who was an old reformist and associate of Mahatma Gandhi in the Quit India movement. Dalit writers from Maharashtra- Babuji Baghuji, Daya Pawar and Arun Dangle also attended the conference. The over whelming participation of Bohra women, in such dangerous situation, was remarkable. This conference had far reaching effects on the community which ultimately realised the objectives and the strength of the reform movement and it gradually started drifting away from the oppressive and exploitative Bohra religious establishment.

The 2nd AllWorld Dawoodi Bohra Conference was again held at Udaipur on 16-17-18 February, 1979. The reformist Bohras from U.K, USA, Kuwait, Pakistan, Dubai and Colombo attended and participated in the conference. Delegates from Gujarat, MP, Maharashtra, Rajasthan and Hyderabad also attended the conference in large number. Eminent personalities like Om Parkash Rawat from Indore, Onkarlal Bohra, Hassan Kamal, PS Nerulkar, Jawahar Lal Rathod and Rajan Mathur were present in the inaugural session.

The outsiders were highly impressed by the participation of Bohra women in large number specially from Udaipur.

Third All World Dawoodi Bohra Conference (AWDBC) was held in Bombay in 1981. The opposition from Syedna's side was at its peak once again. The conference was attended by the most prominent persons like S.M. Joshi, Prof. Qamar Rais, Prof. Imtiyaz Ahmed, Dr. Riyaz Ahmed, Justice Nathwani, Justice V.M. Tarkunde, Mirnal Gore, and Prof. SS Vardhe etc.

Bohra women, in disguise represented the silent majority in the community who supported the reform movement latently, caught the attention of the press.

The Fourth AWDBC was held at Pune on 11-13 February, 1983. Dr. Zenab Poonawala and her husband Taher Poonawala played active role in organising the conference. It was inaugurated by the Vice Chancellor of Poona University. Prominent persons like Dr. Mohammed Hasan, Prof. Aman Chishti, Kuldeep Nayyar, S.M. Joshi and Dr. Baba Adhav participated in the conference. The success of 4th conference had proved that a woman may be capable enough to organize a world conference.

5th AWDBC was organised in Ahemadabad from 22nd to 24th February, 1985. Tayab Bhai Zamindar's family was the organiser. Babubhai Patel (Ex. Chief Minister of Gujarat), Jina Bhai Darji, M.J. Akbar (then editor, Telegraph), Gulam Rabbani Tanba, Dr. Moin Shakir were the prominent participants and speakers at the Conference. By this time the Report of Nathwani Commission had been released, *Kothar* remained unsuccessful in its agitation against Bombay Mercantile Bank, murderous assault on Asghars Ali's life at Cairo (Egypt) had completely damaged Syedna's image even in the eyes of community members as well. Therefore it was not possible for him to incite and moblise the Bohras to oppose the reformists. Consequently Ahmedabad Conference went unopposed. Total 600 delegates participated in which the number of women was more than men. Media coverage was also good.

A Regional Conference was held from 8 to 10 August, 1986 in Leicester (UK). In Ahmedabad Conference it was suggested that a regional conference may be organise in UK so that friends in UK and other European countries could participate in large numbers. Mr. Fazal Kapasi worked in this direction with all sincerity and organised the conference in his home city in Leicester.

More than 400 delegates from UK, Sweden, USA, Canada, France, Holland, Kuwait, India and other places participated. The enthusiasm of the participants was highly encouraging. Their spirit to fight against Kothari establishment influenced reformist greatly. The militant spirit exhibited by the reformists' women during the deliberation in the various sessions impressed the participants. A trust to help the reformist cause was established. In short, this conference in UK had certainly added a new dimension to the reform movement.

6th AWDBC was held at Indore in 1987 immediately after Syedna's *waaz* (Ashoora-Muharram) and demolition of hall in Saifee Colony. It was the first ever conference held in MP (Madhya Pradesh) as is well known, has a large population of Dawoodi Bohras perhaps next to Gujarat. Though visibly there were no reformists Bohra, but with the support of underground sympathizers OmParkash Rawal and Comrade Lagu who keep the banner of secularism, democracy and human rights aloft the conference was successfully organised.

Khawaja Ahmad Abbass (editor of Urdu Blitz) inaugurate the conference. The decision to visit Galiakot visit was taken in this conference. The report of the conference was highlighted by national dailies both in Hindi and English.

The Bohras of Indore, despite provocation from Kothar kept their cool and refused to publicly oppose the conference. Some of them even boldly attended the conference on the quiet.

7th AWDBC was again held at Udaipur on 10th to 12th February 1989. On 22 August 1988 Syedna had cursed the *Khalifas* of Sunni Muslims and had to apologize publicly in the most humiliating situation. Hence the conference in 1989 was the most peaceful.

First All India Bohra Women Conference was held in Udaipur under the joint auspicious of Bohra Youth Girls'Wing and Central Board of Dawoodi Bohra (CBDBC). Dr. Zainab Poonawala and Dr. Zainab Banu, Secretary Girls' Wing, Udaipur were the conveners. It was attended by 500 delegates. During the deliberation in various sessions, the Bohra women were quite critical of certain age old practices like *'Khatna'*, *'Iddah'* (after husband's death) inheritance, divorce etc. in this conference. The decision to hold a women conference was taken in the seventh AWDBC to promote women's thought process and training to speak out about their day-to-day problems.

8th AWDBC was held in Bombay in February, 1991. Before the commencement of the 8th world conference, a procession was taken out with Dr. Shuja Vali and Rehana Lonkhandwala, in chains and their mouth sealed, leading the procession. It was a symbolic representation of bonded slavery of Bohras under Syedna's oppressive rule. The silent procession with placards and banners started from Fort and marched up to the conference hall. The earlier conference in 1981 in Mumbai was opposed by the Syedna most violently but this time was not even noticed by him. Mrinal Gore, Azam Saheb and Aziz Qureshi were the speaker.

9th AWDBC was organised at Aurangabad from 28th to 30th April 1995. This conference was very successful because of Zulfiquar Hussain Bhai's popularity and his respect in General Public in Marathawada. Eminent persons of all religion and various political as well as social organisations were present in the conference. A photo gallery and a medical centre were also inaugurated before the conference.

10th AWDBC was organised at Udaipur from 13th February to 15th February, 1999. It was held in the Silver Jubilee year of the Bohra Youth

Association, which is fighting for freedom from religious tyranny. Surely it was an occasion to look back on the achievements and failures in the last 25 years of struggle. The inaugural session held at Railway Training School Conference Hall. Rajya Sabha member and Journalist Kuldeep Nayyar inaugurated the conference. Justice D.S. Tewatia was Chief Guest while Bihar Minority Affair Minister Lutfur Rehman and Rajasthan Panchayati Raj Mantri C.P. Joshi were special guests. About 400 delegates had participated from England, Canada, USA, Middle East West African and various states of India. The number of women was more than men. To counter the effect of conference the Shababi Bohras organised three days (25-26-27 February) celebration of Syedna's Udaipur visit anniversary.

11th AWDBC was held in Bhopal on February 13-14 in 2001, Madhya Pradesh. L.S. Hardiyaniya Ji was the organiser. Delegates from various parts of the country as well as abroad were present to show their solidarity with the reformists group. Dr. Asghar Ali Engineer, General Secretary of CBDBC in his report highlighted the achievements of the reform movement launched 25 years ago. He also dwelled on the different phases the movement passed through. The orthodox Bohras also participated in the conference. Women presence made the conference lively.

2nd International Conference was organised from 3-5 August, 2001 in Ontario, Canada by the Association of Progressive Dawoodi Bohras of Ontario. The theme of the conference was 'working in partnership'. Saifuddin Insaf and other persons attended the conference from India. The suggestions that came out from the conference were valuable as website formation, book display, youth participation, photography and short summary of key historical figures and events of reform movement, advertisement and marketing – publicity.

12th AWDBC was organised in Surat, Gujarat. Zehra Cyclewala a brave fighter against the hegemony of Syedna was one among the organisers. More than 250 Bohras women and men supporting the reform movement came from different parts of the country and abroad to participate in the conference. The conference was inaugurated by Prof. Mushiral Hasan- then Vice Chancellor of Jamia Millia Islamia University. Swami Agnivesh and Gandhian Narayan Desai were the speakers.

13th, 14th, 15th Conferences were organised in Udaipur only. 13th conference was held in February, 2008 and 14th held in February, 2011. Because of the strategic reason that the reformist Bohras are majority in Udaipur. They have retained the original "Dawoodi Bohra *Jamaat*" with independent democratic functioning and having their control on all the community's properties in Udaipur. Whereas the Syedna's religious establishment has walked out from this original *Jamaat* and has established a separate "Shia Dawoodi Bohra *Jamaat*" and "Burhani Anjuman". It is most commendable that the reformists Bohras in Udaipur are making very good use of the Bohra properties and they need to be encouraged. So the CBDBC decided to hold 15th AWDBC in Udaipur itself and made hat trick by holding the three conferences consecutively in Udaipur.

13th AWDBC was held from 1st to 3rd February, 2008 at Bhartiya Lok Kala Mandal, Udaipur. Before that a seminar on'Communal Harmony' was jointly organised by the University Department of Political Science at Seminar Hall, UCSSH (Arts College) on 'Challenges to Secularism in India' on 1stFebruary, 2008. Rajendra Sachar was the keynote speakers, Dr. Asghar Ali Engineer and Hardeniayjee were the panel speaker. The seminar was chaired by prof B L Mungekar, member Secretary Planning Commission of India.

13th Conference was inaugurated by Rajendra Sachar and co-chaired by B L mungekar, Syeda Hameed and Aruna Roy were guest of honour.

14th AWDBC held in Udaipur from 11th to 13th February 2011 to spread the message of love, harmony and understanding among the Bohras on the both sides of the divide. It was whole heartedly welcomed by all in Udaipur. There was absolutely no adverse opposition from any corner. Huge banners and hoardings giving details of the conference were put up on the main junctures in the Bohra Mohalla and all over the city, several days ahead of the conference. The inaugural function of the conference was held most peacefully at Sukhadia Rangmanch hall and seating of next two days was in the Bohra community hall in the mist of Bohra populace.

The prominent non-Bohra citizens of Udaipur formed a reception committee headed by the Vice Chancellor of Mohan Lal Sukhadia University, Prof. I.V. Trivedi. On 8 Feb., a press conference was held to inform the media regarding the program of the 3 day conference.

A day before on 10th Feb. a national seminar was organised on 'State, religion and Society' so that issues of social reforms could be understood in social and national perspective. Many writers, academics and social activists participated in the seminar. The seminar was inaugurated by Tahir Mahmood and he threw light on the problems and odds reformers have to face.

The conference was inaugurated by Prof. Shahid Mehdi, Professor Tahir Mehmood, Prof. M.S. Agwani, and Medha Patkar were speakers of the inaugural session. Shahid Mehdi said in his inaugural address that all great changes are initiated by small number of people and others follow them. Tahir Mehmood also agreeing with Syed Mehdi said that it is always persecuted minorities who bring about revolution and usher in new social values. Medha Patkar saw the Bohra reform movement in the perspective of people's struggle for liberation.

Since the Bohra reform movement believes in inclusive approach, it formed in its delegate session, three important commissions- Interfaith Commission, Intra- faith Commission and Women Commission.

The Women Commission was formed to raise awareness among women for their rights and gender justice. It would include women of all communities in general and Muslim Women in particular.

Over all this was a historic conference, especially because women showed great enthusiasm as always and also showed keen interest in working for interfaith dialogue. They said "we celebrate unity in diversity. It is our profound belief".

After six years interval15th AWDBC was held on 11-12 March, 2017 at BLKM (Bhartiya Lok Kala Mandal) auditorium, Udaipur. Shri Wajahat Habibullaha, former Chief Information Officer and Chairman Minorities Commission had inaugurated the conference. Padmashri, Indira Jaisingh, former Additional Solicitor General and Senior Advocate Supreme Court of India, Swami Agnivesh and Shri Ved Vyas were the speaker. Prior to the Conference a National Seminar and a Memorial Lectures in memory of Late Dr. Asghar Ali Engineer was organised on 'communal Harmony, Secularism and Democracy' at BLKM on 10thMarch. Dr. Faizan Mustafa, Vice Chancellor of NALSAR University, Hyderabad was the key speaker. Shri Harsh Mandar, former IAS and Irfan Engineer, Director, CSSS, Mumbai were the penalist. The seminar was conducted by Raziya Sanwari. After seminar a play Lashkar Chowk was staged in the evening.

This conference missed very much Dr. Asghar Ali Engineer who passed away in May 2013. The vacuum created by the sudden demise of Dr Asghar Ali Engineer delayed the conference for three years. Saifuddin Insaf was General Secretary of CBDBC at that time. He read the General Secretary's report in spite of his poor health. As per programme the conference was conducted in four sessions. (First inaugural, second and third delegate sessions and fourth election session of office bearers of CBDBCwere held. Mansoor Ali Commander as General Secretary, Saifuddin Insaf on Chairman, Raziya Sanwaree and Irfan Engineer on Vice chairman and Unus Baloowala as Treasurer were elected. Representation of women in

CBDBC has always been very low. Some women are elected to Executive Committee of CBDBC. But from 1977 until now only once a woman was elected as Vice–Chairman. The positions of Chairman, General Secretary and four Secretaries have always been occupied by men.

Application of Mussulaman Wakf Act 1923 on Bohra Wakf Properties

The judgment in the Chandabhai Gulla case was delivered in 1922. Thereafter, the reformist movement lost its focus although scattered efforts through various forums and institutions continued. But nothing much happened from 1922 to 1928. It again gathered momentum in 1928. The Central Assembly had passed the Mussulaman Wakf Act in 1923. The provincial assemblies also adopted it and enforced it is their respective provinces. However, in the Bombay province the Bohra high priest managed to get exemption from the act initially for a period of three years. The reformists were hoping that the application of the Wakf Act would force the high priest to subject the Bohra wakf properties to the control of the Wakf Board and thus would no longer be under his absolute control. The reformists also knew that if the exemption is not challenged in time, the High Priest would manage to get it extended for a much longer period, perhaps even permanently. The reformists, therefore, decided to challenge the exemption.

When the Wakf Act 1923 was before the Legislative Assembly, the Bohra high priest, through whatever leverage he had pressed the Government and the legislature thereupon introduced a section (section 13) in the Act empowering local governments to exempt any community from the operation of the Act. The Act was made applicable to the Presidency of Bombay in 1925, and at that time the Government of Bombay, under pressure from the Bohra high priest, exercising the powers under the said section 13, issued a notification exempting the Bohra community from the operation of the Act. This exemption continued in force till 1931 when the Government of Bombay withdrew it.[8]The reformist Bohras had played an important role in getting the exemption withdrawn.

The Bohra high priest was indignant at the withdrawal of exemption. He organized demonstrations and ordered his followers to take out processions with placards denouncing "gross interference in the religious affairs of the Bohra community". The high priest also won over some Muslim members of the Central Legislative Assembly to support his demand for the exemption but it was refused by it on the ground that this was a matter for the Local Government to decide. The Wakf Act was applied to the Central Province in May 1932 and the high priest had managed to get exemption from the government of Central Provinces right away. Now he enjoyed this exemption in the Central Provinces whereas he lost it in the Bombay Province. In a memorandum submitted on his behalf to the Joint Parliamentary Committee it was maintained that "This exemplifies the danger of allowing matters connected with religion to be left to the sweet will of different Governments and legislatures. What has happened to the Bohra community may happen to any other community. Moreover there is great danger of such interference under the new constitution where all Legislation will depend upon the will of the majority in any legislature. It is therefore essential in the interest of peace and good Government that by a proper enacting of fundamental rights, it should be put beyond the Powers of any Legislature or Government either by legislation or by executive action to do anything which either directly or indirectly has the effect of interfering with religion or religious beliefs of any community".

Thus we see that the Bohra high priest wanted, in the name of religion, to do whatever he pleased. The only result of non-interference by the government would be unhindered exploitation and unrestricted persecution of those who defy the priesthood. Naturally, the reformists pleaded with the government to use its powers, executive or legislative, to curb such exploitation and persecution of dissidents. They formed Dawoodi Bohra Wakf and Trust Welfare Association to struggle for the withdrawal of the exemption of Bohra Wakf properties from the Mussalman Wakf Act, 1923. A memorandum was submitted on behalf of this association to the Joint Parliamentary Select Committee on 6 October 1933 by the secretary I.M. Mandviwala. All the claims of the Bohra high priest were refuted point by point, heavily substantiated by quotations from various religious scriptures and also some important observations of the learned judge in the Chandabhai Gulla case.

An appeal was also addressed to the Honourable Members of the Council of State, the Legislative Assembly and the Legislative Council of Bombay. This appeal was signed by some Muslims, Hindus and Christians as well, besides 407 prominent members of the Bohra community. Among its Bohra signatories were persons like A.M. Kajiji, B.A., L.L.B. (Cant.), Bar-al-Law, Ex. Judge of High Court, Bombay, M.T. Kaderbhoy, Bar-al-Law, President of Anjuman-Zia-ul-Islam, Bombay, Shaikh Faizullahbhoy, S.M. Hamdani, Professor of Theology and brother-in-law of Mullaji Saheb, Ismailbhoy Saiyadi Lukmanji, Professor of Theology and brother-in-law of Mullaji Saheb, Dr. T.M. Kajiji, M.A. (Oxon.) L.L. D.J.P., Bar-at-Law, Dr. F.G. Abbasi, M.B.B.S. and many others most of whom held high qualifications. It was emphasized in the above appeal that "It is absolutely false to say that the application of the Wakf Act is against the religion of the Bohras. Dawoodi Bohras are Mussalmans pure and simple. The Laws of their Religion are strictly according to the Shariat of Islam. All the religious books of the Dawoodi Bohras are written strictly as per commands and injunctions contains in the Holy Quran, strictly according to the Hadees and Sunnate Nabavi, and strictly according to the Teachings, Writings and Khootbas (public lectures) of Hazrat Ali several of which are found in the book *Nehjul Balagha.*[9]

Similarly, the reformists submitted a memorandum in detail to the Governor of Bombay Sir Leslie Wilson. In this memorandum the reformist leaders challenged the Mullaji's contention that there have been no complaints of mismanagement or misappropriation about the charitable trusts under him. The memorandum pointed out, among other things, that "It was only the Mullaji Saheb who has not only not published an account of his management but denied the charities not withstanding that he had under his management as Trustee more than 600 Mosques and 60 Gullas. The Mullaji during the 7 years by various coercive methods got scores of charitable properties and other institutions of the Community transferred to his name or brought under his control."

The above mentioned also pointed out the *modus operandi* employed by the Syedna Saheb to get the charitable properties transferred to his name. Since accountability of the high priest to the community has been one of the major demands of the reformist movement it would not be out of place here to give details of one case showing how coercion was used for transferring properties to his own name. This case pertains to the Faize Huseini Trust, Karachi. I am quoting the memorandum itself:

There is a Trust by name Faiz-e-Huseini in Karachi, which was founded about 35 years ago on a small scale. A trust Deed was really fine condition was drawn up by some honest and sincere good Bohra gentlemen of Karachi. During the last 35 years, its management was so good, and it did such an enormous amount of good to the Community and the Trustees created such confidence in the community, that within the short period of about 10 to 15 thousand rupees, has grown today enormously, become possessed of properties and other things of the value of 30 to 35 lacs of rupees. The trustees themselves carried on their affairs quietly and peacefully without interference or authority over them from any of the three predecessors in title of the present Mullaji. About 6 months ago, when the Mullaji last went to Karachi, he sent round his agents to the Trustees, firstly in asking them to insert a clause in the Trust Deed that the Trustees cannot do anything without first obtaining the Mullaji's permission and that on a vacancy of trustee no trustee could be appointed without his approval. As the trustees had no authority to do this, the Mullaji started coercion. The Trustees to save the Mullaji's molestation and wrath took legal advice and the *advice was that their action would be illegal and they would be civilly and criminally liable* as the Trust Deed prohibited the interference of anyone other than the Trustees. The threat of the Mullaji increased and he demanded that those trustees should transfer the whole concern, including all estate and properties, to his name. As the Karachi legal advisers of the trustees did not advise them to comply[9] with the Mullaji's demand, the Mullaji instructed his solicitors in Bombay on behalf of the Trustees to draw up a deed transferring all properties and everything to the Mullaji's name. When the document arrived in Karachi, the Mullaji's emissaries went to the trustees, coercing and threatening them to sign the deed under the pain of ex-communication. To save himself from punishment of the Mullaji prescribed in the manipulated Misak, the president of the Trustees, Yusufaly Alibhoy Karimji, resigned. Thereafter the feast of the Community was held at the Jamatkhana and a crier loudly proclaimed that no Bohra should go to the Jamartkhana. There were *only two trustees in the Jamatkhana out of nine.* One of them under Meesak said that the "Mullaji was Malik and Dhani and we hereby transfer the whole concern of Faiz-e-Huseini to our august Master Mullaji". Within a minute it was declared that the *Jamat* has passed a resolution, and 10 or 15 Bohras waited upon the Mullaji and told him that by their resolution the whole concern of Faiz-e-Huseini was transferred to him. The memorandum further continued, "Thus the biggest charitable institution is swallowed up by the Mullaji. We humbly request the Collector of Karachi, and Your Excellency and the Government of Bombay will be horrified to learn from the Collector of Karachi what kind of tricks and dangerous games were played by the Mullaji with Faiz-e-Huseini knowing full well the law of the country."[10]

Many more memorandums were given to the Government of Bombay and other officials to press for the withdrawal of exemption from the Wakf Act. These memoranda were given by the leading Bohras of different towns and cities. A petition was presented to Sir Frederick Sykes, Governor of Bombay in Council, Kirkee, by 100 families of Dawoodi Bohra Community residing in Surat. Similarly, about 786 families of Dawoodi Bohras of Central Division gave a petition to him for the same purpose. In a similar memorandum to the minister of education Maulvi Rafi-ud-din Ahmed, signed by many prominent Bohras of Bombay, the following facts were highlighted:

It is astounding and deplorable that the Dawoodi Bohra Community, with its nearly 15 crore of Rupees worth of Wakf properties, bringing in an annual income of more than 15 lacs of Rupees, in the shape of income, rents, profits, etc., does not possess a single High School in the Presidency; not an Hospital; nor a Maternity Home; nor an orphanage; nor an Asylum for widows, the aged, and the crippled, and emaciated. If the income from Bohra Wakf properties were made available for its legitimate and proper use and the Trustees brought under the operation of the Mussalman Wakf Act of 1923, the Dawoodi Bohra Community would possess a high number of High Schools and other such Charitable and Benevolent and Human Institutions, much to the relief of the needy and the poor, and also to the educational and other advancement and progress of the community, and this moreover would relieve the burden of Government, who have not surplus money for nation building purporses.[11]

As a result of all this the government of Bombay appointed a committee under the chairmanship of the collector of Bombay to consider the question of withdrawal. Many prominent Bohras like Abdul Tayeb Maskati, Seth Amiruddin Salehbhai Taiyebji, Dr. Taher Qazi, bar-at-law, Abdeali Qazi (the first Bohra judge of Bombay High Court), Qamruddin Isabhai Vahmi, and others deposed before the committee urging it to withdraw exemption as the community required most of the projection of the Act. The committee subsequently urged the Government of Bombay to withdraw the exemption which was done. One Tayyebali Musajee Koicha also played a leading role in the withdrawal of movement and was persecuted by the Bohra high priest. He was excommunicated and his two daughters who are now past 50 could not marry for that reason. They are presently living in Bandra, a western suburb of Bombay.

Again, after the 1937 elections the formation of ministries under the 1935 constitution, the Bohra high priest, through Muslim members, tried to obtain permanent exemption from the Wakf Act. The reformists, on learning of this led a deputation to Mahatma Gandhi. The deputation also included one Lady Amatullah, who knew Gandhiji from the days when they were in South Africa. Gandhiji was favourably impressed and the matter was discussed in the Congress Working Committee. Maulana Abul Kalam Azad spoke in favour of Syedna but Frontier Gandhi Khan Abdul Ghaffar Khan said that if the Bohra high priest was a Muslim the Act apply to him also and this was accepted. Bhulabhai Desai who was Mullaji's lawyer was also present in the meeting and had to confess that the high priest had forced his followers to transfer charitable properties to his name and was about to do so in case of many more properties.

The latest in the list are the properties of Sir Adam Ji Peerbhoy Sanatorium Trust and Burhani Society, Saraspur, Ahmedabad. Here the Bohra people are residing as tenant on Dawat Property Trust for more than 80 years. The trust asked the residents to vacate their houses as the trust wants to carry out some constructions towards expansion of Dargah area. Some families got stay order from the Civil Courts in 2015. Besides this they have filed petitions in the State Wakaf Board for illegal evacuation and encroachment over the graves of their relatives.

Law Suits

The High Priest Syedna Saheb claims to be not only the religious head of the community but also its sole authority for all secular affairs. Every Bohra is forced to obtain his permission (Raza) before carrying out any activity, religious or non-religious. But the reformists question these powers claimed by the Syedna, which no previous Dai or Imam had ever claimed.

Chanda Bhoy Gulla Case

Well known reformer Shri Ibrahim Adamji Peerbhoy became a party to a suit (OCJ Suit No. 941 of 1917) filed by the then Solicitor General of Bombay province in the Bombay High Court against the then Bohra high priest Syedna Tahir Saifuddin. The suit was filed to compel the Syedna to account for the money collected from the Gulla(cash box) kept at Chandabhoy Seth Mausoleum. It is highly interesting to read the amazing claims made by the then High Priest, 51st Dai Syedna Taher Saifuddin in the suit. He contended that Chandabhoy was not a saint at all and that the mosque was not named after him. He also *stated* that the donation to the Gulla was not charitable and he as a Dai or head of the community had absolute control over the Gulla and that he was entitled to dispose of all such offerings as he pleased. His contention was also that by virtue of his office as a Dai he had power to close it at any time and that Chandabhoy'a tomb could not form the subject of a trust and further that Badri Mahal was presented as a Wakf to him and his successors in perpetuity and all the suit properties vested in him by virtue of his office as spiritual and temporal head of the community. He claimed that the management of these properties had been carried on by his deputies (Amils) who were accountable to him only and the plaintiff had no right to ask for any accounts. To substantiate these claims the judge Martin examined witnesses who said that Mullaji Saheb was not accountable to anyone except the Imam in seclusion and that he is representative of God on the Earth and as such infallible (Kal Masum). His witness further said that according to the levels of this religion the Mullaji is the master of the mind, property, body and soul of each of his followers and that his followers are bound to obey him implicitly and cannot question any of acts of Mullaji.

Justice Martin[12] after rejecting the extraordinary claims of the 51st Dai (SyednaTaher Saifuddin) that the mosque was the subject of a trust for public purpose of a religious and charitable nature and the tomb of Chandabhoy and the Gulla offering were charitable gifts held on charitable trusts for public purposes by the Mullaji. The Court also held that Badri Mahal was purchased partly with the aid of Gulla moneys and that the Gulla charity was entitled to be recouped, the amount utilized towards the acquisition and that pending such recoupment the Gulla charity was entitled to a charge on the Badri Mahal.

Against above judgment an appeal to the division bench of the Bombay High Court was preferred by the high priest. It was appeal No.42 of 1921, however, the only variation made in the decree was that the Mullaji Saheb was given liberty to place at any time another box outside the enclosure of Chandabhoy's tomb and therein are at the absolute disposal of the Dai-ul-Mutlaq or any purpose charitable or not charitable as the said Dai may direct.

This case (1917-1921) exposed the mind and attitude of the 51st Dai Syedna Taher Saifuddin when he made astonishing and absurd claim that he is the God on earth, infallible, immaculate, the master of mind, body, soul and properties of Dawoodi Bohras. None of the previous Dais or Imams or even Prophets ever made such claims.

The Abde Fatima Case

In this case in 1937 A Nikah solemnized by a Muslim Qazi was declared improper and not recognizable by the chief Amil of Bombay Sheikh Salehbhai Safiyuddin. And he served notice both on husband and wife. He addressed notice to the bride as Miss Fatima and not as Mrs. Fatima Abde Ali. The high priest had gone for Hajj but he upheld the contents of the notice on this return.

The aggrieved party then filed a case in the Bombay High Court for defamation. The case came on board in the month of March 1940. According to the plaintiff's Council a marriage in Islam is contractual and it is not necessary to obtain any priest's permission before its solemnization. The high priest employed the best brain to win this case but could not win as the Islamic law was so very clearly on the plaintiff's side. The high priest had to agree to a compromise with the plaintiff's and recognize their marriage. Despite this the high priest continued to harass other couples who dared to marry without his prior permission or consent.

Buxamusa Dadhi (beard) case

The suite no. 7074 was filed in the court at Bombay in 1941. The matter in this case was that the bridegroom was clean shaven and the priest refused to solemnize the Nikah. However he agreed to do this after a refundable deposit of Rs. 200 was deposited with him. The money was to be refunded after the bridegroom grows beard. The bridegroom grew beard but the deposit amount was not refunded. Hence the father of the bridegroom filed the suit. Consequently the judge decreed the plaintiff's claim with costs and Rs. 80/- professional costs against the defendant.

The reformists no doubt registered victory in many of these law suits. But the Bohra high priest converted the defeats into victories each time by false propaganda. Not only that, after every such defeats in law suits, grand victory celebrations - Fateh-e-mubeen were organized keeping the community completely in the dark about the actual judgments. Such shrewd tactics helped in increasing the hold of the Syedna over the community and creating an image of invincibility.

Numbers of legal cases have been filed by the Central Board and other persons against Syedna and Kothar. In Udaipur, Masjid case is historical one. All Bohra Masjids in Udaipur are under the complete control of Reformists. The Syedna and his representatives claimed in this suit that Syedna should have complete control over Masjids of Udaipur in his capacity as the Sole Trustee. His aim was to prevent Reformists from entering the Masjids for Namaz and crush the Reform Movenment. All Masjids in Udaipur, as in all over the world, were built, maintained and managed by local Bohras money. Syedna never gives any money for Masjids or any other Wakf properties, even as Sole Trustee. Before filing the case, Syedna had told his blind followers not to pray in Masjids because all the Masjids controlled by the Reformists have lost *Rooh.(soul)* Rajasthan High Court did not give any relief to Syedna, did not accept his claim that his *Raza* (prior permission) is necessary for each and every activity that the Bohras do, but allowed the orthodox Bohras to pary in one of the Masjids with their own Imam. This was a great blow to Syedna.

Rasool Engineer had taken lots of pains in fighting a case against Syedna and his persistence was really admirable. He has spent so much time, energy and money from his pocket and had pursued the cases with single minded devotion. He even succeeded in getting the Kurla Amil arrested through a court warrant.

Idris Bhai Kingkhabwala from Surat has also taken an admirable step by filing a case in Charity Commissioner, Baroda against Dawat-e-Hadiya and is pursuing his own and spending great deal of time, money and energy on it. Ali Husain Lashkarwala in Ujjain and Kika Bhai Advocate also has filed cases against the *Amil* of Ujjain for declaring *baraat.* Ali Husain Lashkarwala even succeeded in his case and a judgment came against the *amil* in the Ujjain court. Mr. Fida Husain Kapasi of Nasik has filed several cases against the local *amil* and has pursued these cases with consistency. Abid Bhai Merchant fighting the Charni Road Sanatorium case for years with great zeal and determination. His case has given very tough time to the Kothar. Zehra Cyclewala also filed a case against some prominent orthodox Bohras who were harassing her at the behest of Kothar. Mr. Zainuddin Wali and Tayyabi Zamidar, Former Vice Presidents, CBDBC are pursuing a case regarding Qutubuddin Shaheed Mausoleums income in the Charity Commissioner's Office in Ahmedabad and have applied for scheme. Zainuddin Wali obtained court order for burial in two to three cases and as a result succeeded in burying dead bodies. These cases have given great fillip to Bohra reform movement. Recently in Burhanpur three-four families residing in the periphery of Burhanpur Dargah filed cases against the Dargah committee that evacuated them forcefully. The Central Board of Dawoodi Bohra Committee filed a petition in the Supreme Court for reviewing the judgment on the prevention of Excommunication Act delivered in 1962. However the case has still not come on Board.

Relief and Charitable Work during sectarian / communal violence and natural calamity

In December 1914 a piece of blood stained cloth was found in the courtyard of a Sunni mosque in Bhopal (a princely State). It was suspected to be stains of menstrual blood and the piece of cloth to have been thrown from the adjoining Bohra house. This unrest led to rioting and about 120 of the 134 Bohra shops were looted and burned by the Sunni Muslims of Bhopal. This wanton arson and loot drove some 800 Bohras out of Bhopal.[13] The sought shelter in a Bohra Musafir Khana at Ujjain. When the sons of Adamjee Peerbhoy[14] came to know about it they sent their representatives to the Viceroy and the Political Agent in Bhopal and sent telegrams to the Begum of Bhopal demanding compensation for the loss suffered by the Bohras. A deputation of the victims of the riot also met Syedna Abdulla

Badruddin to apprise him of the events at Bhopal. The latter expressed the satisfaction at the action taken by the sons of Sir Adamjee Peerbhoy.

However, SyednaAbdullah Badruddin died on 24 January, 1915 and Syedna Tahir Saifuddin succeeded him. The new Syedna did not like the initiative taken by the sons of Sir Adamjee for securing compensation and rehabilitation of the victims of the Bhopal riots. He sent a barrister called H.A. Husain and resident of Bhopal Zamin Husain to the Vazir of the Begum to convey to her that the Syedna has raised a fund of Rs.10 lakhs for the relief of riot victims and that she need not arrange for the compensation as paid by the sons of Adamjee Peerbhoy. When the Bohras of Bhopal learnt of this step they requested the high priest to withdraw his letter to the Begum of Bhopal asking her not to arrange for the compensation. The high priest gave a verbal assurance to the delegation that he would consult the sons of Adamjee Peerbhoy before taking any step. Despite this assurance the high priest met the Begum's *Vazir* secretly in Surat and settled the matter with him without any compensation money. Not only that, he sent his men to Ujjain and force the refugees staying in the *musafirkhana* to vacate it immediately and proceed to Bhopal.

The riot-affected Bohras however, refused to go to Bhopal without any assurance of their safety. The sons of Adamjee Peerbhoy again came to their rescue and arranged for a special train to take them to Burhanpur. Meanwhile they started negotiations with the political agent at Bhopal and finally secured an assurance from him for the safety and well-being of the Bohras before they returned to that town. The high priest was annoyed at this development and decided to take revenge. He withdrew his Amil from Bhopal and stopped permission for all religious rites. Ultimately the Begum intervened and the high priest agreed to send his *Amil* again. But he never pardoned the sons of Sir Adamjee Peerbhoy for the initiative taken by them for securing relief for the riot-affected Bohras of Bhopal.[15]

During Gujarat earthquake in 2001, the earthquake affected Bohras of Bhuj, Anjar, Morbi, Wankaner, Surendanagar and Limdi the Bohra Youth reformists of Udaipur helped the poor Bohras of Kathiawad. Similarly during communal riots 2002 in Gujarat, the reformist of Udaipur helped them by providing them with ration, dresses, blankets and cash.

Conclusion

Thus it will be seen from the above that the reformists stands for social reform and progress in the Dawoodi Bohra community. They are opposed to Syedna's absolute dictatorship. They stand for human rights, freedom of conscience, accountability and democracy. They oppose un-Islamic practices of social boycott and *raza* which violate human rights. They consider themselves true Dawoodi Bohras and have never challenged any well-established religious doctrines. They are thus not involved in any religious controversies of theological nature. They accept the rightful successor to the 52nd Dai Syedna Mohammed Burhanuddin. Their aim is to usher in social reforms.

Notes and References

Nass: Shias developed a doctrine of '*nass*'. According to this doctrine, a successor for the high religio-political office is specifically appointed by the predecessors without any ambiguity. All Shia sects and subsects follow this doctrine of *nass* in one form or other. Shias thus reject the principle of election by people. The doctrine of *nass* provided the Shias a strong feeling of certainty and a sense of being followers of the holy family and Prophet.

1. Asghar Ali Engineer, *The Bohras,* Vikas Publishing House, 1980, New Delhi, P.266.
2. Ibid, P.180.
3. Vide judgment in Civil Suit No.32 of 1925 commonly known as Burhanpur Dargah Case in the court of 1st class sub-judge, Burhanpur, C.P. published in the booklet form by Tayyeb Ali Bhangarhwala, Burhanpur, October 1931, P.59.
4. Times of India, 2nd April, 1949.
5. Dawoodi Bohra Bulletin, Miladun Nabi, Number, Surat, 27-28, dated 31.5.69 pp.61-62.
6. See Souvenir Charity, Programme Social Cultural Centre, 28.6.75, Surat, under the title, The First Conference of the Reformist Bohras in 1944.
7. Theodore P. Wright Jr., 'Competitive Modernisation within the Dawoodi Bohras Sect of Muslims and its Significance for Indian Political Development', in: *Comparative Competition and Modernisation in South Asia,* (Ed.) by Helen F. Ulrich, B&C Abhinav Publication, 1975, Delhi, P.153.
8. *Vide Musalman Wakaf Act and the Dawoodi Bohra Community: Important Memorial*, 1933, Satya Mitra Press, Fort, Mumbai, P.3.

   Most of the properties of Bohra community in India were build and established around late 19th century,(after1870 when economic prosperity came in due to government's tenders to honest and hard working Bhoras during first and second world wars. Many trusts were built in the memory of their elders by wealthy Bhoras like.

   The Husain Ali Abdul Ali Dholkawala Trust

   The Noorbhai Jivenji Moriswala Trust

   The Naimatullah Bai Maskati Trust

   The Adamji Peerbhoy Trust

   The Mullaha Kalimuddin Amiruddin Trust

   The Lukmanji Bootwala Trust

The Haider Ali Kasamji trust

The Esmail Machiswala Trust

Mohammed Ali Tawawala Trust

The Adamji Mullah hasan Ali Jhanjiria Trust

The Seth Alibhai Alvi Trust

Mullaha Ibrahimji Gheewala Trust

The Abdul Kadar Ebrahim Trust

Ea Currimji Trust and many more

No Dai prior to 51st Dai had ever interfered in the management of these trustsand the members of the community used to take benefits of various mosques, jamatkhanas, Musafirkhanas, Sanatoriums, Madarsas, Schools and Hospitals etc established by these trusts. Their use were either most nominal or free. s.

9. Ibid, P.9.
10. Ibid, pp.24-25
11. Ibid, P.75
12. Vide judgment by J. Martin in suit No.941 of 1919 in the High Court of Judicature at Bombay, 19th March, 1921, P.5.
13. Asghar Ali, Op. Cit., P.169.
14. Sir Adamjee Peerbhoy was a man of humble origin who through his hard work and entrepreneurship became quite rich. However, he remained pious and humble. He was also a great philanthropist who founded many charitable institutions like orphanages, schools etc. He also built the rail to uninhabited Matheran hill station near Mumbai at his own cost in 1907. He was highly respected by the community both for his humility and philanthropy.

    49thDai Syedna Burhanuddin was heavily in debt. He borrowed some money from two Hindu Banias and his own Amil Shaikh Abdul Taiyab. They filed a case and actually his Amil tried to put the Dai into prison for non-payment of the debt. Local Dawoodi Bohra Jamats were quite independent then. They used to collect fund and spend locally. Nothing was regularly sent to Dai.

    Sir Adamjee Peerbhoy organized a first All Bohra Conference at Dhoraji. Among other reforms, it was made obligatory for Amils to remit part of their collections to the Dai.

    SyednaTahir Saifuddin did not take very kindly to Sir Adamjee's sons' philanthropic activities, as in them he saw his rivals, and perhaps more so because their philanthropic activities far exceeded his. Sir Adamjee's sons were well educated and emulated their father in public and charitable activities. Sir Adamjee was a highly successful government contractor mainly supplying to the British army in India. His honesty, integrity and hard work were highly valued by government officers. Hewas made sheriff of Bombay for the year 1897-97. Adamjee Peerbhoy was the first member of his community to become Justice of Peace and Sheriff of Bombay. He died on 11 August, 1913.

    On 13 August, the *Times of India* editorial said: "His wealth was made entirely by his own energy and preserving enterprise. He started life next to none. But as he accumulated the earnest of a hard life he showed in marked degree that trait, which is fortunately characteristic of the modern Indian Capitalist, of generosity in devoting a portion of it to the amelioration of the lot of his fellow man... Moslems will remember his for his beneficiations to their communal interests and all India is indebted to him for the splendid contribution which he made for the prosecution of scientific study at Aligarh. Government marked publicly their sense of his worth when they recommended him for Knighthood and now that he is gone we may thanked thank him as a faithful citizen whose example behooves his successor to emulate."

15. '*Seerat*': Weekly Urdu paper, Mumbai, Jild No.4, Shumara No.44, 26th August, 2010, P.11.

Chapter - 5

Status of Dawoodi Bohra Women

The question of women's status has acquired great importance throughout the world and among all community. The reason is obvious. For thousands of years women were kept in total subjugation in all patriarchal societies. Women in Islamic societies are perceived to be suffering more compared to women of other societies.

The orthodox *Ulama* treat the question of women in Islam with hypersensitivity. They are opposed to any kind of change in general and women's status in particular. They imitate quite mechanically all the provisions in this respect formulated by the *Ulama* more than fourteen hundred years ago. Any rethinking on the issue is no less than a sin. The status of women has become an important question of identity vis-à-vis the west as far as the Islamic countries are concerned and similarly Muslim minorities vis-à-vis majority communities in counties like India. Thus, any change in Muslim personal law is opposed vigorously considering it as a threat to Muslim identity and an unwarranted interference in Islam. The agenda of Islamic revolution in Iran included re-assertion of Islamic identity vis-à-vis the west and it found expression in enforcing chador (a head gear) for women.

In the modern era, education is spreading fast in all over the world. Muslim women in almost all countries are going to colleges and universities in large numbers. These educated women become far more aware of their rights than illiterate women. Thus there is hardly any country with sizeable Muslim population, where women are not seen asserting themselves. Even in the conservative sheikhdom like Kuwait, thousands of women surrounded the Parliament demanding right to vote and right to hold political offices in 2005 and succeeded in winning their rights.

It is important to note that Islam is the first religion in the world which recognized women as legal entity and gave her all rights that man enjoyed.

In addition, Islam's equalitarian message guarantees unalienable rights to Muslim women namely, the right to life, right to obtain education, right to conduct business, right to inheritance and maintain property, right to keep their names (her surname remains same even after the marriage), right to consent in nikah (marriage). Male domination is not at all Islamic, though it is justified in its name. Men use some selective verses from the Qu'ran, ignore their social context and use them to perpetuate their domination. They conveniently ignore the verses empowering women or laying down equality of both the sexes. In fact in verses like 2:219, 2:228 and 33:35 there is clear statement about equality of both the sexes and yet they are totally ignored and instead they quote verses like 4:84 to establish their domination.[1] They even distort the meaning of words like *quwwam* used in above verses to retain their hegemony.

It is interesting to note that while the Saudi government did not allow women to drive cars (allowed in March 2018 with certain restrictions). The Iranian government has started exclusive taxi services to be run by women. Thus Iranian women cannot only drive private cars but can also be a taxi driver. Similarly, the Kuwait government denied its women to vote till 2005. Other Muslim countries like Bangladesh, Pakistan, Egypt and other countries gave them the right to vote long ago. How does one explain these contradictory practices? Are there different Islam or there are differing attitudes towards women? Thus it is not Islamic sources but man's attitude which matters.

The Bohras belong to Shia Ismai'lis sect. The current period is period of seclusion (Imam is in hiding) and hence the present hierarchy of *Dawah al-Hadiyah* (i.e. rightly guiding mission) is headed by *Dai.*The *Dai* is supposed to be spiritual guide and spiritual leader in the absence of Imam. However, from the 51st *Da'i* Syedna Taher Saifuddin on wards, all *Dai* and their establishment (known as Kothar) have totally given up spiritual pursuit. They are using their inherited position and power in exploiting the followers for their own personal and worldly interests. The Bohras are led to believe that their prayers, fasting, Haj or any religious rituals will not be valid if *Dai* is not pleased with them! In spite of this the reformists recognize the position of *Dai*, they do not interfere in religious affairs[2] their demand is about temporal affairs only.

The Bohra in general and Bohra women in particular have superficial knowledge of their religion. Most Bohras can read Quran in Arabic but do not understand a word of it. Bohras are encouraged to memorize some *Surahs* or even whole of Quran but are not allowed to read its translation and *tafseer* (explanation). They are easily exploited becauseof their ignorance.

The holy Book Qu'ran puts women on equal spiritual footing with men. The Bohra women must consider Maulatuna Hurrat-ul-Malika, the Queen of Yemen, whom18th Imam Mustansir made her overall head of Dawat(*Hujja)* in Yemen their role model. She was very brave, very intelligent and learned lady. She was veiled but attended state councils in person and thus mixed with men, and refused to conduct the meetings hidden by screen. After 20th Imam Amir's assassination and at his command, she instituted the *Silsila* of *Dai-ul-mutlaqeen of Dawat-us-sharia* (established the institution of the vice regent of the Imam on Earth). In the history of Fatimi Dawat, she stands out prominently as the mother of all *Duats*. This case study of Hurrat-ul-Malika is enough to manifest the status of women in Bohra religion and faith more than 1000 years ago, even in male dominated Arab society. But gradually with the passage of time and with Indian cultural influence the status of women has deteriorated from free dominating to submissive and confined to home, dependent on men for sustenance and protection.

At present status of Bohra women in India is little bit better compare to other Muslim women because:

(i) Equal liberal and flexible attitude towards women in religious matter: Bohra both men and women uphold the seven pillars (*daa'im*) of Islam (compared to five in other legal schools). These are (i) Allegiance, love and devotion to Allah, Prophets, the scriptures and the Imam (*walayat*), (ii) ritual purification (*taharat*), (iii) ritual prayer (*salat*), (iv) alms giving (*Zakat*, presently collected by the Dai), (v) fasting (*Saum*), (vi) pilgrimage to Mecca (*Hajj*) and (vii) struggle against evil (*Jihad*).

Bohra religious doctrine also espouses the social injunctions of *Shariat*, including both personal and civic laws. It expects women to wear hijab in public (head covering with open face) encourages men to grow beards. According to Shazadi Dr. Tahera Bai Saheba, "in terms of their spirituality, women are addressed as being with soils, just like men as being who has the potential to obtain nearness to God through worship and good deeds just like men. She also draws attention to the women that are held in high spiritual regard such as Maryam (S.A.) and Maulatuna Fatima (S.A.)." Bohra women are allowed to enter in mosques and perform five times prayer there. Similarly during *majalis* (religious gathering) they remain present.[3] The individual (generally man) presiding over a *majalis* is termed the *sadar* (chairperson). He sits in a central space surrounded by male members of the congregation. Women usually sit in concealed enclaves ore in a main space with a divider between them and the men, from they can view the proceedings without being seen themselves. In women only *majalis* a female *sadar* presides. Women do not recite Quran, poetry (*naat, marsiya*), call *azan* in the presence of men in mosque nor can a woman perform *imamat* (lead congregation prayer).

Bohra women can pray in the mosques, visit Bohra shrines and graveyards without any restriction. Other Muslim women in India do not enjoy these privileges. They do not pray in mosque, do not go to graveyard. Previously they were allowed to enter any shrine and Dargah but since Haji Ali Dargah ban, their entry to any shrine / *mazar* became questionable.[4]

(ii) Female domination in family life: Bohra family life is near to Matrifocal[5]in terms of women domination in domestic affairs. Bohra community is a trader community where male members have to go outside home for trading activities from morning to late evening and the female members stay at home, remain busy in household chorus and maintain social relations. In the domestic affairs women have been taking decisions autonomously about replacement of kitchen and home appliances, interior furniture, decorative items and invite relatives and friends for lunch / dinner etc. It is the lady of the house who prepares budget for the family members and try to make saving out of it.

In Bohra family life, daughter and son are equally treated. Gone are the days when there was some discrimination between male and female. Now both get equal education according to his/her caliber, equal health care and nutrition, equal affection and regards and both share equal responsibility in maintaining family discipline. Daughters are never considered as liability. She is brought up as asset. Female child infanticide is never done. Hence sex ratio is higher compare to other communities. Although Human Development Index (HDI) is not available but it must be equal to any developed community.

Family planning is very common and two children norm is generally accepted practice. Joint family life has gradually withered away and nuclear family trend is prevalent everywhere.

(iii) Mobility: The Bohra society does not endorse the view that women should be confined to the four walls of the home and should have no role to play outside. Bohra women go out for shopping, for morning and evening Walk in nearby public parks either alone or with children or with female friends or relatives. They drive cars or ride scooters or bicycles without any objection from anyone.

Bohra women are also free to go to Ziyarat tour with their *sahio* (friends) or female relatives. They stay at Musafirkhana (guest house) on rental basis where both lodging and boarding are provided. Every Bohra shrine has a Musafirkhana. They go for *Hajj* and *Umrah* without *Mehramdar* with tour operators who managed *Mehramdar* by his own.

Purdha /veil which they call *rida* was made mandatory by 52nd *Da'i*, Syedna Mohammed Burhanuddin for adult women outside the home, comprised of a full length shirt (*lehenga* or *ghaghra*) and a triangular garment (*parr* or *pardi*) covering the head and bosom down to the lips; the *parr* has a flap that is sometime used to cover the face. The *rida* is evolved in the present form in the last 30 years or so in order to differentiate them from reformist women who do oppose *rida* as a symbol of anti-women because previously it was not mandatory for common Bohra women. Only the Royal(Syedna) women family members used to wear. In public places they were generally seen with common outfit –Salwaar-Kurta or Sari. 52nd Syedna's ferman made Rida compulsory for Bohra women as symbol of Dawoodi Bohra identity. The reformist women do not wear Rida, hence they are recognized and prevented from entering into Bohra mosque, Dargah and Jamaat Khana.

Rida is not like black burqa which hide every part of the body except the eyes. Rida is made very colourful and attractive, which gives a beautiful look to a woman. Her face and hands are open. Rida is worn by Bohra women only. No other Muslim women wear Rida.

Triple Talaq

Muslim practice of triple divorce which has been a subject of much heated controversy in recent years is not applicable to Dawoodi Bohras. Amongst Bohras, the utterance of the word 'talaq' thrice by the husband has no significance,divorce does not occur. As compared to other Islamic sects divorce is comparatively difficult amongst Bohras. The divorce proceedings are carried out by the 'Amil' (often with the assistance of the Jamat Committee) who initially tries to listen to the grievances of the two parties and makes best efforts at resolving the difference between them. But if all hopes of reconciliation fails, a divorce is allow after considerable time. Before acceptance of talaq by Amil all the valid demands of wife have to be fulfilled by the husband. Amil issues divorce certificate which also includes signatures of two witnesses[6] of the divorce and of husband. The certificate is issued to both the parties. This procedure of talaq prevailing in Bohra community is wholly based on Quranic verse 4:35. The privilege of a Bohra woman to appoint her own arbiter in a dispute with her husband appears to be far more significant.

Maintenance after divorce is granted for *iddah* period i.e. three months or three menstrual cycles although the Quran has not fixed any time limit for maintenance. Neither the amount of maintenance nor the period has been mentioned[7]there are two keywords in the verse pertaining to maintenance *mala'a* and *bilm'aruf*. These have been translated differently by the exegetes, Allama Yusuf Ali translates *mala'a* as maintenance but *m'aruf* as reasonable (scale).[8] Mohammed Asad also translates *mala'a* as maintenance but *m'aruf* as goodly manner. Imam Raghib defines it as anything which benefit but while referring to verse 2:241 of the Quran, he defines *mala's* as something which is given for the period of *Iddah.*[9]

Thus we see most jurists of the classical period interpreted them to mean maintenance of the period of *iddah* and because the supreme court of India awarded Shah Bano maintenance beyond the period of *iddah* the Indian Muslim leaders and office bearers of the Muslim Personal Law Board decried it as an interference in the divine law. However, what is divine is verse 2:241 and the words *ma...* and *bilm'aruf* not their interpretation. In fact, the verse neither sets down time period nor specifies any amount. It has been left to human understanding and the requirement of changing times. Reformists Bohra should extend its time till second marriage of the divorcee. But in Bohra divorce case the practice is of one time settlement, means whatever both the parties agree to give and take the divorce committee endorses it. After that no liabilities of maintenance remains with the husband.

Divorcee woman has a right to remarry of her choice after the witnesses of her divorce are present at the time of *nikah*. In case one of the signatory witnesses has passes away then the other who was present in the court at time of divorce may appear to give testimony. Without witness of the divorce the marriage of divorcee remain postponed till testimony of the witnesses received. For men it is not needed. This again a manifestation of deprivation of women rights on the name of *sharia* laws while the supporter of *sharia* laws explained it in terms of Quranic privilege of man to have four wives.

Mehar: Dower

Mehar or dower money is essential part of Islamic marriage. Without *Mehar* a *nikah* cannot be said to have been properly solemnized. Dower money must be paid or fixed before the solemnization of a marriage. It is the exclusive preserve of the woman or the bride to determine the amount. Also *Mehar* belongs the wife alone. Neither her father nor husband can claim it. She can spend it the way she likes. The Quran does not specify any amount of *Mehar*. It is the right of the bride to demand as much as she desires. It could be nominal or it could be quite substantial. Part of the *Mehar* could be paid at the time of *nikah* which is known as *mahr-i-mu'ajjal* (immediately paid portion of *mehar*) and part of it could be paid at later date or at the time of divorce. This is known as *mahr-i-muwajjal* (deferred portion of *mehar*). Generally at the time of *nikah* both the portion of *mehar* is separately specified. *Mehar* also often acts as a security against divorce though it is not its original intent.

The practice prevalent in Bohra community is of *mahr-i-mu'ajjal*, promptly paid at the time of *nikah* in cash. Generally Bohra bride demands a nominal amount of *mehar* as I demanded Rs.41 as *mehar* in 1975. Now a days the most common figure is Rs.786 or less or slightly more because Bohra community believes in this concept that bridegroom must pay to the bride some amount as a token of his love, truthfulness and sincerity. They do not consider *mehar* as a security against divorce. Some highly educated brides now have been demanding to increase the *mehar* amount in lakhs as deterrent against divorce.

Nikah and the Role of *Wali* (guardian)

Marriage is a social contract in Islam. During *nikah* both the bride and bridegroom can stipulate conditions for marriage. It implies that women are free to enter or not to enter a marriage contract. However, traditionally the women herself is not allowed to negotiate her marriage. She is given into marriage by her guardian (*wali*) who generally happens to be her father. In his absence, her grandfather or brother acts as the guardian.

Though the *wali* does so with her consent and the consent is given in the presence of two witnesses. But coercion in such a cases is not ruled out. Hence some Muslim countries have deleted the requirement of *wali* from *nikah*. They emphasized that mere consent of bride during *nikah* ceremony where she remained present behind the curtain is sufficient and her signature on *nikahnama* as well is essential.

In Bohra community the bride is not required to be present at the time of performing *nikah*. Prior to *nikah* ceremony two trustworthy gentlemen go to bride's residence with printed *nikah* forms in which they fill the required details, including the *mehar* amount demanded by the bride, after the bride clearly gives her consent for the marriage. She is then required to sign the Nikah forms. *Amil* performs the *Nikah* in presence of many people, by checking the *Nikah* forms signed by the bride and bridegrooms, confirming who is bride's *wali*, confirmation by the two witnesses in front of all about brides consent to this marriage and after confirmation by the bridegroom and *wali* about the conditions of the marriage.

Though polygamy is perfectly lawful, it is seldom practiced among the Bohras who are, by and large, monogamous. No polygamy, no domestic violence and adherent to family planning (generally two child norms) are some other reasons which make Dawoodi Bohra women more dignified and respectful.

Hundred per cent women literacy with encouraging higher education

"Seeking knowledge is mandatory for every Muslim man and woman." (*Hadith* Prophet Mohammed PBUH). Unfortunately this *Hadith* has been ignored by Muslim in India as elsewhere in South Asian countries. The level of Muslim female literacy rate and also enrolment of girls in primary / upper primary is low and dropout rate is high. For example in Rajasthan Muslim constitutes the second largest religious community. But on literacy rate it is on the lowest place. Jain community has the highest literacy rate (94.7%) in the State while Muslim has 56.6% literacy rate in total, male have 71.4% literacy rate where female having only 41.8% literacy rate. The gender gap in education among Muslim community is 30 per cent. Girls enrolment up to primary 30.5%, middle level 14.2%, secondary 9.5%, senior secondary 3.9%, graduation 2.4% and madarasa school 3.8% only.

A study commissioned by the Ministry of Women and Child Development (2007) found the main factors contributing to low enrolment and high incidence of dropout among Muslim girls were a combination of poverty, absence of separate girls' schools, conservative attitude and early marriages.

Surprisingly among Dawoodi Bohra community there is hundred per cent literacy rate both in male and female. Higher education in girls is very encouraging and in some cases more than boys. It may be a role model for other girls in general and Muslim girls in particular. In addition to Bohra women's education, Bohras ranks high in gender development index and gender empowerment index. There are number of women MBBS doctors, engineers, CAs, Ph.Ds, university professors, journalists, office assistants, advocates and school teachers. Women entrepreneurs are on rise.

Prior to 'literacy mission' Bohra community had achieved the target of 100% literacy rate in women too. A common Bohra tries his best to send his daughter and son in the basic school of the locality. If needed,he does not hesitate to send children for tuition and spend maximum of his income on education. Meritorious children are encouraged to appear in competitive exams such as ZEE, NEAT, PMT, PET, RAS, IAS though success rate remained very low because without reservation they have to competein general category only. The choice of Bohra children's school status depends upon the income of the family from missionary English medium private school, government school and community school respectively.

It is said that Syedna Tahir Saifuddin, 51st *dai* empowered women in the community by encouraging them to pursue education, advising them about the importance of their role in their families and simultaneously encouraging them to pursue professions in which they maintained their dignity and respect (*lihaaz*). He established numerous schools for girls to encourage their parents to educate them. He also encouraged his own family to pursue secular education in addition to *dini ta'leem*. Syedna Qutubuddin's wife SakinaBai Saheb was the first girl in Saifee Mahal to attend Cathedral High School with Syedna Tahir Saifuddin's *raza* and to pursue higher education further. Syedna Tahir Saifuddin also admitted girls to Jame'a Saifiyyah and encouraged them to pursue *Dawat ilm*. On his Golden Jubilee as *Dai,* Syedna Tahir Saifuddin established a youth organization in *Dawat* for young men *Shabab-ul-Eidiz Zahabi* and also one for women *Bunayyat-ul-Eidiz-zahabi*.

Syedna Mohammed Burhanuddin continued the legacy of encouraging women's education and grant *raza* to so many in the community to pursue education and respectful careers while fulfilling, their primary duty to nurture and to bring up their children. When Syedna Mohammed Burhanuddin established a college student organization for boys (*Talibb'ul Kulliyatil Muminun*) he also established one for girls (*Talibatul Kulliyatil Muminaat*). He also established Burhani Women's Association.

At present 54th *Dai* Tahir Fakhruddin continues this legacy. Emphasizing the empowerment of women in Bohra community in a press meet in March 2017 in Mumbai he referred Maulatuna Hurratul Maleka and said "in our community there is no glass ceiling in the role women play in society."

The other claimant of 53rd *Dai*, Syedna Mufaddal Saifuddin – a school dropout himself does not believe in imparting higher education to women. Recently in a religious sermon (*vaaz*) he appealed *mumineen* (people of faith) not to send daughters and wives for job outside home particularly at call centre on night duty. He also asserted for early girls marriages and *khafz* (women's circumcision).[11]

Better Economic Status

Poverty among Muslims in India is well known. Sachchar Committee Report does underline the poverty of Muslims in general and among Muslim women in particular.A report by National Council for Applied Economic Research (NCAER) has brought to light some astonishing figures, according to which three out of ten urban Muslims are poor i.e. officially come below the poverty line (BPL) living on a monthly income of Rs.550 and less. The rural Muslim comes below down the scale. One in five rural Muslim comes below poverty line with an average monthly income of Rs.338 throughout the year.[11] Going deeps down the fact, the 'Pew survey' showed that Muslim spend Rs.32.70 a day while Sikh is on the top spendingaround Rs.55.80 a day.

However Muslim women are facing "dire abysmal poverty" in India. But Bohra women are somehow outside the BPL periphery as described earlier that Bohras are in business and well to do community. Beggars are found in this community of course and some people may be in the lower income group but working of so many charitable institutions here and there within the community help them from time to time.

There is a tradition to give pocket money to wife, daughter, mother and bachelor sister depending upon the income of father or husband. She can spend it the way she likes or save it for any emergency. Besides pocket money she earns *salam* and *eidi* (gift of Eid) from her family male members. These amount make them economically independent somewhat.

Bohra women are self employed in stitching, knitting, embroidery, rida making, patch work, zari work, topi making and lace weaving. There is no restriction for Bohra women to go outside the home for work. In contrast, Muslim women do not enjoy this, as obscure cleric comes up with fatwa that women should not work outside home, making their economic situation worse and complicated.[12]

The trend of women entrepreneurship is on rise. A feeling of self-reliance boosts Bohra women to work in leisure hours. The kitchen liabilities come down as community tiffin systems[13] provides the cooked food to every household on a nominal monthly contribution (Rs. 3000 per head for month for one time tiffin).

In rich Bohra families, the wife, daughter, mother and sometime sisters are kept as business partner to meet out the partnership firm's requirement. Similarly Bohra woman owns property, either gifted by her husband or received from father's property. Bohra gifted her husband. In addition, in Some cases they also gain from their own earnings.

Friendly attitude with outer world: Believe in peaceful co-existence (*Jio or Jeene Do*):

The social, cultural and public interactive spaces in India can be very daunting for the Muslim. The general sense of unease among Muslims can be seen on a number of fronts – in the relationship that exists between the Muslims and other socio-religious communities (SRCs) as well as, in the variations in understanding and interpreting them. One of aspects their understanding relates to patriotism. They carry double burden of being labeled as "antinational" and as being "appeased" at the same time.[14] While Muslims need to improve on the socio economic development of the community. In General Muslim's complain that they are constantly looked upon with a great degree of suspicion not only by certain sections of the society but also by public institutions and governance structures. This has a depressing effect on their psyche. Many also felt that media tends to perpetuate this stereotypical image of the Muslims. Being identified as a Muslim is considered to be problematic for many Muslim women in burqa complain of impolite treatment in the market, in hospitals, in schools in accessing public facilities such as public transport and so on.

The attitude, behavior and relationship with other communities make Bohra community somehow different from the mainstreaming Muslim communities. They tend to be peaceful community and do not generally take part in politics. They try to buy their peace by generally supporting ruling party.

Women in general are the torch bearers of community identity. So when community identity is seen to be under siege, it naturally affects women in dramatic ways. Women sometimes of their own volition, sometimes because of community pressure, adopt visible markers of community identity on their person and on their behavior. Their lives, morality and movement in public spaces are under constant scrutiny and control. A gender-based[15] fear of 'public' experienced to some degree by all women is magnified manifold in the case of Muslim women. The lines between 'safe' and 'unsafe spaces' become rigid. Everything beyond the walls of the home is seen unsafe and hostile –markets, roads, lanes and public transports, schools and hospitals, police stations and government offices, especially in a communally sensitive situation. Violent communal conflicts, in which there is large scale targeted sexual violence against Muslim women has spread affect even in regions of the country not directly affected by the violence. Recently, Asifa's rape murder case in Jan. 2018 is tale telling that to dislodge the Bakarwal[16] community from Rasha area in Kathua district, Jammu

Kashmir. Sanji Ram with SPO Deepak Khajuria and his juvenile nephew hatches a plan to kidnap the daughter of Yousuf Bakarwal, Asifa who often came to the forest behind Ram's house to graze her horses. On 10th January 2018 when they spotted Asifa enquiring from a woman about her horses, the culprit tells Asifa he had seen the horses and leads her to the jungle. There they drugged Asifa and rape her. Then they locked her in temple and gang raped her for five continues days and on 15th January they killed her and body dumped in jungle and after 2 days body found by a local. After then the case was blatantly communalized. The Jammu bar association, with the active support of Bhim Singh's Kashmir Panthers Party, was enforcing bandhs and taking out rallies "in favour of the rapists and murderers". Members of the 'Hindu Manch' marched through the streets of Kathua with the tricolours in support of the arrested persons. While the women's organizations and others opposed the Hindu fundamentalists and demanded quick justice to Asifa. After Nirbhaya, Asifa's rape-murder case once again ignite the emotions of all people of India as well as whole world.

It established again that during conflict times sexual slavery of women is common as in Japan where Korean women had to be "comfort women" for Japanese soldiers. The enemy's women become the site for conquest. So too in India whether during partition or Gujarat or elsewhere the female body is violated as the marks of the 'property' of the man.[17] Women's bodies not only represent honour, but it is the symbolic marker of the boundary between 'us' and 'them'.

Bohra community believes in 'live and let live' and try to avoid conflict and violence between the communities.

To sum up the status of women has to be spelt out in its tangible indicators. A woman's status is always seen in comparison to that of her counterpart – the man. Whether she enjoys the same freedom and the same dignity or honour as that enjoyed by a man, are crucial here. Freedom here includes the freedom of movement, of association, of dress and mannerisms, of economic and other pursuits, of speech and faith. The honour and dignity she enjoys may be in the domestic sphere among the extended family or in neighborhood, in public place like the market place, offices or mosques or in public conveyances like the railway or buses. The prestige she enjoys may also be classified into different spheres of activity such as social, religious, economic and political.

The status of the women therefore has to be understood with reference to the condition of life. Reference to values; be they religious or secular may not give us a correct lead, because values are not in practice shared uniformly or fully by all the sects of Indian Muslim. Hence the Bohra women being educated and well to do in all spheres of life possess a better status in comparison to mainstream Muslim women.

Notes and References

1. Asghar Ali Engineer, *Islam challenges in 21st century,* Gyan Publishing House, New Delhi, 2004, P. 108.
2. *Hujjat* means that her word was to be considered as law by the people residing in these territories.
3. Burhan Magazine, Vol.132, *www.bohraweb.tripod.com, http://universe. byu.edu/ 2013/3122/living according to Muslim women.*
4. Recently in Mumbai the trustees of Haji Ali Dargah prevented women from entering the inner sanctum where they have allowed for years (till June 2012). A steel barricade had been put up at the entry of inner sanctum preventing the entry of women devotees (*zaireen*) while most of those who visit dargah are women. BMMA (Bhartiya Muslim Mahila Andolan) filed public interest litigation (PIL) in the Mumbai High Court and the Court gave judgment in favour of women to give equal access like men. It had held that the trust had no power to alter or modify the mode or manner of religious practices of any individual or any group. See – Qudsia Contractor, "Muslim Women and the Challenge of Religion in Contemporary Mumbai", *Economic And Political Weekly*, Oct 28, 2017, Vol.42-43, pp. 81-87.
5. Matrifocal- Matrifocal societies are those in which women, especially mothers, occupy a central position. This term does not necessarily imply domination by women or mothers.
6. Two persons must be made witnesses thereof. These witnesses should be pious and truthful and protect the interest of the weak, i.e. the wife.
7. See the Quranic verse 2:241.
8. Abdullah Yusuf Ali, *The Holy Quran,* Hyderabad, Vol.1, P.63.
9. Imam Raghib, *Mufradat-ul-Alfaz al-Quran,* Tiras (Iran), 1343 Hijri, P.461.
10. A ghetto is a part of a city in which members of a minority group reside, typically as a result of social legal or economic pressure.
11. Vidhi Rathi, *www.quora.com, www.minorityaffairs.gov.india.com.*
12. Sayeeda Saiyidain Hameed, *Voice of the voiceless: Status of Muslim women in India,* National Commission for Women, 2000.
13. Tiffin system is a supply of cooked food to every household on the pretext that *Barakat nu Jaman* (blessed food). Previously it was mandatory to deposit Rs.3000 per month per household but many household rejected the cheap quality of food so now it is voluntarily to subscribe the tiffin. The tiffin has introduced after regime change in 2016 by the present Dai Syedna Mufaddal Saifuddin. Critics allege that the tiffin scheme is an income generating scheme of Kothar (Syedna's administration).
14. Sachar Committee Report, 'Social Economic and Educational Status of Muslim Community of India, Prime Ministers' High Level Committee, Government of India, 2006, P.11.

15. Ibid, P. 30.
16. The Bakarwals are a tribal community. Ethnically they are Gujjars. The backward Gujjar community is recognized under the scheduled tribal category in the States of Himachal Pradesh and Jammu & Kashmir. Their counterparts in Himachal Pradesh are entitled to forest land under the Forest Rights Act 2006. This has been a long pending demand of the J&Ks Bakarwal community and CM Mehbooba Mufti promised to enact this law. Bakarwal are sees as Muslim since they live on the border.
17. Sabula Meena Gopal, 'Body Gender Sexuality: Politics of Being and Belonging,' *Economic and Political Weekly*, April 24, 2010, Vol.XLV, No.17, P. 44.

Chapter - 6

Women's Assertion

The struggle for women's rights is a part of the struggle for human rights because women are equal partners of men in integrating human civilization. Desire for autonomy and freedom is an important attribute of every human being, including women. But women in India, since ages; had been considered as non entity whose only obligation is to serve all members of the family. Her status in almost all communities and cultures simply depends on the biological fact, which restricts her to perpetuate the familiar role. She is expected to deny her 'self' and compromise as well as sacrifice life, which is a natural phenomenon in patriarchal society, which consequently relegates women to the secondary position. So they started analyzing their innermost yearnings for self-emancipation, which made them to move towards self-assertion.

The impact of social reformists, activists as well as spread of education has set a new pattern for the prevailing Indian tradition. Raja Ram Mohan Roy the great Hindu social reformer while describing women said:

> "Woman is the earth, ether, sound; woman is the microcosm of the mind, the articulation of space, the knowing in knowledge; woman is fire. Movement, clear and rapid as the mountain stream, the woman is that which seeks against which is sought. Woman is kingdom, solitude, time. Woman is growth, the God's inheritance."[1]

During the struggle for freedom Gandhiji first incorporated and legitimated women's power in his non-violence disobedient movement. He realized the strength of women power and constructed a separate niche for them in the public arena. So, as a result women realized their own ability and power. They organized themselves into organization of women such as AIWC (All India Women's Conference) and NFIW (National Federation of Indian Women). Women participated whole heartedly with civil disobedient movement of 1930s. Equal participation of women on equal terms in the freedom movement made society realize the necessity of women's participation and rights. After independence India became a democratic country. So, legally Indian women got equal rights and status. But still each and every woman could not enjoy this equal legal status. There are still some communities and groups of people who really do not want to be aware while during the period women strongly participated in Telengana agitation of 1955. Sahada and anti-price rise agitation in Maharashtra of 1972 as well as Anti-alcohol agitation in West India in 1978.

In above background if we analyse the Dawoodi Bohra women's participation in reform movement we find that due to some drastic norms and traditional ingrained in the society had made women to think and feel themselves subjugated, oppressed and weak. In fact they were unaware of their own identity and process. But with the spread of education among women and the eruption of reform movement in Dawoodi Bohra community in Udaipur, Rajasthan, the Bohra women came out from their shells and openly took part in the agitation against religious hegemony.

Phase-I

After the World War I, in the eastern world, nationalism and not religion was the controlling factor which determines the whole direction of the life and thought of Asia. Before the War, pan-Islam was the guiding spirit for the Muslim world. Easterners now looked westward, since the models of nationalism were in the West. In the quest for success, measured by modern or western national standards, the East was compelled to break old ties from new alliances which were no longer determined by the dictates of religion. Islamic countries such as Turkey and Egypt made efforts to harmonize religion and progress and tried to imbibe the spirit of secularism in individual thought (Wood small, 1930).[2] Sweeping changes occurring in several Islamic countries had an impact on the Muslims of India.

Among the Bohras the first demand was the establishment and spread of Western style education for boys. This was followed by a desire to improve the socio-economic status of the community. This was manifested in the demand that the clergy be made accountable for the enormous funds collected from the community in the form of taxes, endowments and offerings at shrines and a corollary of this demand was challenging the high priest's exemption from the Mohammedan Wakf (Trust) Act of 1923.[3]

The time frame for the first phase was between 1917-1930. During this period women by and large played a passive role, extending moral support to their family men and withstanding the rigors of social isolation.

Phase-II

In the general process of redefining Eastern life on a modern basis, the emancipation of women became a critical indicator of the progress of Muslims. Hence the mid and late 1930s' concern of the reformists with the question of women is a direct result of the changing role of women in other Islamic countries. Other contributing factors are, the progress made in improving the status of Hindu women by Hindu social reformers and women's organizations and the impact of liberal Muslim thought in India as exemplified by Sir Syed Ahmad and the Aligarh movement. The All India Muslim Women's Association at their conference held in 1929 sought to promote the educational and social interests of the women of the Muslim community.

The early 1930s saw the establishment of the Bohra Youth Association for cultural and educational purposes in Karachi. In the mid-1930s, the Association took up issues concerning women's education, abolition of *pardah*, and the need to draw women out of the confines of their homes to play a more public role. This period also saw women coming forth directly for the first time to participate in the movement. They wrote, gave speeches and assumed a more companionate role with the family men in the struggle for reforms. It must be mentioned here that questions of women's emancipation remained secondary to the movement. Progress made by women of other communities in Western India and changes in the role and status of Muslim women in the Middle East – other than the reformists' struggle against the clergy's power became a vehicle for examining gender inequality among them. The second phase stretched approximately from 1930 to the beginning of the Second World War.

The period between 1946 and 1950 was characterized by a lull in reform activities and this could be attributed to the pre-partition riots, followed by the partition of the country and an uncertain future for the Muslims who remained in India.

Phase III

Regarding the third phase of the movement, the adoption of the ideology of nationalism, even ostensibly non-political movements came to acquire a political colour during the independence struggle (Heimsath, 1964). This political colouration was also manifested by the Bohras who demanded decentralization and democratic rights. Independent India was characterized by rapid urbanization and planned economic development. A series of new social legislations, undermining several traditional values and extending protection to 'weaker sections' was also passed. Together with this was a firm commitment to socialism, secularism and democracy (Oommem, 1977).[4]Each of these elements could have influenced the nature of the demands and the arena of conflict between the clergy and the reformists.

In the third phase after independence lasting roughly between 1950 and 1970, the demands revolved around democratization, decentralization of power and greater individual autonomy. For example the reformists demands greater say in managing the affairs of the local *Jamaat* (council) by having members duly elected to it rather than appointed by the clergy (*Amil*).

After independence not only the nature of the demand, but also reach out and extent of the movement underwent a dramatic change. In addition to simply filing court cases, publications, posters, pamphleteering, processions and direct action were also resorted to. The struggle received nation-wide publicity.

The aims of the movement were justified in terms of an Islamic framework, e.g. according to Islam, tax contribution is for the benefit of the poor and needy, and not to enrich the "royal family" of Syedna Sahib, education is a right granted to both sexes and women need not to observe strict *purdha*.

Phase IV

A silent socio-economic revolution was taking place in Udaipur from 1947 onwards. During this period a large number of highly educated professional and intellectual people (both male as well as female) came into being among Udaipur Bohras. They were naturally much more aware of their individual rights and democratic privileges. They began to resent priestly domination over the secular sphere too in the name of religion. They formed Bohra Youth Association to promote education, welfare and other social activities, which was led by Ghulam Husain (a highly popular social worker enjoyed the confidence of Udaipur Bohras).

Before and after Galiakot incidence (in which Syedna's henchmen committed atrocities and molested Udaipur Bohra women), Udaipur[5]was in ferment and became a hot bed and breeding ground of the activities opposing tyranny of Syedna's establishment. A new independent thinking rebellious *Avtaar* of women as anti-establishment and pro-democratic rights had emerged.

Bohras were in majority in four municipal wards of Udaipur. The local priest (*Amil*) usually nominated candidates for these wards. Candidates nominated by the *Amil* have the *Raza*, that is the permission and blessings of Syedna and all Bohras are expected to vote for them. Syedna's prior permission is required for each and every religious and non-religious mundane activity by all Bohras. Anyone flouting Syedna's Raza is punished, harassed and socially boycotted. In 1970 the local Congress unit requested the *Amil* to nominate four candidates to whom party tickets could be given for the ensuing municipal election. Bohra Youth Association (BYA) recommended four popular social workers to the *Amil* but he nominated Syedna's henchmen on the advice of one Zakir Kurawarwala who was openly patronized by the high priest's establishment, in spite of allegation of corruption. It was also alleged that Zakir Kurawarwala and Syedna's administration had mutual vested interests in maximizing financial gains for themselves at the cost of Bohras. There was much anger against this among the Bohras in Udaipur.

Elders in Bohra community tried hard to persuade the *Amil* to accept the BYA nominees but he remained adamant. Therefore, BYA took the very unusual step and put up four independent candidates against the candidates supported and blessed by the Syedna Saheb. Bohras were made to believe that it is a sin to do any religious, mundane or secular activity without prior permission of *Da'i*(Syedna), and Allah (God) does not accept even Namaz, Roza, Haj etc. of a Bohra if prior permission of *Dai* is not taken for these activities. Syedna issued a firman requiring every Bohra to vote for his nominees. Syedna's administration was shocked and angry when these rebel candidates won[6] with overwhelming majority. Syedna considered this a threat to his absolute control over the life and property of his submissive Bohra followers all over the world.

The BYA's independent winning candidates were admitted to Congress Party. As a reward Congress co-opted one Bohra lady, namely Hamida Haidry against two women co-option quota (in case no women candidates were elected in Municipal Board prior to 74th Constitutional Amendment Act which gives one-third women reservation in all urban self-government bodies).

This was an encouraging step towards Bohra women empowerment. Hamida Haidery was social activist and was working for the up liftment and empowerment of women at that time.

During her tenure as a Councilor she actively mobilized Bohra women for higher education and work outside home. She played an important role in setting up and organizing Bohra Youth Girls' Wing and remained founder secretary until her migration to USA. The Girls' Wing is an offshoot of Bohra Youth Association. The members of Girls' Wing went door to door to promote membership for Udaipur Urban Cooperative Bank Limited which was founded in 1972 by Bohra Youth Association. It made good progress and RBI granted license to it within a short span of one year. This bank served the needs of a large member of needy Bohras. All this was in sharp contrast to the activities of the priestly establishment and its coterie which did nothing but extract money from the people for the benefit of his large extended family. The high priest brought pressure on Gulam Hussain (eminent leader of BYA) to disband Bohra Youth Association and the Urban Cooperative Bank Limited as well because the Bohra Youth Association and the Bank were established without his permission. The argument that the interest was forbidden in Islam and so banking too cannot be permitted does not hold water because in Chanda Bhai Galla Case, the fifty first *Dai* confirmed that he gave and took bank interest. It may be noted that the *Dai's* family had no hesitation in depositing money in banks and lending it on interest. The motive here was to break the backbone of the Bohra Youth Association. Gulam Hussain on behalf of the Youth, refused to oblige the High Priest.

Seeing that the Bohra Youth Association and Urban Cooperative Bank continued to function, the high priest sent one of his son, Prince(Syedna requires Bohras to call his extended family members Prince and Princess)Qaid Jauhar to Udaipur in 1973. On 23rd February he called a meeting of *jamaat* in Vajeehpura mosque and announced the dissolution of the Anjuma-e-Najmi which was a very popular and performing *jamaat* committee. He reconstituted a new *Jamaat* committee with those people against whom the Bohras of Udaipur in general and the Bohra Youth in particular, were waging their struggle against corruption. Earlier Qaid Jauhar had agreed to give due representation to the nominees of the BYA. This unilateral and undemocratic act sent a wave of indignation among the Bohras and about1000 people surrounded the *Jamaat* office next morning where the executive council nominated the previous night was in session. These people demanded that the committee be dissolved and elections be held to elect new members of the *Jamaat* committee.

Sensing the mood of the people Qaid Jauhar promised to consider their demand sympathetically. The people were jubilant and they took out a procession to celebrate the victory. However, Qaid Jauhar had different ideas up his sleeve. Next day when some elderly people went to see him in support of the Youths' demand for holding elections for the *Jamaat* committee, they were beaten up by some toughs trained in Burhani Akhara. This news spread like wild fire and thousands of people including women soon gathered there and surrounded Qaid Jauhar's residence. These people were now more determined to press for their demand to hold election for the *Jamaat* committee. Qaid Jauhar summoned the police for his "protection". The district Collector and other authorities rushed to the scene but found the crowd peaceful. When they listened to their demand for democratic elections for constituting the *Jamaat* committee, they were convinced of their case. The district authorities were hard pressed as the President of India Shri V.V. Giri was visiting the city the same day. They, therefore, intervened and requested Qaid Jauhar to accept the reasonable demand of the people gathered there as they would not be able to continue police bandobust there for long. It is said that around 90 per cent of the Bohras – men, women, old and young alike – had gathered on that day. Thus the high priest's representative was forced to dissolve the committee nominated by him.[7]

After his announcement the people dispersed peacefully in a jubilant mood and that night a meeting was held in Boharwadi to celebrate the victory of the democratic forces. This meeting was also attended by large number of people. For the high priest's representative it was an unprecedented situation as he had never witnessed such a defiant Bohra crowd before. They were just used to facing faithful and obedient followers standing with folded hands before them and prostrating and kissing the high priest's hand and feet. Qaid Jauhar was shocked and enraged. The Bohras of Udaipur had violated the "sanctity" of the high priest's family and thus committed an unpardonable "sin". On 26 February, 1973 he left Udaipur for Galiakot – a small village 75 miles away from Udaipur very famous for a holy shrine of a Bohra saint Syedi Fakhruddin Shaheed.

The High Priest came to Galiakot on the death anniversary(*urs*) of the martyr saint. On this occasion a large number of Bohras from various towns specially gather there. Udaipur Bohras also visit the shrine in large number on this occasion. Many women from Udaipur had come to Galiakot in advance so as to occupy in time the available rooms in the *musafirkhana* near the shrine. Their men-folk were yet to arrive. Many of these women were quite unaware of what had happened in Udaipur. Meanwhile Qaid Jauhar came from Udaipur accompanied by Syedna's henchmen Zakir Husain Kurawadwala and some of his followers and gave an exaggerated account to the high priest of what had happened and how his orders were defied by the Bohras of Udaipur who were once considered to be the most loyal, submissive and obedient followers in the whole of the Bohra world.

Galiakot Incident

The plan was put into action on 28 February and 1 March. A Hindi pamphlet published by the Bohra Youth Association says: "It was in the month of Muharram 1400 years ago that Imam Husain was deprived of water and food for three days before being martyred in Karbala. On this basis these vested interests fabricated a false story and told the large gathering (of the visitors to the shrine) that the people of Udaipur, like the enemy of Imam Hussain, did not give food and water for three days to the Shahzada Saheb (the Prince Qaid Jauhar) and insulted him. The fanatic blind followers were thus incited for a savage violent attack on the supporters of the Bohra Youth Association in a preplanned manner under the watch of Syedna. When the attack began, there were very few men from Udaipur as they had not arrived as expected. So their wives, sisters and mothers became the main targets of attack. According to a victim, "they were pulled out of their rooms (in many cases they were pulled by their hair)and brought before the crowd outside. While being pulled out they were spat upon and dust was thrown in their eyes. Their clothes were torn and they were molested. Many of these women ran away three to four miles into jungles to save their honour. Many tried to catch any available vehicle. However, they were hounded out everywhere, beaten and molested. I met many of these women in Udaipur, who narrated these nightmarish experiences with tears in their eyes. I could still see the horror in their eyes many years after this incidence.[8]

What was most shocking for these women was that all this happened in the presence of the high priest himself. These women, when attacked, shouted "*maula bachao, maula bachao*" (i.e. our lord save us, our lord save us). But the high priest allegedly did not stop the hooligans from attacking the innocent women. On the contrary many priests in white robes and members of the high priest's family were heard shouting "kill these bitches, don't spare them, dishonor them", etc. These women till then had great faith in Syedna Saheb. They had believed that he was unaware of the misdeeds of the corrupt elements around him and that he was innocent and the embodiment of mercy. But that day their faith was shattered and they were shaken out of their complacency when they saw the tyranny of Syedna and his henchmen. Then onwards they became staunch supporters of the Bohra Youth Association's reform movement for democratic reforms and the cleansing of the community of corrupt practices perpetrated by the High Priest's establishment.

Some women who could not escape were kept confined in a few rooms and next day they were brought to the mosque near the shrine and were made to take an oath that after returning Udaipur they would not disclose what happened with them. These women were also compelled under the threat of violence lurking over their heads – to curse their near and dear ones who had taken part in BYA's reform movement. Some people from

Udaipur approached the district authorities of Dungarpur and got these women released from the clutches of their oppressors.

The priestly establishment then declared full-scale war on the supporters of the Bohra Youth Association. They declared *baraat* (social boycott) of all these Bohras. The permission for offering congregational prayers in the mosques in Udaipur was withdrawn (unlike other Muslims, the Bohras are made to believed that the congregational prayer can be led only by a person permitted to do so by the *Da'i* and no one else), as also permission for other activities like marriages, in order to harass and persecute them. Moreover, throughout India as well as other countries a priestly fireman was issued – mostly by word of mouth so as not to involve them in any legal complications – not to maintain any contacts with the rebel Bohras of Udaipur, to totally boycott them and not allow them entry into mosques, *jamat khanas*, religious shrines and other communal properties like rest-houses, etc.

These measures created panic among the Bohras in general, and people of Udaipur in particular. Many Bohras from Udaipur had relatives in cities like Bombay and other places. According to this *firman*(order) these relatives also could not keep any contact with them or else they would also face a similar fate. Only a few Bohras from Udaipur who held identity cards were allowed entry into mosques and other places. This regimentation undoubtedly brought pressure on many people some of whom tendered an unqualified apology to the high priest. We will discuss this in more detail later.

The events took a violent turn after the Galiakot incident. Zakir Husain Kurawarwala and others who had taken part in attacking and molesting women in Galiakot found it difficult to enter the city of Udaipur for fear of reprisals. The *Amil* of Udaipur, Nauman Bhai also could not enter the city as he was instrumental in attacking and provoking other Bohras to molest those women. A violent mob chased him away from Udaipur. Shababis (Shabab is an Arabic word for youth, the name given by Syedna to his orthodox followers,) organized themselves for planning attacks. Some persons were allegedly sent by Syedna's administration from Bombay to participate in planned attacks against the followers of the Bohra Youth. Thus violent occurrences became a daily affair in Udaipur. The peaceful Bohra community, due to manipulation of certain vested interests, was drawn into a whirlpool of conflict. As a result of that hundreds of cases had to be filed in the district and session courts.

Mohan Lal Sukhadia, former Chief Minister of Rajasthan and the then Governor of Tamil Nadu, tried to intervene in the dispute in order to resolve it. He sent some office bearers of the City Congress Committee of Udaipur to Rampura with a personal letter of recommendation to talk to the Syedna. However, Yamani secretary to the Sayedna, did not permit any such visit saying that he had no time. Thus they returned disappointed from Rampura. Then Sukhadia persuaded the Youth leaders to go to Rampura to resolve the dispute. Thereupon about 750 persons (all male) from Udaipur hired the buses for Rampura – a town in M.P. and went there to meet the high priest to apologize and for reconciliation. This journey was undertaken on 12 April 1973. A mass marriage was taking place in the mosque when the party from Udaipur reached Rampura. To begin with the leaders from Udaipur were not allowed to meet the Syedna at all. Thereafter about 10 persons were called by Yamani, the Syedna's secretary, he adopted a very stiff attitude and the people of Udaipur were told that Syedna will not forgive them. the other hand, the Bohras of Rampura did not allow the guests from Udaipur to rest at a suitable place. They were not even allowed to draw water from a nearby well. The people of Udaipur were thus deliberately humiliated. Seeing no other way they left Rampura and came to Kukreshwar, near a mausoleum of a Bohra saint. All the Youth leaders of Udaipur then took a pledge collectively not to tender an apology to the high priest individually under pressure. They decided that they will stand by each other in the face of severe persecution. This humiliation made the Udaipur Bohras even more determined for reforms and they all raised the slogans '*jiyenge to shaan se, marenge to shaan se*' (we will live with dignity, we will die with dignity). These people returned to Udaipur without any hope of reconciliation with the Syedna's establishment.

Syedna, who claims to be all knowing spiritual leader, wanted to make an example of Udaipur Bohras so that no other Bohra would think of revolting or disobeying him. But his action misfired completely and exposed his materialistic nature.

The violent incidents between two factions continued and the women became more determined than over to fight against the priestly establishment which was using violence to crush their movement for democratic rights. The time frame for the fourth phase was 1970 to 1973.

Phase V:

After the disgusting episode of Galiakot and thereafter rejection of *mafi* (apology) in Rampura a period of terror was started by the *Shabab* against the reformist Youth group.

It may be noted that BYA's reform movement is for the benefit of all Bohras, including Shabab or blind followers of Syedna. Shababs are forced to oppose reformists by Syedna under threat of social boycott. Shababs and Reformists both are victims of Syedna's oppression! Shababs suffer more as they are exploited and made to clash with Reformists on behalf of Syedna's establishment, while Syedna's extended family continue to live in luxury unaffected!

When a Bohra dies, he is not allowed to be buried without Syedna's *Raza.* Syedna would refuse Raza for the burial of his blind follower even if there is a single reformist relative in the family, unless the relative fall in line. Reformists would approach the local *Amil* to seek *Raza*, on his refusal clashes would occur and he would ultimately be forced to give *Raza*.

During the violent conflicts period the Bohra women, who normally remain confined to their houses, showed great valour and determination to fight driven by inner conviction when faced with a dangerous situation.

The women's participation gave much more stability to the reform movement. Previously in other places lack of support from women has been the main weakness of this movement as the mother or the wife forces her son or husband to surrender when faced with social boycott and complete isolation.

After the declaration of social boycott all the members and supporters of Bohra Youth were deprived of the right to enter into any mosque, *JamaatKhana* and *Qabrastaan*. However, reformists were in majority in Udaipur and they controlled all Mosques, Qabrastaan, *JamaatKhana* etc. So when Youth people asserted their right to enter a mosque for praying, Shababs created intra-community riot situation obeying Syedna's order.[9] Syedna withdrew *Raza*(permission) for praying in all mosques of Udaipur and asked his followers not to go to mosques, *Jamaat khana,* etc. controlled by Youth. Shababs were forced to rent private halls for prayers and all other activities.

Freedom from Raza

More than two hundred couples could not get married because Syedna refused to give *Raza* even after two years of pleading and waiting.

Performing *nikah* without Syedna's *Raza* was very tough problem to solve because Bohras were made to believe that *nikah* (marriage) performed without Syedna's *raza* will be invalid and child born out of it will be illegitimate. Therefore, efforts were made to persuade Syedna to grant permission of *nikah.* A delegation consisting of nine women and seven men met the then Prime Minister Mrs. Indira Gandhi to help solve this problem .She sent Saleh Bhai Abdul Kader, a Bohra MP from Bombay to Syedna Mohammad Burhanuddin to persuade him to give *Raza* but he refused to meet even the Prime Minister's envoy. The delegation of brides also met the President Fakhruddin Ali Ahmed on 17 April 1974 but nothing came out of this either.

Da'i Syedna Taher Saifuddin and his successors made Bohras firmly believe that Allah (God) will not accept their *Namaz, Haj*, prayers, Nikah or any pious act if done without Syedna's *Raza* (prior permission). Bohras have to pay certain amount to Syedna or his *Amil* every time he seeks Syedna's *Raza*. *Raza* is denied to dissidents. All dissidents are humiliated and compelled to apologize and pay large amount as fine to obtain Syedna's *Raza*. *Raza* is used as an instrument to make money and as a weapon against the dissidents or to control the Bohra community.

Majority of Bohras have very limited knowledge of Islam and its principles because they are not allowed to read any religious literature without Syedna's *Raza*. Social Boycott by Syedna encouraged Reformists to look elsewhere for guidance. Their interaction with dissident Bohra scholars and other Islamic scholars opened their mind. With time they realized that *Raza* indirectly implies that Allah depends on Syedna's permission before accepting any Bohra's prayers. This is akin to *shirq,* which is greatest sin Allah never forgives. After this realization it became easy to abandon and discard the practice of seeking Syedna's *Raza.*

Ultimately a *Samuh Nikah* (collective marriage) of 106 couples was performed on 16th March 1975 at Udaipur without Syedna's *Raza*. And this day became 'Independence Day' in Bohra Youth reformist history. 106 couples got married after an arduous struggle for more than two years. There was unprecedented crowd on the day of the mass marriage. The *pandal* which had a capacity of 25000 proved hopelessly insufficient for the purpose. Police had a difficult time controlling the crowd. However at no stage there was breach of peace. Another unique feature of the mass marriage was that the marriages were solemnized in the presence of the priests belonging to all important religions in India. The Bohra high priest declares even the *nikah* performed by a Muslim Qazi as *haram* (illegitimate). On that day three Muslim Qazis performed several *nikahs*.

After solemnization of 106 couple it became easy to start congregational prayers without Syedna's *raza* (permission) in all mosques controlled by reformists. The first Imam (who leads *namaz*) was Sheikh Ahmad Ali Raj former Professor at Al Jamea-Tus-Saifiyah, Surat. It was a great day in reformist history that in a Bohra waqf mosque *Namaze Imamat* could be performed by a person other than Sydena's appointees. Gradually the necessity of *Raza* in performing *Namaz-e-Imamat* all other activities vanished from Bohra reformists' religious beliefs. Bohras finally felt liberated from the shackles of *R*aza after the solemnization of Nikah of 106 couples by Bohra and Muslim Muftis, Qazis and Maulvis without Syedna's *Raza*.

The *Shabab* group abandoned all Bohra establishment like *sabil* office, maternity home, *Qabristan*, *Jamaat Khana* and new *Musafir Khana* (under construction) except Tayyabiyah Sr. Sec. School. Bohra Youth Association took over management all these properties that boosted Bohra Youth movement.

The reformists leaders in order to give shape to the movement in that critical period decided to form a central organization, namely The Central Board of Dawoodi Bohra Community (CBDBC). An ad hoc committee was formed with Nauman Contractor[10] as the chairman and Ismail Attarwala as General Secretary. The Bohra Youth of Udaipur also declared its affiliation to this central body. A sub-committee was appointed subsequently to draw up constitution on a democratic pattern which was to be ratified in the World Dawoodi Bohra Conference.

Office bearers were to be elected as provided for in the constitution after its adoption along with the members of the executive committee. It must be noted here that the Central Board was formed to provide a democratic alternative for the secular affair of the community. It was not a religious alternative to Syedna. For this reason the Central Board made it very clear that it had no reservations about accepting the religious leadership of the high priest. It was only opposed to his total domination over the secular affairs and personal lives of the Bohras.

The first All World Dawoodi Bohra Conference was held on 17-19 February 1977 at Udaipur. There was an element of uncertainty as the priesthood had started their mechinations to sabotage the conference at any cost. They wanted to take advantage of the emergency in the country to get it banned under the pretext of hurting the religious sentiments of the Bohra community. It may also be noted that as the priestly establishment wielded great influence with the ruling politicians in general and the Muslim leaders associated with the ruling partly in particular, the emergency had gone in Syedna's favour. The reformists' activities were directly or indirectly suppressed, especially in Udaipur. Fortunately emergency measures were relaxed and general elections announced and government found it rather embarrassing to ban the conference outright. Hence the conference was held on scheduled dates with certain restrictions as not to hold inaugural function in a *pandal* for security measure and the conference was curtailed by a day. It was wound up after two days deliberations but the whole agenda had been covered. The draft Constitution was adopted and for the first time all persons irrespective of sex got right to vote and right to elect. The Constitution accords complete autonomy to local *Jamaat.* In the conference, office bearers and 60 members of executive committee were elected comprising members from Udaipur (Rajasthan), Gujarat, Madhya Pradesh and Maharashtra in India and Canada, Kuwait, Yamen, Pakistan, U.K. and Ceylon from abroad. One woman – Mehfuza Sanwarwala of Bombay was elected as Vice President. This led to women empowerment. The entire priestly administration spread lies and false information among the Bohras that the conference never took place due to their opposition and that only a few persons held a closed door meeting for a couple of hours and called it a conference. But when the National Dailies and Rajasthan provincial newspapers published its report and the priesthoods bluff was called off, it became highly embarrassing for them, so in order to divert the attention of the Bohra from the conference, a series of fake 'miracles' at the tomb of various Bohra saints were widely publicised. Still the forces of change are far stronger than those of status quo.

In 1977 Congress lost the Lok Sabha election, Indira Gandhi could not save her own seat. First Non-Congress government of India of Janta Party formed under the leadership of Morarji Desai. This regime change went in favour of Bohra reformist and an investigation conducted by Justice Nathwani Commission (Dawoodi Bohra Commission) appointed by the Citizens for Democracy (CFD) to enquire into the alleged infringement of Human Rights of the members of the community in the name of Bohra High Priest. The High Priest as usual cried of 'religion in danger' and 'interference in Shariah' and organized worldwide demonstration against the commission demanding ban on the commission. The commission made publicly clear that its scope of investigation is to find out whether the allegation of violation of Human Rights of the members of Bohra community were true as the guarantee of freedom of religion enshrined in the Constitution of India does not permit any religious head or his agents to suppress the freedom of conscience and freedom of expression on the members of the community and their right to criticize the behaviour of those in authority. When the report of this commission was made public in1980, it shocked the world outside and newspapers and magazines wrote articles for months questioning, "Should Syedna have secular power?"

Encouraging women interacting cooperation and participation before Nathwani Commissions' investigation team and women's presence in large number during World Conference remained the chief characteristics of this phase. Morarji Desai took the oath of first non-Congress government at the centre. A wave of social justice and progressive thinking had been seen here and there. In this changed atmosphere Bohra reformists received great support from progressive writers, human rights activists and journalists (except some Urdu journalists who were paid by the Syedna). It is also important to note that most of the *ulama* took the side of the Syedna, sadly extended full support to all that he was doing and condemned the reformists. The period of V phase was between 1973 to1980.

Phase VI (1981-2000)

After the publication of Nathwani Enquiry Commission Report and three World Conferences the story of *Kothar*'s (Syedna's administrative body) terror against reformist was quite hair-raising one. What the Catholic Church did to Martin Luther in medieval ages, the *Kothar* was doing the same to reformists Bohras. The reign of terror continued for a quarter of century. Yet the reformists, with few exceptions, remained firm and did not yield to *Kothar*'s pressure. The reformists Bohras both under the leadership of the Bohra Youth as well as Central Board of Dawoodi Bohra Community could be justly proud of their firmness and unflinching resolve. The denial of entry in shrine at Galiakot by Syedna in its retaliation ceased. Ban on Syedna's entry in Udaipur Municipal area remained at the centre stage of agitations during the period.

Various world conferences organized by Central Board during the period brought many eminent citizens from different walks of life on its platform and their support to the reform movement. It was also instrumental in taking support of leading human rights organizations and prominent academics all over the world. Thus the reformists had ears in all sections of people including bureaucracy and government. Also, Asghar Ali (General Secretary, Central Board of Dawoodi Bohra Community) could convey reformists' main concerns to all major universities in India, U.K., U.S.A., Canada, Germany, Thailand, Malaysia, Indonesia, Egypt, Lebanon and several other countries with his academic excellence and persuasion. Thus the reform movement won over a sizeable section of the academic community. This completely demoralized the *Kothar* which was forced to change its tactics.

It was Citizens for Democracy (CFD) a leading human rights organization from India which set up famous Nathwani Commission to enquire into the violation of the human rights of Bohras. Again a second commission was set up in the early nineties by CFD and 'Indian Peoples' Human Rights Commission' which also completed its hearing and produced its reports. However, gradually Bohra reform movement emerged as one of the human rights protection movement and got wide acceptance outside Bohra community as a movement for social justice, communal harmony and gender equality. Both electronic and print media has been giving space of its events and activities.

The struggle for Galiakot Ziyarat

All Bohras require Syedna's Raza for visiting any Bohra shrine. These are controlled by Syedna as Sole Trustee. All *Raza* are denied to reformists because Syedna has declared social boycott against them. The struggle for the entry into Galiakot Dargah became a national issue when the decision taken at Indore conference to organize a visit to Galiakot shrine on 1st March, 1987 and celebrate it as Black Day[11] by organizing a blood donation camp there.

Accordingly quite a few people from Bombay, Ahmedabad, Godhra, Surat etc. came to Udaipur before 1st March1987. Mr. Gulam Hussain had informed the Chief Minister of Rajasthan Shri Harideo Joshi as well as the District authorities of Udaipur of the intention of the Bohra Youth Association, Udaipur to visit Galiakot shrine. The Chief Minister of Rajasthan sent a message to proceed to Galiakot.

However, the crafty *Kothar* moved fast and Syedna himself was brought to Galiakot to frustrate reformists' attempt to visit Galiakot. It would be recalled that it was on 1st March, 1973 that the valiant and fearless women from Udaipur were brutally attacked and molested in Galiakot by the goons of *Kothar*. This brutal assault on ladies was most shameless in the history of Bohra community. Once again the crafty *Kothar* was at its game in 1987. It put pressure on the Chief Minister not to allow the reformists to go to Galiakot. The fear of losing Bohra votes in the Banswara constituency made the C.M. of Rajasthan to dance to the *Kothar's* tune.

The Syedna who came to Galiakot was declared State guest and Harideo Joshi issued a secret order to the district authorities to disallow the reformist Bohras from proceeding to Galiakot. Accordingly the bus owners who had rented their buses for the purpose were told not to proceed to Galiakot otherwise their permits will be cancelled. It was matter of great shame for the Government of Rajasthan and district authorities to behave in this flagrant manner violating the very fundamental norms of democracy just for few votes. It was very unfortunate that certain powerful vested interests and religious bigots control votes and dictate their terms to perpetuate their stranglehold over the system.

BYA organized protest in the form of *dharna* from1st March to 5th March1987outside the office of Udaipur collector. A delegation of five members met Chief Minister and Home Minister of Rajasthan in Jaipur but nothing come out of it. Asghar Ali Engineer then decided to offer an indefinite fast (*Aamaran Anshan*) along with five others including two women – Dr. Zenab Banu and Zulekha Sadri Wala. This was a first occasion in Rajasthan when Muslim women sat on hunger strike on road with shoulder to shoulder of men.

The women showed extraordinary enthusiasm in the matter. Hundreds of them sat on Dharna regularly. The reform movement acquired a new dimension with this struggle.

The fast unto death began from 5thMarch 1987.After three days the administration agreed to allow reformist to proceed to Galiakot but it proved to be a fraud. Fast was got broken most fraudulently and again buses were not permitted to go to Galiakot.

This annoyed all agitating people in general and women in particular. The angry women of reformists' *gheraved* district Collector and Superintendent of Police (SP). The *gherav* continued for 12 hours which was a glorious struggle by the brave women of Udaipur.[13]The public action committee which was formed for the mediatory role took it as great failure on their part and to compensate three of them sat on hunger strike unto death on the same spot. Gulab Chand Kataria, member BJP (former Home Minister of Rajasthan); Himmat Seth, member of Janta Party and Late Meghraj Tanwar, member of CPI as prominent representatives of political parties in Udaipur expressed their solidarity for reformist cause and sat on hunger strike. In a sense the Galiakot agitation turned into a *jan andolan* and became a common cause of all secular and democratic people of India.

While these people showed solidarity with reformists the government played deception. These prominent citizens were also taken for a ride and the visit had to be called off after courting arrest some 50 kms from Galiakot.

More than 100 men and women from Udaipur went to Jaipur at the end of March 1987 to demonstrate before the Vidhan Sabha which was in session. A *dharna* was staged there for five days (from 31stMarch to the end of session 4th April1987). Looking at the zeal and courage of Bohra women agitators' many women's and other organization namely, Rajasthan

University Women Teachers Association (RUWA), People's Union for Civil Liberties (PUCL), Rajasthan Progressive Women Foundation, Bar Council of Rajasthan, and Youth Forum etc. came to their support. Reformist women's delegation met home minister, Gulab Singh Shaktawat and requested him to "Honour and support women who have come out from their conservative shells on the road to get their fundamental and other constitutional rights. They are agitating against tyranny in the name of religion."If government supports them, the message will spread among other women also and they may be encouraged to raise their voice against injustice on the name of culture and religion." On the floor of the house all the opposition parties supported Galiakot Zyarat movement by raising question during 'zero hour' and question hour.[14]

BJP MLA Ganshyam Tiwari raised it under rule 295 and blamed Home Minister Gulab Singh Shakhtawat and transport ministers Heera Lal Devpura that both of them favoured Syedna- a religious tyrant against reformists. Home Minister had promised to give official statement on Bohra issue on 4th April1987. Unluckily the session began on 4th April with women problem which continued from zero hour till the end of the day. Thus Home Minister avoided giving statement in a preplanned way. It showed Congress Governments' favour of Syedna and indifferent attitude toward women rights, secular principles of the Constitution and the progressive thinking the Bohra reformists. As soon as the Speaker announced the end of the session, Pushpa Jain of BJP and Manakchand Surana of Janata Dal immediately appealed the government to at least give statement on the demands of agitating Bohra women on Galiakot but in vain. The agitators who were sitting in visitors' gallery stood up and started shouting slogans against Syedna's illegal ban. This was also first time in Rajasthan Vidhan Sabha's history that women agitators had demonstrated on the floor of the house within few minutes after declaration of the end of the session. Failure in getting entry in Galiakot Dargah made the Bohra reform movement more vibrant, exposed ugly face of social boycott. Feeling the cruelty of social boycott, Smt. Mirnal Gore introduce a bill against social boycott in Maharashtra Assembly in its Nagpur session which began in late November 1988, it came up for discussion on16th Dec, 1988. It was very unfortunate that the Sharad Pawar government took a very negative stand and refused to support the bill. The bill was thus defeated. However it was healthy sign that many congressman also spoke in favour of the bill. In All World Conference, 7th 8th, 9th and 10th the Galiyakot issued remained on centre stage. To counter the ban on Galiyakot Zyarat, women of Udaipur declared ban on High Priest's entry in Udaipur city. Syedna who used to visit Udaipur every two years, could not enter Udaipur for 25 years (1973-1998). Considering the determination and passion of agitating Bohra women, local administration could not allow High Priest Syedna Sahib to entre in Udaipur Municipal boundaries. Bhero Singh Shekhawat the then leader of the opposition had supported the movement from the day one and when he was in second term of Chief Minister of Rajasthan of a coalition government (1990) he did not agree to Syedna's wish to visit Udaipur. He publicly stated that the reformists have all the rights to Galiyakot Ziyarat. Therefore, Syedna will not get permission to visit Udaipur until he allows reformists to enter Galiakot Shrine.

Kothar (Syedna's establishment) tried to break this reform movement, especially in Udaipur by tactical manoeuvre. It threw a trap and unfortunately some people walked into it but it was an insignificant minority (less than 1%). It sent representative to Udaipur who announced that the supporters of Bohra Youth Association can visit Galiakot for Ziyarat. Many people, including me, were against visiting Galiakot without thorough discussion with the Central Board (CBDBC).

Girls' Wing was also against Galiakot move. I being Secretary of Girls'Wing wrote an open letter to the *Jamaat* secretary "to have patience and avoid hasty decision, because there may be many a slip between lips and the cup. Still, if you have already decided to proceed, please proceed with road show." But Gulam Husain, Ibrahim Sahib and some other senior members insisted on silent move. On 26thOct, 1997 about 1500 reformists including women and children boarded in 20 busses and 15 cars for Galiakot, where they were treated well, they performed Ziyarat to their full satisfaction.

This paved the way for the Syedna to visit Udaipur to break the movement from within.

In its meeting in Ahmadabad on November 10, 1997, the central executive committee decided to enter into talks with *Kothar* only if the talks were between the authorized representative from both sides and minutes of meeting or any agreement duly signed by them so that no one goes back on one's commitment. It was also made clear that there is no questions of compromised on basic principles i.e.,

- Freedom of individual in secular affairs.
- Democratic election of local *Jamaats* without interference from *Kothar.*
- Accountability on the part of Syedna for the funds collected from the community.

- Scrapping of *Mithaq* and *Raza* which are in no way integral part of *Ismaili* faith.

The reformists, it was made clear in the meeting were prepared to talk only on above conditions. A high power committee was also constituted in Ahmadabad to meet and take decisions in the event of negotiation or other developments.

The high power committee met subsequently in Udaipur on 1st March 1998 and reviewed the situation. It was then that the Syedna's visit to Udaipur was announced. The committee held a wider meeting of reformists and constituted a core committee to handle the situation during the visit of Syedna and also established a control room to be manned by the member of the core committee to counter rumors and constituted a volunteers force to contact people in Udaipur and explained the official position so that reformists were not misled in anyway.

Syedna's Udaipur Visit: a Lucid Test of Reformist

Syedna Mohammad Burhanuddin arrived on 7th March 1998 by a chartered plane and then went to the 'Railway Training ground' by helicopter. According to the newspaper the total turn out of followers from all over the world was around twenty thousand.

But the eyewitnesses say it was not more than 7 to 8 thousand. Syedna did not want more outsiders in Udaipur because the Bohra Community's properties were in the hands of the reformists and it was difficult to provide lodging and boarding to outsiders. Followers coming from outside were two to three thousands who were pushed out the very next day.

Syedna did not inaugurate the Moiyedpura Mosque as the mosque is under the control of court receiver.[15]On his arrival in Udaipur, Bank cheques of Rs 51 lakh 52 thousands were distributed to various non Bohra educational and social organizations to show his generosity and win their favour. For Bohras he announced a 'Saifee-Burhani Qarze Hasana Trust' and contribute Rupees one crore ten lakhs from his own pocket to this trust. He distributed gold coins of 20 gms to press reporter and many more to the editor and sub editor of the local newspaper in order to get only their version published in news from. He had already spent crores of Rupees[16] for making Udaipur visit possible.

Functionaries of government of Rajasthan were invited to Saifee Mahal, Bombay on the occasion of *Idul-Fitar* and costly gifts were given by Syedna for ensuring his personal security and for gaining favours from various government department. With the power of money, Syedna had succeeded in extending his visit from four days to twenty days.

The reformists had promised not to interfere in Syedna's functions and to maintain peace. In spite of constant provocation from Syedna's side they kept their promise. Strategically *Shezadas* and *sheikhs* went from house to house, from morning 8:00 a.m. to sunset for persuading reformists to give *Mithaq*(oath of allegiance to Syedna).Though during this house to house visits they faced great humiliations by reformists women, who had been suffering the wounds of social boycott imposed by them in last 25 years. Announcements were also made over mikes in every Mohalla to avail this last opportunity and come for *Mithaq*.

After making all efforts to pursue reformists for *Mithaq*, on 18th March, 1998 Syedna organized a grand function of *Mithaq* at 'Taya Estate'. He expected that more than 500 people would come for *Mithaq*. Interestingly the press released to that effect was issued in advance. But totally 43 person could be brought in closed cars to take *Mithaq*. The 'Paratkal'(local newspaper) reported on 19th March that out of these people many remained silent or did not say Naam (yes) and few were even weeping during *Mithaq*. They even did not do *matam* with other people after *Mithaq*. This shows the compulsion under which even these handful persons, out of more than 7000 reformists in Udaipur had given *Mithaq*.

Hence the reform movement had not been weakened a bit by above development. But *Kothar* published the event as *Fateh Mubeen* (great victory) as usual. They even compared it with *Fateh Macca*.[16] They spread rumors among fanatic blind followers that all reformists have taken *Mithaq*, and they have come back (*ghar vapsi*) to Dawat's fold. The ground reality was that even the few one who crossed the floor felt a sense of guilt and hesitated to grow beard or put on Bohra topi and rida. Real spiritual leaders never indulge in falsehood and deception.

Another evidence of the strong position of reformist might be seen in the result of Udaipur Urban Cooperative Bank Limited's election 1998 in which Bohra Youth achieved a sweeping victory over pro Sydena's candidates which was a clear verdict against betrayal. All candidates of Syedna were defeated as in 1973. Founding directors of the bank who betrayed and shamelessly walked over to *Kothar*'s fold faced the wrath of the banks' shareholders in the election. All their candidates were defeated though they tried various tricks to win the election. They kept the date of election on 10th of Ramadan so that the fasting Bohra Youth voters especially the women members would not turn up for casting their vote in great number. They also changed the venue of polling station to Bhandari Darshak Mandap instead of *Jamaat khana* as it used to done all previous years. The Election

Day was a Monday, an off day for the employees of Hindustan Zinc Ltd. On whom Ibrahim Ali thought he can depend for support. They even went up to the extent of bogus voting, stealing ballot papers, employing *gunda* elements etc. they made all possible desperate attempt to win this election. Why? Because *Kothar* was interested in winning despite the fact that Syedna had issued an order in writing to dissolve this bank in seventies.

Syedna's aim of his Udaipur visit was to lure the reformists to surrender and to accept that Syedna is the owner of their property, life and soul, but he failed miserably. 10th World Conference was held in Udaipur on 13-14 Feb, 1999 after Syedna's Udaipur visit. The Central Board thus saluted the determination of the people of Udaipur specially women who resisted all allurements of the *Kothar* and remained steadfast in their resolve.

The period between1989 to 1999 is known for political instability. During this time seven Prime Ministers had taken oath and a period of coalition governments was prevalent. Rise of communalism and spread of Hindu and Muslim fundamentalism in the form to 'Shah Bano'[17] Ramjanam Bhoomi and Mandal Report became the pivotal point of Indian Government and politics. Religious identities took precedence and women's rights were relegated to margin. The two issues that divided women and inhibited alliances among the women's movements were the Uniform Civil Code and the reservation of seats for women in Parliament and State Legislatures. Certain women's organizations even opposed state intervention in introducing secular laws.

The period (1980 to 2000) was also characterized by a hot period in reform activities and this could be attributed to the communal riots ignited after Babri Masjid-Ramjanm Bhoomi controversy, followed by identity politics. This influenced the conservative Bohras also to preserve their Bohra identity. *Kothar* made it compulsory for Shababs to sporting beard, wear *Saya, Kurta, Pyjama, Topi* and *Rida*. Reformists are free to wear any dress according to occasion and place.

Bohra Youth Girls' Wing played a very assertive and aggressive role in the evolution of women entrepreneur and made women economically self-dependent. A co-operative store was established by women and registered under Rajasthan Cooperative Act. This was successful and gradually many women entrepreneurs flourished in Bohra locality.

This period is also known for a successful "All India Bohra Reformists' Women Conference" for women empowerment. The conference was organized in Udaipur Rajasthan on 12-13 October 1989 under the auspices of Central Board of Dawoodi Bohra Community (CBDBC) and Bohra Youth

Girls'Wing, Udaipur. This meet was the first of its kind in the reform movement in Bohras. Women delegations from Bombay, Surat, Godhra, Malegaon, Pune, Ahmadabad, Neemach, Aurangabad and Hyderabad participated on women related issues. The conference began on12th October, *Bara Wafat–Milad-un-Nabi day* (birthday of the Prophet Hazrat Mohammed (PBUH). This day was chosen because Prophet Muhammad liberated women from subjugation, gave them rights. In Arab tribal society of that period, women were considered property of men.

The Bohra reformists hold a conference every two years to highlight the despotic rule of the Syedna in these name of religion. However in the conferences, women's problems remain low key as women hesitate to air their views and grievances. In this context this conference deliberated on women's developmental issues that women feel part of the mainstream and come out of the narrow confines of religion, custom and language. Deprivation of women's rights and strategy for its resolution were the other objective of the conferences.

Dr. Usha Bambawala, in the Department of Development, Communication Research Project in the University of Pune, was the Chief Guest. She inaugurated the conference and highlighted the different developmental issues of women, explaining that there are two levels in which the development takes place; one, at the private and the other at the public level. Self-respect, relationship with other family members, own health etc. comes in the private life of a woman. While being a citizen of a democratic country and economically an independent entity falls in the public level.

Ms. Kaushalia Bhatia, Project Director, Women's Development Authority, Rajasthan who presided, said that all women are oppressed and face the same problems. They should help each other, join others welfare organizations and work hand in hand for the up liftmen of women. Ms Sushila Agrawal professor of political science and Director of the center of women's studies, Rajasthan University, pleaded that women should, work against exploitation, social evils and empower themselves with education and gain self-reliance.

In the two days conference, total eight sessions took place on different women related themes like women and social reform movement; women and social consciousness, women and social problems - marriage, divorce, maintenance, *iddat*, children's guardianship, women and communal harmony; women and social change. Serious discussions went on, in every session and related resolutions passed as well, which were later sent to different governmental department for consideration and hopefully implementation.

During the sessions the participations of women remained encouragingly high. Women dared to speak out on the issues of *iddat*, *khatna*, *talaq*, *virasat*, communal harmony and social change. About 600 women attended the conference.

The conference recommended the formation of the action groups in different towns and cities and formation of a central action committee to implement suggestions and opinions expressed in this conference which ended on a happy note of optimism. Dr. Zenab Poonawala of Pune and Dr.Zenab Banu of Udaipur coordinated the conference. Women enthusiastically followed the deliberations of the conference and there seemed a change in their outlook and mindset.

It provoked the former Professor of Al Jamea-tus-Saifiyah, Surat, Sheikh Ahmad Ali. He distributed a hand bill with the heading- *'Ek Zarooree Aam Ailan and khas Tanbia'* (An important announcement and warning). He strongly condemned the deliberation of women conference and resolutions which were published in "Bohra Chronicle" and "Mumbai Samachar" and termed it anti-Islamic and anti-*shariyat* and declared that no Dawoodi Bohra can support it. Sheikh Ahmad Ali was one of the four Professors of Jamea who were harassed, humiliated and expelled by Syedna's brother Shahzada Yusuf Najmuddin on the suspicion that they do not consider the Syedna a properly appointed legitimate *Dai.* Sheikh Ahmad Ali was a true Bohra scholar and used to preside over religious functions of the reformists and give sermons and religious guidance in Udaipur.

Sheikh Ahmad Ali was held in high esteem by all Bohras in Udaipur as he was one of the teachers of Syedna Burhanuddin Saheb. His orthodox views prevailed and the reformist's zeal came down and no further discussion and meetings of follow-up could be organized and women's empowerment efforts reached at a low ebb again particularly in Udaipur.

But in Bombay reformist women led by Maryam Bai Contractor and Batool Bai Kagzi showed a great deal of interest and organized a series of demonstration against the Bohra priesthood and their exploitation of women. Mrs. Nafeesa Neemuchwala, Rehana Merchant, Hussaina Blockage, Saira Rangwala, Kubra Contractor, Masooma Ranalwi and several other women took enthusiastic part and distributed literature on Bohra reform movement. These demonstrations were held near Church gate, VT, Santa Cruz station and Kurla station. These demonstrations drew large crowd of passed by who were then informed about the exploitation of the Bohra priesthood.

During the demonstration women also collected more than 500 signatures of Bohra and non-Bohra Muslim women on a memorandum to Prime minister in Bombay. Similarly about 1000 signatures of Bohra and Muslim women were collected on the memorandum in Udaipur and sent to the Prime Minister of India V.P. Singh. Zainab Poonawala with six ladies from Bombay, Mehfuza Taj and ten ladies from Udaipur and Dr. Sakina Habib from Delhi met the Prime Minister V.P. Singh and demanded that a law banning the social boycott be introduced in the Parliament.

A press conference was also held in Delhi after meeting the P.M. All this was prominently published in major newspapers.

In short women's assertion and active participation made this phase very important in reformist history. Without women's proactive, aggressive participation (during Galiakot *Ziyarat*, Syedna's Udaipur visit, call for *mithaq* and betrayal by some top leaders) reformists could not have beaten *Kothar* in their machination, deception, bluff etc.

Phase VII

The period begins with new millennium 2001 to present day. It deals post Udaipur visit of Syedna Saheb which intended to crush the reformist movement.[18] But *Kothar* failed to achieve any of their objectives. The Bohra priesthood continued to be on the offensive to maintain its highly authoritarian grip over the community. On the other hand the reformist had succeeded in proving that the Bohra priesthood has been violating the democratic and human rights of Bohras. Reformist stands for non-interference in seculars affairs of individuals.

Reformists, in spite of all odds, have remained steadfast and peacefully active into constructive activities in the public interest. They have been making all efforts to unite Bohras from both sides of divide created by the imposition of social boycott (*baraat*). Five world conferences have been organized in various cities –Bhopal, Surat, Udaipur in India between 2001 and 2018; and four mini conferences in foreign countries - USA, Canada, London etc. They brought many eminent citizens from different walks of life on its platform and got their support. Prof Mashirul Hasan said in Surat, "I have come here to express my solidarity with flag-bearers of a small army who are fighting against suppression in the Bohra community."[19] Well known freedom fighter and Gandhian- Narayan Desai said in the same conference, "I will call this a fight against dictatership."[20]

Elections for the office bearers of the CBDBC and members of executive committee are regularly held in the last session of every conference.

It is widely acknowledged today that communal virus is spreading like a plague in our country and that this has acquired menacing proportions. What is worse even our mainstream politics is fast getting communalized. The unfortunate result of this is that substantial issues confronting the country like poverty, unemployment rising prices, corruption etc. have been side tracked and non-issues like Ramjanam Bhoomi - Babri mosque controversy, triple talaq, personal laws etc. have become focus of public attention. The entire electoral processes are getting communalized and instead of real merit of the contestants, their caste and community has become main consideration. The reformists are committed to democratic secularism and are actively involved in promoting communal harmony in multi religious society. The reformist also believes that communal harmony can be established in society provided, there is equal respect for all religions (equal respect is more important and carries positive attitude than mere tolerance which carried the sense of obliging others).

Therefore in every world conference while strongly condemning recurrence of communal violence, CBDBC calls upon the State and Central Government to take effective steps to stop violent communal irruptions and ensure safety and sanctity of life and property of the people. It also urges upon the political parties to desist from resorting to the communal politics and earnestly take up and strive for solution of real issues confronting the people. They should desist from alliances with communal and fundamentalist forces from any community, majority or minority.

Sad demise of Dr Asghar Ali Engineer

During this period the reformists suffered irreparable loss as they lost many[21] stalwarts of reform movement. Dr. Asghar Ali Engineer, former Secretary General and the chairman passed away on Tuesday 14th May 2013 after a period of short illness. It was a huge shock and monumental irreplaceable loss for Bohra reform movement. The reformists lost a great dynamic leader, an honest reformists[22], a loyal soldier of communal harmony, a truth teller, a prolific writer and tireless fighter of injustice. He took up the reformist cause in the early seventies and was involved right until his last breath. He gave shape (body, mind and soul) to the movement. He wrote in every issue of 'Bohra Chronicle' - mouth organ of Bohra reform movement. He went on fast unto death (indefinite hunger strike) when necessary. He regularly organized World Bohra Conference and reiterated the goals and strategies of reform movement.

He gave a dynamic direction to the Bohra reform by making it a fight against injustice, persecution, protection of human rights and social change.

He made it a common cause for all persecuted peoples and not Bohras alone. He struggled for bringing the atrocities and inhuman practices of Bohra clergy in public eye by arranging seminars and conferences on record in black and white. He wrote the most important book THE BOHRAS besides 52 books covering many issues and many papers and articles, including those for scholarly journals. He edited Indian Journal of Secularism and a monthly paper, 'Islam and Modern Age'. He also published Secular Perspective every fortnight. He left no stone unturned for appointment of an enquiry commission headed by legal experts and Islamic scholars which was most vehemently opposed by Sydena Saheb as he knew that such inquiry would expose his misdeeds, atrocities and running a government within the Government. The powerful Sydena Saheb used all the religious, social and political forces at his command but could not silent the torchbearers of reform. The high priest and *Kothar* felt desperate and in sheer desperation they started physical violent attacks on Asghar Ali, by hired goons at places like Calcutta, Hyderabad, Cairo (Egypt), Bombay etc. but he never used any derogatory words for Sydena Saheb. The last and most deadly attack was attempted on Asghar Ali in 1987 instigated by Syedna Saheb himself. His home and office were also ransacked. He was hospitalized for many days. Under political pressure few Bohra attackers were arrested. During the hearing in the court Asghar Ali had said, "They are slaves of Syedna Saheb and they do whatever they are instructed to do, including murder I have nothing to say against them. If you can arrest and punish the main culprit and the master mind, do it".[23]

Asghar Ali won the Right Livelihood Award (an alternative to Noble Prize) and the National Communal Harmony Awards of Government of India, Hakim Khan Suri Award of Maharana Mewar Foundation. He was also recognized as one of the top 500 most influential Muslims in the world.

Close to his heart was the struggle for gender equality in Islam. He wrote number of books and articles on the subjects and pleaded passionately for the rights of women in Islam. He was the voice of women in reformists groups. He addressed issue which violates the practice of honour and dignity of Bohra women like *khafaz*, the practice of *iddat* after the death of husband, inheritance, divorce, guardianship etc. He wrote a booklet in Urdu on 'Aurto ke Qurani Huqooq'(Rights of Women in Quran) for ordinary women who cannot understand the Quranic teaching. He tried to hold women sessions separately during world conferences. In his last Bohra conference (14th) which he organized and attended in 2011 at Udaipur, he suggested for the formation of WOMEN COMMISSION along with interfaith and intra-faith commission. Under the banner of women commission, three four seminars/

workshops were arranged for raising the women's voice in decision making. But after his passing away the situation had taken 'U' turn because the roots of patriarchal society is alive in Bohra community also. The demise of Asghar Ali is set back to Bohra women empowerment.[24]Saifuddin Insaf, a face of a Bohra reform movement also passed away in October 7, 2018 in Mumbai. He edited the reform movement mouthpiece, the Bohra Chronicle for over 25 years of 50 years of its existence. He edited it till the week before he passed away. At the Bohra Chronicle, Insaf was one man army. He quit his job in 1995 to dedicate his life to the reform movement. His poem "*chup na rehna*" became the song of the movement. Like Asghar Ali Engineer, he always encouraged women's voice. He wrote regularly on women's issues like FGM, cruel practice of *Iddat*, veil and divorce. However women lost another crusader of women empowerment.

Women's Protest during Syedna Muffadal Saifuddin's Udaipur Visit in 2013

Even before ascending the throne of *Da'i*-ul-Mutlaq of Dawoodi Bohars in 2014, Muffadal Saifuddin started striving hard to get greater control over the Bohra community. He realized that the reform movement within Bohra community would remain a big hurdle for the complete subjugation of the community. Therefore, he tried to weaken the reform movement in general and in Udaipur particular. He was also under the impression that after the death of Dr. Asghar Ali Engineer at central (CBDBC) level and committee of youngsters who were elected for local Udaipur *Jamaat* would work more enthusiastically. Hence he planned to slam reform movement by hook or crook. He made a trip to Udaipur in Dec, 2013to try to suppress the reformists and slacken the movement. An appeal was published in 'Rajasthan Patrika stating that Syedna Mohammed Burhanuddin and his successor Aali Qadar Muffadal Saifuddin appeals to the brothers of Bohra Youth to forget all previous disputes and return to the fold of the community.

The secretary of the reformists Dawoodi Bohra Jamaat (DBJ) asked for clarification of a number of doubts arising out from the appeal but he left Udaipur without replying to DBJ's letter.

Women's protests became the important events during that visit. Actually, their agony and heart breaks continued from yester years when they were kept away in isolation from the entire Bohra community's religious festivals and family celebrations.

Reformist women came out on the roads to speak out and manifest their anger and wrath. They demanded answer to their long pending questions, borne out from social boycott and other atrocities. They had been asking "Can you bring us our teenage years back when we were deprived of love and affection of our grandparents and other kith and kin?","Can you unite those couples who were separated in the wave of social boycott?", "Can you heal up the wounds of single parenting?" Also can you express regret for what happened in Galiakot forty years ago as the wounds of public molestation of women are still alive in our minds and souls (*dilo-dimag*)"?

The women got divided into 4-5 groups, one surrounded him at Syedi Lukmanji's *Mazar* at Vajeehpura and waved black '*duppatas*' in front of him. They yelled and screamed for their sad stories could be heard by all.

The second group encircled his *kafila* (caravan) when he came out from Moiyedpura mosque after *isha Namaz*. The aggrieved women did not allow him to proceed further until the voice of all poor victim women was heard. The *kafila* could move after an hour with the intervention of ladies police.

At the colony of Basti-Ram, near the house of Sanwar Wala, where he was invited for *Ziyafat*[25] (dinner) the enormous group of hostile women kept reciting a poem *"chup na rehna chup na rehna dosto', chup rahe to dushmano ke hosle badhjayeng*e' (Do not keep quite friends, else the morale of the enemies will be higher). There again with the help of police force they could move to the dinner place.

Rift in Syedna's Camp

Mohammed Burhanuddin- 52ndDa'i passed away after cardiac arrest on 17th Jan, 2014 at Malabar Hill. Before this Dr. Asghar Ali Engineer (in 2013) and Sheikh Ahmed Ali Raj (in 2009) who lead the reformists in secular and religious matters respectively had also died, which caused leadership crisis in reformists group and it was expected that it would bring a change in the relationship between the two camps of Bohra community. In spite of that a rift evolved in Syedna's camp on the question of real successor of the 52nd*Da'i* after the death of Sydena Mohammed Burhanuddin Saheb. On the one had Syedna Khuzema Qutubuddin,*Mazoon*(2nd in line of hierarchy for 50 years) claimed he was privately appointed by Burhanuddin Saheb on Dec10, 1965 (17thShaban, 1385 Hijri) while conferring him the title of *Mazoon*. And for 50 years all Burhanuddin's sons prostrated in front of him, showing allegiance, loyalty and respect to his position, until they finally grew up. On the other hand his second son Muffadal Saifuddin claimed that nass[26] was conferred on him on July 4,

2011 by his father, the late Syedna, after he was hospitalized in London following a stroke. Mufaddal Saifuddin also claimed that he had been officially anointed successor and had the supporters of the majority of the community. It may be noted that Syedna's administration controls Bohras through *Amils* in each town. The *Amils* were in control of Mufaddal Saifuddin during the last years of Syedna Mohammad Burhanuddin Saheb.

Khuzema Qutubddin filed a declaration suit to the effect in Bombay High Court[27], seeking declaration that he was the 53rd *Da'i* and for possession of all the community property, including being the soul trustee of the community trusts and the properties that were attached to the office of *Da'i*and for orders restraining Muffadal Saifuddin from claiming to be the 53rd *Da'i* and directions that he had over the properties.[27] However this suit was pending in the court, Khuzema Qutubuddin passed away in March, 2017 in USA. His elder son Taher Fakhruddin claimed that he was appointed 54th *Da'i* by his father. Bombay High Court allowed son Taher Fakhruddin to continue his suit for *Da'i Mutlaq* title.[28] Thus Dawoodi Bohras have two Dais 53rd Muffadal Saifuddin and 54th Tahir Fakhruddin concurrently . Both the camps tried their best to get more and more supporters in their favour.

The reformists are neutral in this dispute. Reformists are keenly observing the attitude of both the claimants about gender equality and justice

Politically the period witnessed four governments at center-Atal Bihari Vajypaye led NDA-3 government; Manmohan Singh's UPA-1 and UPA-2 government, and the Narendra Modi's (NDA) government. Anti-incumbency, and presumption of non-performance corruption, unemployment, price rise, devaluation of Rupees, farmer's suicide, scams and women security, etc. played important role to bring change in government in 2014.The BJP won an overwhelming majority of seats with just 31 percent of the popular votes in 2014. BPJ's biggest electoral asset was the disunity among political parties.

This made Narendra Modi a superman both at party and government level. PMO became a pivotal point round which the whole political administrative machinery revolves. A new trend of majoritarianism is seen on Indian political horizon. And a rising tide of hate is surging in the form of mob lynching throughout India, of toxic speech and attack on religious minorities mostly Muslims.

In the name of NRC (National Register of Citizen) in Assam 40 lakhs of people have been declared intruders to polarize the voters. It is alleged that names of Muslims are being removed from the voter lists all over the country. This is not for the first time in India's history that minorities are being targeted. Grave incidents of mass violence against minorities recurred periodically through 70 years of India's freedom. But these attacks often deadly and brutal were still bound by geography and by time. They occurred in particular area, had a beginning and an end. The current spate of lynching, by contrast, communicates a deadly warning that people from the targeted community are not safe anywhere, any time. They can be attacked in their homes, on trains on public roads or at work.

Wake up call for gender justice

An upsurge in gender equality movement was observed as the apex court delivered verdicts after verdicts in favour of gender equality and justice which have laid a foundation for future judicial reform in the country. Following is a description in brief for some of the landmark verdict of 2017-18:

(i) Equal rights for LGBT: The court decriminalized homosexuality and said, criminalizing gay sex is irrational and indefensible and India's LGBT community should be recognized as equal citizen. Section 377 is irrational, arbitrary and incomprehensible as it filters the rights to equality for LGBT community.[29]

(ii) Adultery no longer a criminal affairs: Supreme Court five judge constitutional bench has unanimously struck down section 497 of the Indian Penal Code dealing with the offence of adultery and holding it as manifest arbitrary, archaic law which is violation of the rights to equality and equal opportunities to women. It makes perfect sense as clearly the Supreme Court is saying that, "men and women within marriage are equal". Chief justice Dipak Mishra commented, "Offence of adultery treats women as chattel dents their dignity".[30]The judgment was welcome also because it does away with a law that was blatantly patriarchal and treated married women as the property of their husbands.

(iii) Women can enter Sabrimala: Questioning the legality of Travancore Davaswam Board's decision to ban entry of women between 10 and 50 years into Lord Ayyappa temple at Sabrimala in Kerala. The Supreme Court in its verdict said that temples are public places and there could not be any discrimination on the basis of gender, sex and age at places of worship and women should be given access as it is their fundamental right. If man can go then female can also go. Both male and female can be denied access on the ground of health, morality and public order. What applies to male also applicable for female.[31] this landmark verdict has not yet been enforced on ground. Women (10 to 50 years age group) are not allowed to enter in the temple after the judgment as well. The women till date are fighting for their entry and the orthodox patriarch denied it with the patronage of ruling party (BJP).

(iv) Struck down triple talaq: On 22nd August 2017 a five member constitutional bench of Supreme Court struck down triple talaq, calling the practice unconstitutional and in violation of Act 14 of the Indian Constitution which provides the equality before law. Three out of five judges in the panel concurred that the practice of triple talaq is unconstitutional. The remaining two declared the practice to be constitutional while simultaneously asking the government to ban the practice by enacting a law.

This was metamorphosed into a convenient stick in the hands of majoritarian forces to beat the Muslims with. It was politicized to the extent that it became a topic of heated debate during the UP election as it was the only last problem facing Muslim women. Prime Minister Narendra Modi expressed his concern about the plight of Muslim women who needed emancipation. He said it is his government's responsibility to give Muslim women justice by enacted a law. A Bill entitled 'The Muslim woman (Protection of Rights of Marriage Bill, 2017) to criminalize the practice of instant talaq was introduced in Parliament but that could not be passed in August 2018. After that government brought an ordinance making triple talaq a punishable offence in September 2018 as a huge steps towards "empowering Muslim women". A sentence of three years can be awarded to those who indulge in instant triple talaq – the offence is non-bail able i.e. only a Magistrate and not the police can grant bail. Bail can be granted only after hearing the wife. Maintenance and allowance to the wife is decided by the Magistrate.

To replace the ordinance, The Muslim Women (*protection of rights on marriage*) Bill 2018 was introduced in Lok Sabha and passed during winter session but could not be introduced in Rajya Sabha till the end of the session. It was brought back in the form of ordinance on 19th Feb. 2019.

The NDA government's contradiction on its stand on controversial triple talaq on one side and the ban on the practice of *khafz* or women *khatna* (FGM/FGC) prevalent in Dawoodi Bohra community on other side. Narendra Modi during an interview to NIA on 1st Jan, 2019 said, "triple talaq is not religious and a matter of gender equality while Sabrimala is a religious tradition." Similarly the government did not support Dawoodi Bohras Muslim women's plight on *khafz* (FGM).

An ongoing case (PIL- Sunita Tiwari v. Union of India (09-July 2018) in the Supreme Court on whether female genital mutilation (FGM) practiced among the Bohra Muslim community should be banned. While a survey conducted by the Bhartiya Muslim Mahila Andolan (BMMA) has shown that of 4,710 Muslim women from the economically weak strata 78 per cent had been given unilateral divorce by their husbands, a petition by Speak Out on FGM has stated that at least 90,000 women from the Bohra community – across the economic strata have maintained that they have been cut and want the practice to end[31]. In response to the said PIL the Union Ministry of Women and Child Development (MWCD) held that there is no official data by NCRB or study that supports the existence of FGM in India. It was expected that the court would decide the case before the retirement of Chief Justice Deepak Mishra who was hearing the three judges bench and like other judgments related to gender justice and gender equality, FGM be banned by the apex court. Unfortunately on 24th September, 2018 the Division Bench referred the case to a Constitution Bench. The Division Bench held that the case necessitates an assessment of whether FGM is an essential religious practices.

FGM is performed on girl child at the age of seven without her consent. FGM is born out of a social structure that privilege men over women, and the practice is rooted in the belief that women's bodies and their sexuality are a dangerous, negative influence on society. FGM then is a symbol of misogyny and gender inequality.[32]

Supreme Court on March 26, 2018 also examined the validity of polygamy[33] and '*nikah halala*'[34] and several other Muslim practices while hearing a petition by two women's organizations and BJP leader Ashwini Upadhyay. The petitions argued that the prevalent practice of polygamy and *nikah halala* were unconstitutional and should be declared illegal. The judgment is awaited.

Secular activities and mainstreaming of reformist women

A delegation of reformist women was invited by Swami Agnivesh – then anchor of Lok Sabha T.V. show – 'Vichar Manthan' to discuss upon 'women's role in religious reform movement'. Seven members of Girl's Wing Udaipur under my leadership and three male members travelled to Delhi to reach Lok Sabha T.V. studio. The discussion with Swamiji remained very fruitful and it was telecast from 10 July 2009 to 17th July 2009.

A women group had joined Peace March 'Karwan-e-Aman' at Ajmer and marched with it from Fountain Circle to Ajmer Dargah in Dec, 2009. The Babri Masjid was demolished on 6th Dec 1992, so a peace march – 'Karwane Aman' from Ayodhya to Ajmer was organized with the intention to spread communal harmony among the people. Dr. Asghar Ali Engineer and *Mahant* of Ayodhya Ram temple were leading the Karwan-e-Aman. The management of dargah committee welcomed the Karwan and a public meeting was organized in dargah compound in which social organizations like People's Union for Civil Liberties (PUCL) and other participated. Media also covered the event in full.

Impact of awareness due to reform movement was wide in open with the violent demonstrations in Madras (Chennai) by the blind followers of *Kothar* against the sale of Musallah spaces during Ramzan in Oct 2008. On September 3, 2008 the Deccan Chronicle reported that "Dawoodi Bohra Muslim women and men in the city reportedly damaged at least two cars of mosque authorities on Tuesday when Bohra women were denied iftar snacks (fast breaking snacks) as they did not pay a monthly rent of Rs.1500 per prayer mat (musallah space). Praying in the Mosque is free all over the world except in Mosques controlled by Syedna. Azan from any mosque is an invitation to all to come and pray. Mosque cannot be commercialized, ... Fatima, a 20 year old Dawoodi Bohra girl who was asked to get out of the mosque along with 60 other women who could not afford the rent." Such violent demonstrations of women were reported from Mumbai, Dahod, Rajkot, Ujjain, Burhanpur, and Bhopal too.

Year 2010 saw quite a few things to be proud of. The young and popular Bohra reformist, Rehana Banu German Wala was elected as a Councilor of the Udaipur Municipal Board from ward no.48. Rehana Banu was the candidate of the Congress party. Two other Bohra candidates from the orthodox *Jamaat* also won seats in the Municipal Board elections. Muslim Ali Bandook Wala from ward 47 and Nafisa Saif from women ward 55. The entire Dawoodi Bohra community both reformists and orthodox group came together and supported the three Bohra candidates. The community was then well represented on the Municipal Board. It was heartening to notice that the community that was divided on the issue of Municipal elections again got united on the same issue. But after election the divide remained as usual.

Rehana Banu was elected again in 2015 as Municipal Councilor, but on BJP's ticket. She became chairperson of water supply committee and performed well on this post.

Conclusion

It must be remembered that the reformists themselves made belated beginning regarding the question of women's emancipation. The men were able to carry out an active public role precisely because women look care of the private one. In the first third of the twentieth century there were conflicting pressure on women to uphold tradition on the one hand and break out of traditional practices on the other hand like, *Raza*, *mithaq* and *baraat*.

With the beginning of new millennium they made further progress,due to the impact of women empowerment upsurge all over India, the Bohra women began to flourish and develop more vocal in their expression more aggressive in their agitations and more firm in their stands.

Notes and References

1. Raja Ram Mohan Roy, *The Serpent and the Rope,* Orient paper back, Delhi, 1986, P.35
2. Wood small, R. *Muslim Women Enter a New World*, George, Allen and Unwin, London (1983).
3. The application of the Wakf Act would force the clergy to subject the Dawoodi Bohra Wakf properties to the control of the Wakaf Board and would no longer be under his absolute control (in the name of sole trustee) consequently he will have no power to prevent any Bohra person to enter in any Bohra Wakf property like Masjid, *Musafir Khana, Jamaat Khana, Kabrastan* and Bohra *Dargah.*
4. (i) Oomen, K.T., 'Sociological issues in the analysis of social movements in independent India', *Sociological Bulletin,* Vol.26 (March 1977), pp. 14-37.

   (ii) Heimsath, C., *Indian Nationalism and Hindu Social Reform,* Princeton University Press, Princeton, 1964.
5. Udaipur a small picturesque city of Mewar in Rajasthan. It being far from the city of Mumbai and had very little to do with anti Syedna group at that time.
6. Men and women, old and young alike voted for the Bohra Youth Association candidates who stood for democratic functioning. Certainly the verdict at the polls was significant in more senses than one. It should also be born in mind that the verdict was certainly not against the religious sanctity of the high priest and *Dawat-e-Hadiya* (The holy mission) represented by him. It was rather against the corrupt practices of certain individual's patroised by the high priest's establishment.
7. My mother and younger sister were among the victims. They narrated the eye witness happening in Galiakot.
8. Zenab Banu-'Galiakot se Galiakot tak' (Hindi booklet) published by Khan Mohammedji Sugra Bai Trust, 1979.
9. Of course this cannot be categorized with the communal riots between Hindus and Muslims or sectarian clashes between Bohras and the Sunnis or Bohras and

Ithna- Ashari- Shias. It was between Shabab (orthodox Bohras) and Youth Bohras (who were agitating for democratic and civil rights).

10. Noman contractor, a self-made industrialist, was the senior most reformist leader. After sons of Adamji Peerbhoy his contribution was most significant in sustaining reform movement against very heavy odds.
11. On 1st March. 1973, forty six years ago the helpless Bohra women were mercilessly beaten up and publicly molested in the presence of the Bohra High Priest Syedna Mohammad Burhanuddin in Galiakot. Bohra Youth Association, Udaipur commemorates 1stMarch as '*Black Day'* and organizes blood donation camp for remembering the blood stains of Galiakot.
12. The Syedna was alarmed at this development and personally rushed to Galiakot on 26th February, and collected large number of fanatics and hire lings to let loose violence on the reformists.
13. *The Times of India,* Bombay, March 13 1987; *Free Press Journal* March, 13 1987 p. 4. *Mumbai Samachar,* 13 March, 1987, *Nav Bharat Times* 8-3-1987 *Navjeevan* 7-3-87; *Navjyoti*, 7-3-87.
14. The debate went on for half an hour. The government had to cut very sorry figure. However there was no doubt that the government could not avoid the responsibility for long.
15. For this visit Syedna promised to donate one crore rupees to the Chief Minister- Shri Bhero Singh Shekhawat for the construction of a super specialty hospital. A cheque of Rs .Fifty One Lakh, Fifty Two Thousand was given before the entry in Udaipur. On 19th March, 1998 in a public reception function, Syedna had given cheques to some reputed civil societies of the city as a token of support in their respective missions. Such as Vidhya Bhawan Society, Two Lakh Rupees; Manav Seva Samitee One Lakh Ten Thousand Rupees; Mahila Parishad One Lakh Rupees and Mahila Mandal Fifty Thousand Rupees had granted.

    All this money was community's hard earned money which *Kothar* collected in the name of religion at a time when community was going through hard times, due to crash in financial market world over, the head of the community was indulging in lavish extravagancy.
16. The visit of Syedna at Udaipur most shamelessly compared with the historic conquest of Mecca (Fateh Macca) by the Prophet in a circular on the letter head of Dawat-e-Hadiya and Al-Vazarat-e-Saifiya has been sent to Amils all over the world.
17. A divorced Muslim women appealed for maintenance under Article 125 of Indian Panel Code (IPC)in 1985. There was a backlash from the orthodox in Muslim community as the judgment that provided for her maintenance and emphasized a Uniform Civil Code was seen as an infringement of religious freedom and undermining Shariat, the religious laws. The political mobilization of the community ensured the passing of Muslim women (Protection of Rights on Divorce) Bill in 1986 which exempted Muslim women from Article 125 of the code of criminal procedure. BJP and its allies called it minority appeasement. Rajiv Gandhi Government then issued order to open the gate of Ram temple for worship and also granted permission for *Shilanyas* for countering the criticism of Muslim appeasement.

18. Saifuddin Insaf, '*Kothar*'s miserable defeat in crushing the reformist movement in Udaipur', *The Bohra Chronicle*, 1-4-1998, P. 5.
19. Melvyn Thomas, 'Bohra reformists come together to fight fundamentalism', *The Indian Express News Line,* Saturday, Feb 5, 2005
20. Ibid.
21. The following reformist leaders passed away on the mentioned dates :

    Sept 30, 2003 Mohammed Hussain Haidry, President of Dawoodi Bohra Jamaat, Udaipur.

    26th Feb, advocates Yahya Ali; June 2008 Sheikh Ahemad Ali Raj; Dr Abbas Alvi, Secretary, Dawoodi Bohra Jamaat, Udaipur; Saleh Mohammed Nayab Sahib, the Editor of All World Bohra Journal; Mehfooza Bai Sanwari, Hussain Udaipuri, President of Bohra Youth; Asgar Bhai Pachisa, Tahir Bhai Rangwala and many other in Udaipur.

    July 7, 2008 Hussain Bai Hamdani died at Ontario, Canada, July 26, 2008 Hussaina Bai Sanchawala died at Surat. 8th Oct, 2008 Zulfiqar Hussain passed away in Aurangabad. March 29 2009 Ahemad Ismail Ji Lukmani died in London. Oct 11, 2009 Shafaqat Hussain Anjumin Malegaon, Jan 26, 2010, Fizza Bai Fida Hussain Jeevanji died in Ontario, Canada. Feb, 2010 Zehra Tahir Ali Paliwala died at Tanga, Tanzania the granddaughter of Sir Adamji Peerbhoy; Mehfuza Haidry June 2, 2010. Shoeb Ranalwi expired at Mumbai on 26th Aug.2010, Ismail Bhai Attarwala Ex-Chairman (BDBC) at Mumbai in 2014.

    11th July 2016 Mansoor Taj expired at LA, USA.
22. The Vice President of India, Mohammed Hamid Ansari had deeply condoled the passing away of Dr. Asghar Ali Engineer. In his condolence message he said, "Engineer's valuable contribution towards promoting secularism and inter-faith harmony are particularly noteworthy. His liberal rational views, based on his deep understanding of Islam and Islamic jurisprudence, are most pertinent in our time."

    Hilal Ahmad, In Economic & Political Weekly (EPW) argues that apart from his contribution to secularism, human rights work and reform within Muslim communities, his abiding legacy would be towards establishing an emancipator form of intellectual politics which remained analytically open but grounded on politically committed arguments.

    Executive Director Right Livelihood Award Foundation Sweden wrote "Asghar Ali Engineer tirelessly promoted the universal values of tolerance, equality and justice in all his writings and speeches."

    Many newspapers, individuals and institutions around the world marked his death with obituaries.
23. *The Bohra Chronicle,* 1-7-2013.
24. He was celebrated voice of liberation theology. This is very same approach adopted to strive for the rights of Muslims women. When the more conservative section of the Muslim community was opposing the Shahbano Judgment Dr. Engineer supported the judgment and demanded codification of Shariyat laws. He argued that Islam is being misinterpreted by the priests for vested interests and the Quran gave women irrefutable rights, Thus inroads to this end must be

made by being equipped with correct facts and knowledge of the Quran. With his vast knowledge and passionate views, firm but not rigid, he compelled the other persons to think rationally which-him was so popular in trainings or lectures. His attitude made dialogue and learning easy for so many youth and women across colleges and communities.

25. Ziyafat – A Banquet – lavish feast in honour of Syedna. A rich Bohra invites Syedna Saheb and his family members on dinner at his residence, called *Ziyafat*. The acceptance of *Ziyafat*is granted only after the settlement of *Nazrana* (a huge amount) between the sponsored and the invitee according to the economic status.
26. Nass - A lawful declaration of successor by the *Dai.*
27. Suit called suit No.337 of 2014; plaintiff Taher Fakhruddin Saheb Alias Taher Bhai Qutbuddin versus Muffadal Burhanuddin Saifuddin (defendant)The High Court ordered the petitioners and the defenders to submit testimony and evidence supporting their claims. The verdict is expected to be delivered soon after the trail.
28. Such a situation was initiated in 1591when the 26th Syedna- Dawood bin Ajabshah died. A spat broke out between the successors and a case was filed at the Royal Court of Akbar. The court declared Syedna Dawood bin Qutubshaha as the new Syedna. But the community split into two Dawoodi Bohra and Sulemani Bohra (the follower of Suleman).
29. *Times of India,* Sep 6, 2018.
30. Dhananjay Mahapatra, *Times of India,* Sep 28, 2018.
31. Pallabi Munsi, *The Indian Express,* Jan 8, 2018.
32. Lakshmi Anantnarayan, Shabana Diler, Natasha Menon, *The Clitoral hood A Contested Site, Khafz* or female genital mutilation / cutting (FGM/C) in India (A Project Report in collaboration with we speak out Nari Samta Manch, 2018).
33. Polygamy is the practice of being married to more than one woman.
34. Nikah Halala refers to the Islamic stricture to remarry and they get a divorce before being able to marry her first husband again.

Chapter - 7

Redress From Social Boycott to Women Empowerment: Some Case Studies

The reform movement in the Bohra community owes much to the role of women. In fact the main weapon of the Bohra priesthood is social boycott which is disastrously effective in this small and well-knit community and this weapon's coerciveness is made to be felt through women. The women become its main victim. Sociologically it is not difficult to understand why it is so. In Bohra society women are usually highly ritualistic and in fact, it is women who perform most of the rituals very meticulously. Men being busy in their business or professions are less scrupulous about these rituals. In Bohra society many women don't work outside home and hence they have much more time to spend on these rituals. Again, since women do not work outside home, they need something to keep themselves busy with and the religious rituals not only keep them occupied but also give profound satisfaction and solace.

The Bohra community like any other Indian community has its own lifecycle rituals starting with the birth of child. In these life-cycle rituals women, needless to say, play a key role. Many of these rituals are performed outside home in a congregation. If the priesthood declares boycott against any family its womenfolk are deprived of participating in these congregational rituals. Nothing could be more tormenting to them than this deprivation. Since very few Bohra women work outside the home participating in these congregational rituals provides the only venue for social life. In the event of social boycott this isolation from collective social life is felt very acutely. Even for those women who work outside home, psychological upbringing necessitates at least to some extent participating in the congregational rituals. The Bohra priesthood in order to maintain its grip over the womenfolk in the community is devising new congregational rituals. What was unknown until recently is common practice now, thanks to shrewd strategies followed by the priesthood. When anyone from the community takes part in the reform movement or expresses sympathy with it, the priesthood immediately declares social boycott against him/her. Mostly they happen to be men. The moment wife, mother or sister of that boycotted person comes to know about the boycott, she panics and puts all possible pressure on him to go and apologies to the priesthood in order that the *baraat* (i.e. social boycott) be withdrawn. The whole family is thrown into turmoil and he is compelled to tender apology on most humiliating terms to the local priest. If the offence is 'graver', the local priest is not authorised to pardon and the person concerned has to go to Bombay and prostate before the Syedna, the lord (i.e. the high priest). Because of such pressure from women even some of the stalwarts among the reformists had to tender apology and withdraw from the movement.

Thus the Bohra priesthood finds it easy to exercise pressure on men through women who are helpless victims. Even if they show readiness to bear isolation with fortitude and courage, the worst form of pressure is put on them threatening to dissolve the marriage itself. There are many cases in which longstanding marriages were dissolved when the husband or the wife remained recalcitrant. In one case a woman in Baroda was required to pronounce curse on her reformist brother, when she (she had two children at that time) refused to oblige the priest, the marriage was dissolved. The woman was an Associate Professor in medicine and could stand on her own legs.

In the early seventies, the women of Udaipur showed exceptional courage in standing up against Syedna's atrocities after the Galiakot episode. The entire Galiakot episode has recorded in detail by Nathwani Commission Report.

Reformists' women told their stories; they wanted to raise the spirits of others so they may be inspired to give their best. They have expressed their bitter experiences of social boycott to help others to get through their own difficult times. As they reflected their past experience to give a message to other women – "Don't be afraid to speak up" and "advocate for yourself".

In this background I have conducted several case studies of young and old Bohra women to illustrate how the Bohra reform movement inspired them and make them stronger to turn social boycott into women empowerment. They were co-operative enough to prefer to write their story in their own language and I have included them as received.

Razia Sanwari

I grew up in Kolkata (then Calcutta), third of four siblings, a Dawoodi Bohra by birth. My Dad was a humanist at heart, gentle and kind by nature. More importantly, for him religion was merely a way of life. He taught us to first be good human beings because, he said, this was the base of all religions. He was naturally our idol! We children looked up to him and hung on to every word he uttered because, we believed, he spoke nothing but wisdom.

On the other hand, there was my Mom…religious without understanding religion and pious without understanding piety. Her take on the *Da'i* of the Dawoodi Bohras (then Syedna Mohammed Burhanuddin) - he was the God on earth who must be followed blindly.

Therefore, as kids we were subjected to a great deal of confusion at home! There was my Mom telling us to do *sajdah* (kneel before) and kiss the feet of the Syedna whenever he was in town and on the other hand, my Dad scoffed at even the thought and reprimanded us if we did so. We wondered why the disparity in thoughts when all we could see around us was an insane sort of worshiping for the High Priest.

When small I had even begun to believe that this was the God we had always been praying to. It was only when I reached puberty and had to give *misaq* that I realised this gentleman and everything associated with him (whether the *Kothar*, the Amils or his policies) were highly debatable and he was no saintly figure we had been led to believe he was.

In the metropolitan city I lived, Syedna Mohammed Burhanuddin was a regular visitor and you need no two guesses to say why. The big crorepati businessmen of the city were always inviting him over from Mumbai after quoting astronomical sums as salaams. I remember my Mom dragging us to the masjid and to those homes where *ziyafats* were being held and where the salaams would be taken. Usually I came back from these events overawed and also a trifle annoyed with my Dad for criticising the Syedna. I was blinded by the holy aura surrounding him, the purity of his white robes, the gentleness of his demeanor, the raised hand blessing his followers and the awed frenzy around him!

Came 1973 and the Udaipur incident happened. Soon we got the news that all our relatives there had been termed *'washamras'* (non-believers) and were facing social boycott for having gone against the Syedna. Mom was hugely upset while Dad rejoiced that finally the world was awakening. I still didn't know whose side to be on.

We visited Udaipur every once in two years and having no house of our own in the city, we always stayed with our mother's relatives. But the visits after the Udaipur incident proved to be quite traumatic. As usual we put up with our relatives who were also facing social boycott (*baraat*). But Mom was scared that if the *Kothar* found out we had put up with the 'Youthis' we would be socially ostracized back home in Kolkata, too. This fortunately did not happen then but a few years later, when my sister and I went to Udaipur to attend a cousin's marriage all hell broke loose. My parents were called to the local Amil's office and reprimanded for having allowed us to attend a Youths' marriage. And that was not all. We were then told that we were henceforth barred from attending all *Jamaat* functions till the Amil got the green signal from the *Kothar* in Mumbai.

A call for social boycott from the powers-that-be had a devastating impact on my family. For my Mom it was one of the most traumatic periods of her life. All our relatives in Kolkata stopped meeting us and talking to us. There were two reasons for this. Either because they were scared of going against the *Kothar*'s diktat and being boycotted too or because they actually believed we were in the wrong and should therefore be shunned.

Our Bohra neighbours, who had always been so close to us, began to avoid us like the plague whenever we bumped into them in the building. Mom was devastated and Dad too was disturbed by the way our Bohra friends were behaving with us both on the social front as well as in business circles.

After a traumatic six months of repeated pleas and apologies, we were 'readmitted' into the Bohra social circle. Yet, Mom found it very difficult to visit the masjid after the lifting of the 'ban' because she was conscious of people staring at her and whispering amongst themselves.

A couple of years later the social boycott was reinforced upon our family following the marriage of my elder sister into a reformist family from Udaipur. The irony of the situation was that her marriage was not attended by my parents but conducted under the supervision of my reformist relatives in Udaipur. Despite this, the Amil from our city imposed *baraat* upon us, alleging my parents had attended the wedding. This was a huge lie and had been fabricated and conveyed to the *Kothar* by a few trouble-maker Udaipurites residing in Kolkata. This time the social boycott was for nine months.

Mom was grieving twice... once because she hadn't been present to see her daughter married off and secondly, she was being shunned by neighbours and relatives alike because of the social boycott upon us. Again repeated pleas to the Amil fell on deaf ears. The family suffered because my mother was suffering. For us siblings, it did not matter much because we had our own social lives among our classmates. My father anyway stayed away from the *jamaat*.

But my mother had already been made accustomed to the *jamaat* life (a social tool employed by the *Kothar* to keep Bohras worldwide in its grip) and was finding it difficult to stay away from it. Well, this was exactly what the *Kothar* wanted. Get the people on such a high that they find it impossible to live without it... thus always toeing the line.

When the *baraat* was finally lifted, all of us had become completely disillusioned with the ways of the *jamaat*. I, for one, was fed up and found the whole thing such a farce. My two brothers, too, were going my father's way. And now, after the two traumatizing boycotts, even my mother was getting bitter about the whole social system which the Syedna had imposed upon us.

While the Udaipur reformists fought against the *Kothar* in a group of thousands, we struggled alone in Kolkata!

It was then that, going against all odds, I too got married to a reformist Bohra from Udaipur. It was a natural consequence of the past events in my life which had left us all bitter and disillusioned. Having seen the shallowness of this society run by the *Kothar*, I was finding the whole thing suffocating and couldn't wait to get out. This time, too, my parents did not attend the wedding and my Youthi relatives in Udaipur took care of everything. Despite being happy about marrying a reformist, I was shattered emotionally for I was far from home and going through all the premarital nerves without my parents and brother to help me through.

Since then it became one furtive game for us all. Whenever my sister and I visited our parents (after marriage, the two of us were based abroad) it was a hush-hush affair. It was always a short trip in which we were confined to the house. A quick meeting with our parents and we would leave. Since we had become Youthis too, we could not be seen outside with the family because of the fear that if any of the snoopers from *Kothar* happened to see us, our parents and rest of the family stood to be harassed by the *jamaat*.

And so life went on…

Today, my two brothers have also moved to the reformists group and are based abroad as also my sister. I am a journalist having worked for local Kolkata publications and then the Gulf News in Dubai for 13 years. Currently, I am based in Udaipur with my spouse while my son pursues journalism in Mumbai.

For the past few years, I have been actively involved in reformist *jamaat* work in Udaipur and am also an active critic of the practice of FGM among Dawoodi Bohras. I brought out the All World Dawoodi Bohra Journal on behalf of the Dawoodi Bohra Jamaat and am on the organising panel for the Golden Jubilee celebrations of the reform movement. I am also a director on the board of the Udaipur Urban Co-operative Bank, an institution founded by the reformists of Udaipur, and the vice-chairperson of the Central Board of Dawoodi Bohra Community (the first woman to hold this post).

Today I live a life free of all social pressures. I am a free individual, I think independently, do as I deem right without allowing anyone to dictate even my thoughts, leave alone action. And I look around me at the so-called 'believers' and wonder what keeps them from getting the taste of freedom. After all we have only one life!

Shamim R.V.

I was born in the same year when social reform movement was born. I did my Kindergarten at "Bohra Youth School", which was opened and run by reformist group Girls' Wing to support education for kids whose parents can't afford costly tuition price of private schools.

My Elementary education was at Tayyabiyah School, run by Dawoodi Bohra group (followers of Syedna). There were only 2 kids from reformist group in the entire class. Since my Grandpa was first Sheikh Saheb who led religious events and prayers for reformist without *raza*, so I was always a target of the class, whenever there was a conflict in the community. Many times I was cornered out or singled out by other girls and boys, and that's where my fighter attitude was seeded. "Fight wrong, Follow truth" was running in my blood and I never gave up among peer pressure. I was good at academic and never been shy of stage performance, so I was dear to all my teachers and in the midst of all the hatred and peer pressure, I continued to do my best. I moved to RMV School for my middle and high school, where I learned many other values, including religious harmony, giving back to community and adopted my childhood hero "Mother Teresa".

My Grandpa was appointed in East Africa on behalf of Syedna as a teacher, so my Mom side family was strong supporter of Syedna and served them very well. At the time of reformist movement, my Grandpa decided to follow truth, so stayed with reformists and led them in *waaz, namaaz, nikah*, haj and other religious events. My grandpa led first Hajj journey of reformist without *raza*. At that time the only means of journey was via ship and used to be very strenuous journey. One of my uncle and aunt remained with Syedna's followers and discontinued relations with their parents and siblings. My grandma found out right before boarding the ship through their common friends that her son said 'my parents had died', even though they were alive. That news gave such a shock to my Grandma that she couldn't survive and passed away at Makkah. My Grandpa completed Hajj and came back empty handed. It was the beginning of demise of my Nanaji's house. In next two years, my Nanaji died and two years after my uncle died during another conflict between Youth and Shabab. He met with an accident, while returning from news office after giving a day's account of conflict.

I never met one Mama and Maasi in my life. In 1998, when Syedna Saheb arrived in Udaipur so does his entire crew and followers, so my uncle also came with his family to Udaipur. He came to visit us, but when he came to our door and asked for my Mom, all I could say "Mom there is someone to meet you at door". I didn't even know that he was my real Mama. He was there to pitch in favor of Syedna Saheb and asking us to take his *Misaq*, but he couldn't convince us and then again we never heard of him or his kids. I never met one of my Maasi and if she will come face to face, I wouldn't be able to recognize her. It's really sad. I have seen through conflicts how my neighbor used to say mean words and how they find comfort in seeing Police hitting young men, kids and ladies. Life was all disrupted through constant conflicts and fight.

I am proud of my family that they never gave in and continue to follow the righteous path. I can see how our community grows together, stronger and build our own *jamaat*, masjid, dispensary, school, and bank and made ourselves self-sufficient. Emphasis was always on education and giving back to community so now we have many scholars, achievers all around the world and care for our community.

I could see, if I needed to make a difference in this world, all I have is power of education, so I never stop learning and studying. I was the first female Chartered Accountant of our community. Then after marriage I moved to USA and earned Certificate of Public Accountant. Though I had 5 years of experience on my resume and CPA certificate, it wasn't easy to find job in USA. I walked into one of Indian CPA office and asked him to allow me to work as a volunteer, but he filed for my work visa and I started job with minimum hourly wages. On my first job over here, I helped creating a Bohra Youth Association of North America Inc, a non-profit organization, which raises funds for education and medical purposes. It's a small community of our own and we celebrate all our holidays together. It was a rocky beginning of my career in a new country, new culture and whole new office environment. To add the cherry on top, it wasn't just my accent, but I have never spoken English while I was in India and here English was a basic communication language. It was a challenge, but my fighter attitude kept me going and 19 years down the road, now I am working and managing various teams of accountants along with developing talents and providing career advice. While career and life start getting settled, I was tested again and faced a moment of life and death for my son. That's when I learned more about Organ donation and how one Organ donor can save many lives. We were fortunate to be in a country of medical advancement and close to the best children Hospital in America so my son could receive 3 chances of life via transplant. Since then it became mission of my life and actively advocated the organ donation to all my friends and family.

It is my dream that how we were fortunate to live in a country, where organ donor awareness and transplant facility is available to common man, I wish in my own hometown Udaipur, lives can be saved in future with organ donor awareness and better transplant facility. Two years ago on a casual conversation with family, where I asked them to walk near Fateh Sagar with a banner to promote Organ donor awareness, but with help of friend and family, it turned into a movement, where, Bohra Youth Medical relief society came forward to help the cause. I got in touch with MOHAN Foundation and other activist in the same area and glad to see the progress year by year. Where is a will, there is a way.

This life changing experience also taught me that humanity is above religion race and ethnicity and its better for all of us to forget our small differences and come together for better cause. Now a days, I see both groups are reaching out to each other and *baraat* is not as stringent as it used to be. Though I am still missing family members of my one uncle and aunt, but rest of the families is constantly in touch and we respect each other's belief and participate in family functions and live harmoniously.

Sharifa Attarwala, Wife of Ismail Mohammed Ali Attarwala

I am one of the very few fortunate women whose mother's side of the family and husband's side of the family were mostly on the reformist side of the community and therefore have not experienced first-hand pain of separation from loved ones. Nonetheless, the pain of social boycott has affected each and every one of us in some way or the other.

My young brother died in the early years of this movement and when the sting of social boycott was at its peak. He was denied to be buried in the Dawoodi Bohra cemetery because he was a reformist and I, his sister, was married to Ismail Attarwala. After more than 24 hours and under heavy police protection, he was buried in the community cemetery.

My dear father was asked to leave a masjid because I, his daughter, was married to Ismail Attarwala. My 11 years old daughter was harassed and boycotted by her entire school for six months, because her father was Ismail Attarwala. I share my husband's pain when my mother-in-law was in coma in a hospital when some in the community wanted to use this occasion to bring my husband to bend down to the Da'i and request for *mafinaama- misaq*(forgiveness) from him. But he did not knee down with my support. His mother died in Udaipur and he did all the burial rituals with help of reformists of Udaipur.

On a Social / Community Level: I was one of only four young girls who passed matriculation at the time when young girls / women of Muslim community were not allowed to venture out of the house. This was a proud moment for the community and all four of us received recognition and felicitation from the then 51, religious head of the community / Dr.Taher Saifuddin. During my school days and later during my college days, I met and became friends with some young girls from the Syedna's family and I visited them occasionally. Thus, I have seen this family closely but never doubted or questioned their leadership of the entire Dawoodi Bohra Community. All of my friends from school days and college days were staunch believers of the *Da'i*, some of them from the *Da'i*'s family, whom I met occasionally but after the social boycott I lost all of them.

On an Individual level: I already came from a progressive family, as both my parents believed in higher education for all children – sons and daughters alike. When I got married, my husband was not only very progressive but also highly educated in the religion, Islam. He taught me true Islam. He awakened me that Syedna need not to interfere in the personal and secular matters of his followers. If he does the followers have the right to question him. To understand this basic reason for the reformist movement, I become a crusader of the movement as my husband was. With him I also had participated in rallies, *dharna* and conferences in Bombay. He was elected the first General Secretary of CBDBC. So he spent most of his time on reform movement without much concern of me and family. I took on a larger responsibility of raising our children and I also took care of the business while he remained away, involved in the movement.

Religion plays a very big role in how you live with your family, how you raise your children and how you live within your community. Within a religion, your own community is on a micro level within which you would like to live and follow its traditions. But, in the absence of the closeness of a community, we got the opportunity to experience and understand broader perspective of religion. We have opened our eyes and minds to Islamic teaching. We sent our four sons for higher study in U.S.A. When necessity arose, I used to go to U.S.A. to look after them and also found out Business Avenue there. I had started family business of fragrance there. Slowly it flourished. Sons joined it and we could establish our factory there. I after getting Green Card became citizen of U.S.A. My husband is no more. I live with my son's family in California, U.S.A.

Zehra Cycle Wala: One Against all

My name is Zehra Cyclewala. I am 60 years old, and have lived in Surat for most of my life. I was born in an orthodox lower middleclass Dawoodi Bohra Family. My parents had five children and I was the youngest child. In the mid-1980s, soon after I completed my education. I did my graduation in Commerce. I Joined the Saifee Cooperative Society in Surat, a bank established in the 1960s by a group of Bohra traders. It was inaugurated by the Bohra head priest Syedna Burhanuddin himself, and enjoyed his blessings. I started work then as a clerk and gradually, rose to become its manager.

From the very beginning, the Saifee Cooperative Society gave and took interest. The Syedna naturally knew of this, and he had no problem with it. Although some Muslims believe that even bank interest is forbidden or *haraam* in Islam. However two years after I joined the bank, the Syedna issued a *fatwa* claiming that bank interest was forbidden and demanded that the Bohras working in our bank leave their jobs at once. All the staff of the bank was Bohras at that time. Because the Bohras believe the word of the Syedna to be almost like divinely-inspired law they hurriedly complied with his order and quit their jobs I was the only one to refuse. After all, I thought when from the time the bank was established till the Syedna had issued this fatwa the bank had been giving and taking interest and the Syedna knew about this all along how come he had suddenly decided or realized that such interest was *haraam*? The Syedna himself had inaugurated the bank, and when he did so he had no problem with it dealing in interest. There are something fishy in this fatwa, I felt.

Despite enormous pressure to leave the job, I refused. I lived with my mother Fuliben Taher Ali in Surat, and was the sole source of her support because my father had died when I was 20. I simply could not do without this job. So despite the Syedna's order I carried on. The District Cooperative Society Board appointed a non-Bohra administrator- a man called Mr. Daruto run the bank and I worked under him. My defiance of the Syedna's orders was not liked by the Bohras of Surat, and soon complaints about me reached the Syedna's religious establishment- the *Kothar*.

The eldest son of the Syedna, Qaid Jauhar came to Surat and met with me, and insisted that I must resign. 'Why should I? I asked. I told him that a branch of the Bank of Baroda functioned in a building built on a plot of land owned by some Bohras in Surat and that this bank dealt in interest. The bank paid rent to the Bohra owners, who, in turn, parted with some of it to the Syedna's establishment, through the Syedna's local Amil or representative. 'Why don't you stop taking rent from the Bank of Baroda?' I asked. Qaid Jauhar was shocked by what he regarded as my impudence. He told me that I asked too many questions, and said that this was improper.

As I said, by this time there was enormous pressure on me to quit my job. The Bohras believe that the Syedna is a divinely-appointed man. To displease him, they believe, is a sure way to land in hell. To refuse his order, they think, is to disobey and revolt against God. This is what the Syedna has made them believe. Hence, they thought that my refusal to quit my job was no ordinary revolt-but that it was nothing than a defiance of the divine will. And so, in a short while, a campaign was launched in Surat to excommunicate me. My house is in the middle of the Saifi Mohalla, a Bohra locality, hardly five minute walk from the Jamia Saifia, the Bohras' biggest learning centre. All my neighbours were fellow Bohras. Soon after I was excommunicated, they all stopped speaking to me. Even my relatives were forbidden to have any interaction-even on the phone-with me.

Yet, even in the face of this ostracism, my mother insisted that I must not give up. 'Don't you quit your job,' she said you have to stand on your own feet your community is not going to help you when you need it.' I did what she said after all I was no longer young and it was not easy for me to get another job if I quit my job, who would feed us?

The Syedna has a powerful weapon that he readily deploys to shut up anyone who dares protest against his oppression. Anyone who speaks out against his crass corruption (on the basis of which he and his vast family have become enormously rich by levying all sorts of taxes on the Bohras) or dares to criticize his dictatorship is at once excommunicated. This is called *baraat*. A Bohra who is thrown out of the community's fold by the Syedna can have no social relations at all with any other Bohra, not even with his or her own family. Numerous spouses have been forcibly divorced, against their will, because one of them dared to differ with or raise his or her voice against the oppression and corruption of the Syedna and his henchmen.

And so, I, too, was declared to have become a *muddai* or apostate, and was subjected to *baraat*. Even my closest relatives, barring of course my mother, with whom I lived with, stopped talking to me. When my mother and I walked on the streets, Bohras used to spit at us. Many would utter abuses and curse us. I refused to take this lying down. After all, I was always assertive even as a child, and could not tolerate nonsense. And so I filed a case against almost 20 Bohras who used to torment me and my mother in this vulgar way. This was in 1989 I won the case, and my tormentors came to me asking for forgiveness.

Meanwhile, the Syedna's men continued to try to force me out of my job. They entreated Mr. Daru, the newly-appointed administrator of the bank, to throw me out, but he refused because I was good at my work. When I discovered that several rich Bohras of Surat, including some who had been office bearers in the bank, had taken loans and had defaulted on payments, I took them to court, and the court forced them to return the money that they owed. This greatly incensed these men, and, using the enormous political influence that the Syedna wields, they pressurized the government of Gujarat, which was then controlled by the Congress, to remove the administrator of the bank and appoint someone else in his place, who they hoped would do their bidding. They managed to do so, and Mr. Daru was replaced. Mr. Daru's only 'fault' was that he had refused to agree to their demand to expel me from my job.

Now that the Syedna's men had succeeded in forcing Mr. Daru out of the bank and that the new administrator was a pro-Syedna man, I felt that my own job was under threat. So, I sent letters to top officials, including the Chief Minister of Gujarat, informing them about what was going on. Thereupon, I was suddenly demoted to the post of accountant, on the instigation of the Syedna's men. I approached the court in protest, which issued a stay order, declaring that I should not be removed from the post of manager. The new administrator of the bank pursued the case in the higher courts but even the high court confirmed the stay order which was in my favour.

However, because the majority of shareholders of our bank were Bohras, and because they believed every word of the Syedna to be divine law, they voted to suspend me despite the court's stay order. This was tantamount to contempt of court. And so, for three years, from 1989 to 1991, I could not go to office. It was at this time that I began meeting with other women-Hindus, Sunni Muslims and Christians-who had also suffered in their own ways and who were trying to speak out against their oppression. We formed a support group and tried to help each other cope with our difficult situation. It was these women who inspired me to refuse to let the board of directors of the bank off the hook. After all, by voting to suspend me they had violated the court's orders. And so I lodged a contempt of court case against them, which dragged on for two years. In the end; the court ruled in my favour. The directors of the bank begged the court for mercy, and I was reinstated as manager, while 15 Bohra men were suspended from the bank's board of directors. Till then the bank had been in the hands of the Syedna's cronies. To stabilize the bank and to make it more broad-based, I appointed several Hindus, Sunni Muslims and reformist Bohras as members of the society, and so it became much more cosmopolitan.

The Syedna's men kept sending me messages, saying, 'Repent and you will be forgiven.' But what I did I need to repent for? It was not me, but they, who had done wrong. They should have repented, not me. I refused to tender any apology although I had to face, and still continue face, brutal social ostracism. After all, my struggle was not for myself alone, but for the many Bohras who live under the cruel tyranny of the religious establishment. It was a struggle for truth and justice.

In 1991, my mother fell sick but no relatives could come to see her for fear of being excommunicated. She, too, had been excommunicated by the Syedna, because she lived with me and refused to accede to his orders that no Bohra should have anything to do with me. She knew that having been excommunicated she would not be buried in a Bohra graveyard. Still even on her deathbed, she stood like a rock behind me, insisting that I must never surrender to injustice. Shortly after, she passed away. No Bohra came for her funeral not even her other children, my siblings. The Bohras of Surat refused to bury her in the community's burial ground. I insisted that she would be buried there and nowhere else, because I was a Bohra and I had my rights, and my mother had been a Bohra, too. The Sunni Muslims of Surat offered to let her body be buried in their cemetery. I thanked them but I declined their offer, saying that if I accepted their offer, it would be conceding defeat in the struggle against the Syedna's religiously-sanctioned tyranny.

News about my mother's body being thrown out of the Bohra mosque soon spread throughout the town, and so, in the dark hours of the morning, and under police protection, a crowd of some 10 thousand Sunnis and Hindus collected at the Bohra graveyard and ensured that my mother's body was laid to rest there. Not a single Bohra came for the funeral.

Sometime in the 1990s, a local Bohra leader, Yusuf Bhai Badri, who was then Secretary of the Bohra Jamaat of Surat and a close confidante of the Syedna, had taken a loan from our bank, but because he had not repaid the loan, interest on it had mounted and he owed the bank almost double the principal. He refused to pay back on time and I was compelled to take him to court. The court issued a warrant ordering the seizure of the property of his guarantor a Bohra industrialist called Haider Bhai Hazur. I went to Haider Bhai's house with the court order, along with some policemen. When I got there and he saw me, he said, 'How dare you come here? You are an apostate!' I told him that he had to repay the money, otherwise the court would take action against him. Scared of what might happen to him, he asked for three days to pay up.

Just as I left his house, some Bohras began screaming like mad men, alleging that I had abused the Syedna. They began hollering out to the Bohras around to come out and beat me up. Soon a huge crowd collected and surrounded me, including many Bohra women. Somehow, I managed to escape. I ran to the nearby Mahidarpura police station, but the crowd of Bohra men and women, more than 5000-strong, rushed there as well, following me. They started raising slogans, crying out, 'Give us Zehra Cyclewalawe will kill her!' The Bohra Amil of Surat, Syedul Khair, son-in-law of the Syedna, was leading the crowd. 'Come out and we shall hammer you!' he shouted.

Inspector Khan of the police station said to me, 'Ask them for mercy and they will let you go, or else they might kill you. Why create a fuss about refusing to say just two words in apology?' But I refused, saying, 'I would rather die but I shall never ask them for mercy. After all, what wrong have I done?' The policemen did nothing to control the crowd or stop them baying for my blood. Instead of beating them with lathis or tear-gassing them or even registering a case against them, they lent them their support. Such is the enormous power of the Syedna's establishment.

Although I was perfectly innocent and the crowd was at fault, a false case was registered against me, claiming that I had abused them! I tried to lodge a formal complaint in the police station, I was not allowed to and, instead, I was put into the police lock-up, where I had to spend the entire night. The next afternoon, I was taken to the court. A huge crowd of Bohra women gathered there. They demanded that I be sent to jail. But the magistrate refused, saying that it was a bail able case and so I was released on bail.

Because it was no longer safe for me to stay in the Bohra locality, where I had my home, I shifted to a Hindu locality for a couple of days. The Bohras had spread all sorts of false news about me, claiming that I had caused a disturbance by abusing the Syedna, so I went to the offices of leading newspapers in Surat to tell them the truth. I said, 'You have been fed on wrong propaganda and, without doing any investigation, you have published false things about me. Now you have to publish my version of the events or else I will go on hunger-strike and will lodge a complaint with the Press Council.' The journalists heard me out and the next day they published my story.

As I said, instead of supporting me, the police had taken the side of the Bohras, and so as soon as I was let off by the court I, along with several of my women friends of the 'Surat District Mahila Sangh', a women's group of which I was one of the founders, went to meet the Police Commissioner and told him how badly the policemen had treated me. I don't know what I would have done without the help of these women colleagues-who were mostly Hindus and Sunni Muslims. With the help of the Police Commissioner, a case was lodged against a group of Bohras who had attacked my house when I was in the prison lock-up, and eight of them were arrested. But I was not satisfied with this measure and lodged a writ petition in the High Court against the policemen and the Bohras who had assaulted me. I complained about how the police had refused to lodge a case of rioting against the Bohras, and, instead, had kept me locked up in jail Some policemen came to me and asked me for mercy but I refused. If I relented, I thought, how would these people, who are paid to help the victims of those who violate the law, learn that they cannot refuse to abide by their duty?

Soon, my case was heard in the High Court, which ruled in my favour and came down heavily on the Bohra rioters and the police. By now things had become so tense that I knew that some enraged Bohra could easily kill me, and so the court ordered that I be given police protection 24 hours a day. And so, two armed police men were given to me, who accompanied me wherever I went. This carried on till 2006.

In 1998, the Rotary Club of Surat decided to hold a function to honour me for my struggle against the tyrannical Bohra establishment. They announced the event in the newspapers. As soon as the Bohras of Surat heard about it, they arrived in a huge horde outside the Rotary Club and began shouting slogans against me and the Club's decision to honour me. The men who runs that Club got scared on seeing them, and so, just a day before the event was to be held, they told me that they had called it off. When my colleagues in the Surat District Mahila Sangh heard of this, they were enraged. They went to the Club and told the men there, 'You have dishonored and insulted Zehra, although you had announced you would honour her!' The next day the news was splashed in the papers. But we did not stop at that. Through a lawyer, we sent a notice to the Rotary Club saying, 'If you don't apologies within three days, we will lodge a defamation case against you.' The Club folks got nervous, and they asked me to forgive them. 'We will never do this sort of thing again with any woman,' they promised. I told them, 'We accept your apology, but you must issue an advertisement in the press to this effect, and you must also add that the orthodox Bohras forced you to cancel the programme.'

The advertisement came out in three news papers; it must have cost the Club a lot of money! but we women were glad. After all, we did all this not so that I could salvage my name but so that organizations like the Rotary Club would learn not to cave in to the pressure of reactionaries and that they would stand up for justice, which they claim they are committed to.

Because I had taken on the Syedna's henchmen the police and influential organizations like the Rotary Club for siding with the tyrannical Bohra establishment many newspapers had reported about me. This further incensed the Syedna's blind supporters. One of them, a certain Mustafa Dodia, tried to trap me. Later, it was discovered, he had been paid by the Syedna's men to do this. One day, he lodged a false complaint against me in a police station, claiming that I had tried to kill him. He got together a group of Bohras and they went on hunger-strike outside the police station, demanding my arrest and the removal of the police protection that the court had granted me. I was not one to take this lying down, of course I reacted by lodging a complaint in the police station against Dodia alleging that he had demanded the removal of police protection so that he could kill me. His demand, I added, was tantamount to contempt of the orders of the court, for the court had ordered that I should receive police protection. Finally, Dodia was forced to withdraw his false complaint. The crime branch investigated his complaints against me and found them to be completely concocted.

Initially, I was the only Bohra in Surat to speak out against the tyranny of the Syedna and his men I had no idea that there were other Bohras, in other cities, even in other countries, who were fed up of the extortion and the corrupt dictatorship of the Syedna and his family in the name of Islam, and who were agitating against all of this. Slowly I came in touch with these reformists. News of my struggle reached them and they contacted me. They were inspired by my lone battle, and felt that I had something to tell other Bohras, to teach them that standing up for truth, for values, for principles was true surrender to God, and that the supine surrender to a corrupt priesthood, which the Syedna insists on in the name of Islam was its complete contradiction. In 2001, a group of reformist Bohras invited me to Canada to speak on my life and to help galvanise the Bohra reformist movement in the West, where a number of Bohras live In 2005, I was invited to an international convention of reformist Bohras in Birmingham, England, where my biography, titled One Against All, written by the noted Bohra reformist Yunus Bhai Baluwala, was released in the same year. I insisted that the reformist Bohras of India organize a convention in Surat, which is where the major Bohra madrasa is located. Some people were scared to do this in the very den of the Syedna, as it were, fearing that they would be attacked by the Syedna's cronies, but we went ahead. 12thAll World Bohra Conference in 2005 was organised in Surat. I was the co-organizer and it was quite successful conference.

I began my struggle and my public life in the Saifee Cooperative Society in Surat, and I still work there, now as its manager. Our business has expanded considerably over the years And, I must say, despite the torrent of hatred that has been directed against me all these years, many Bohras who refuse to countenance any criticism of the Syedna now come to me with requests for loans. Although I am still officially excommunicated from the Bohra fold many Bohras come to my office to see me. They cannot invite me to their homes on family functions, of course, because of the Syedna's orders. My brothers and sisters too, cannot meet me. If they dare too, they stand the risk of being excommunicated.

I keep attending reformist Bohra conferences wherever they are held. I am also invited by secular women's groups to speak, and in this way I have had the chance to travel to various parts of India. Hindu and Sunni Muslim groups also invite me to their meetings, and I am grateful to them for their support. Wherever I go 1 talk of the central role of women in promoting reform and resisting tyranny in the name of religion, which is an affront to true spirituality. I also keep stressing the need for communal harmony. From my own personal experiences, not from reading fat books, I know how deeply inter-related patriarchy, communalism, violence and priestly tyranny are.

I owe a lot to my mother, who stood firmly by me when I was ex-communicated. For that, she was thrown out of the community herself, but she refused to budge. She kept insisting, 'Zehra! Never cave in to tyranny. Keep your head high. This is what God wants.' Some Bohras from Surat, blind followers of the Syedna, offered me 50 lakh rupees if I issued an 'apology' to the Syedna, and even said that this would enable me to rejoin the Bohra fold. I remembered what my mother always told me and said to them, `I will never do that, no matter how much money you offer as a bribe. I know that by offering me money you want me to shut my mouth, to stop speaking out against the tyranny of the priests, to stop the Bohra reform movement.' Had I accepted their offer, my reputation as someone who has always stood for certain principles would have been in tatters and people would then say, 'Zehra has sold herself for money.' But since I have never cowed down to their threats and blandishments, I can, as my mother always told me to, hold my head high, and so, after I leave this world, people can say, 'There was a Bohra girl called Zehra who shook the Bohra community and dared to challenge the tyrants within it.'

In memory of my brave mother, and as a small token of appreciation for all that she stood for, recently I set up a charitable trust in her name. The trust has five trustees-a Hindu, a Sunni and three reformist Bohras. The trust offers modest financial assistance to the needy. We dream of doing many things in the future, one of them being to establish a common graveyard for people of all religions and communities so that people who are tormented and oppressed by their religious leaders, like my mother was, can find a final resting place there. Recently I have started a new project "Help after death" in August, 2018 from Indore. It is my passion now I spoke in Indore infront of underground reformists group and received amazing support. 150 Bohrasof non-reformist group registered and they have started formulating the committees. So that if any Dawoodi Bohra funeral is stopped by *Kothar* for any money or other matter its committee will come into action by involving police and media to help in funeral ceremony as per Bohra faith and rituals, I think this project would encouraging the orthodox to speak out against the *Kothar* in the matters they do not like to obey as the fearful question 'Who will bury me?' Is solved now. I havealso started to visit Bohra Dargah in Surat and Galiakot in Dec., 2018 without *rida* and without identity card. But they did not dare to stop me. I do not know whether they will allow other reformist ladies in Kurta-Salwar outfit, though I am on their rescue.

Sometimes, people ask me 'if the Syedna and his henchmen are such tyrants why do you reformist Bohras not convert to another religion or to another Muslim sect? Why do you insist on remaining Dawoodi Bohras?' I reply to them, saying, 'this is precisely what the Syedna wants, because if we reformists quit the Bohra fold, he will be able to rule just as he pleases, without any opposition whatsoever!' That is why I insist we must remain within the Bohra fold and continue to struggle for our rights, for true internal democracy. I think Islam, if correctly understood, tells us that this is precisely what we should do.

I have lived a long life of struggle. I have had to face terrible odds. All through, it was not desire for personal revenge or power that goaded me to take on the Bohra establishment, but an irrepressible commitment to justice. That is something basic, or ought to be, to all human beings. I simply cannot compromise on this. Some people may say that I was too obstinate or even vindictive, that I should have compromised instead of taking people to court, staging demonstrations, and lodging police complaints. But I tell them, 'If we keep quiet and cave in, tyrants will continue to play with our lives. Surely, speaking up against tyranny is a fundamental duty and right, is it not? Surely this is what Islam, properly understood, should inspire us to do.

And this is what the Bohra reformist movement is doing The reformists are appealing to the world to see the trickery behind the 'pious exterior of the Syedna and his cronies, who are misusing and misinterpreting religion to extort money from the Bohras and enforce a stultifying form of slavery on them, on their bodies and minds, all in the hallowed name of Islam. This is how the Syedna and his family have become among the richest in all of India. Anyone who dares to speak out against this tyranny is automatically thrown out of the community.

I appeal to the Government, political parties, intellectuals and, social activists, and to people in general to see through this charade of the Syedna and his cronies, who have been twisting Islam in order to promote their own interests. I ask them to stop supporting and patronizing these men. I appeal to people to listen to my voice to the voice of a Bohra woman who has seen through and struggled against the tyranny of the Bohra establishment for decades, not to fall prey to this nefarious propaganda.

Dr. Kaneez Fatima Sadriwala

I Dr. Kaneez Fatima Sadriwala was born on 18th July 1970 in Udaipur during the time when there was unrest among the Dawoodi Bohras and a movement was about to come. My father's family was in the reformist society named 'Bohra Youth' and my mothers' family in the orthodox Bohra group named 'Shabab'. My mother was boycotted by her family numbers including her father and mother. So my mother did not go to her parents' house in day time as Udaipur Bohras customs in that time.When I was in the age of 8, my father Abdul Hussain marched to heavenly abode. My mother Shireen RV was left alone, with three daughters and a social abstain to meet her own parents. During stern *iddah* period her parents could not look after her freely, because we were boycotted and orthodox treated us outcaste. She joined Hindustan Zinc Ltd. after the compilation of *iddah.*

Time passed by, the three young daughters were bought up by the joint family, until the family kitchen were separated in year 1988, Shireen RV was gifted a portion of residential building by my grandfather where she built her house, married two daughters single handedly. She got tired with the time and ultimately thereafter she took *misaq* and joined the Shabab group, as her parents were there and misaq was the only solution to reunion with her parents. Thereafter she married her third daughter in Shabab group. During the marriage ceremony we two sisters of youth group had distantly participated because our social boycott was in force. Till then she was in job at Hindustan Zinc Ltd., thereafter took voluntary retirement as she fulfilled the liabilities of three daughters to an extent.

First realization

I realized the 'Youth-Shabab' divide only when my father died in the year 1980, and my maternal grandfather and grandmother (*nanaji and naniji*) came to console my mother. It was the first time I had ever seen my *nani* in my *dadi's* house. I realized the gap only when she came, but above that what hit me most was the sudden disappearance of *nani* as other people came flowing into the house. The whole house was full, people said consoling words to me, patted me, but my eyes were searching my *nanaji* and she was nowhere to be found.

One day I was at my maternal grandmother's house (though we were not allowed to go, but people ignore breech by children) and all the family was getting ready to go somewhere, I asked where everybody was going and why am I not going with them, why my mother is not going? My *naniji* told me they were going to a 'Hall' for *Jaman* (food), and I or my mother could not go because we were in 'Youth' group and did not belong to their group. My innocent little brain could not diagnose the jargon even after her explanation. I watched them go with thousand questions and longing eyes and somehow I knew my naniji also had tears in her eyes. I was left to bear the pain and also to tolerate all by myself, yet a determination had creeped in to know the reason behind this abnormal behavior.

I asked my loving paternal grandfather whom I fondly called 'bajisa' or 'dadaji'', why they didn't take me, why my mother never goes to my Nani's house, why my nana never comes to our house, why my nanaji shy's away from talking to you, though he respects you a lot, why my nanaji doesn't talk to me in public, as if I am a stranger where as we are best buddies at home, he loves me a lot and plays with me all the time. My nanaji's younger brother is always annoyed with me and shuns me awaythe moment he sees me. I was scared of him and slowly started hating him for no reason. His eldest brother loved me a lot and his behavior never changed, at home or public. Three brothers but all the three behaved differently. All this left me puzzled but made me a keen observer.

Yet, I was the favorite of everybody, may be because I used to run errands for everybody, and may be because I had lost my father at a very young age and they pitied on me or if God knows better, there was any other reason. But amidst all this I was a lost child. I was silent, observant, studying people's behavior and slowly could understand their stand which eventually empowered me to become humble, courageous, patient, knowledgeable, sincere and mischievous. Along with all those virtues shaping my character I also became adamant.

Attack on Moyyedpura Mosque

Being born in the Youth shabby era, I had been a part of suffering, pain and hardship. In fact, all the curses a divide brings, be it a small family, a joint family, divorce of parents, death of parents of loved ones or on a larger platform be it society (Bohra, a small *Shia* sect) or a country, hardship is hardship, time may heal but marks remain.

During those days I was active with Bohra Youth Student Welfare Society. *Shabab* group had entered the Moyyedpura masjid that day. BohraYouth had control overall the mosques and shrines during those days. They were managed and governed by 'Youth' group not knowing much about the history of the Bohras at the age, I just went inside the mosque among the group of protestors, Bohra youth supporters, to see what was happening inside the mosque. I saw shabby people were shouting slogans against Sheikh Ahmed Ali Raj, Sheikh Yaqoob Ali Raj and BohraYouth were shouting slogans against *Kothar*.

Some Shabab people wearing white Kurta-Payjama had shovels, axes etc. with them and they uprooted floor of mosque- which during those days I never understood.

I was one among the mob who did nothing except being present there. Next day when I went to my nani's house as usual, she sternly asked me

'Why did I go to the mosque protest yesterday?' I was stunned as I thought that nobody would know about my presence, not timid by nature, but usually remaining silent and not cross questioning girl, I behaved contrary to my nature and asked her, who told her.

I had seen a neighbor from Shabab in the mosque and I was sure that she must have told my nani. I was very annoyed, not because I went there, not because she complained about me, just because may this act hurt my nani, and the neighbor's daughter had a chance to blame my nani.

Impact of that incident on me

As I witnessed the hatred among people from both side I felt *shabab* were more aggressive and Youths were on defending foot. But the logics I heard from the Youth were more realistic and justified and I really hated those men who dig up the flooring of the mosque. I could not believe my eyes that the social hatred could go to such an extent to destroy a mosque, house of God, but the fight among my own thoughts continued. I was in no position to discuss or ask any question to anybody and tried to solve the happenings around by myself, but those were the days which filled me with emotion of patriotism for youth, for now I had learnt the difference between orthodox and progressive thinking. And I preferred standing with the progressives. They talked about democracy, right to speak, right to enter to any Dargaha like Galiakot, which was banned for the Youth group, These discoveries and forceful personalities and their fight back, by debates and verbal abuses, found position in my thoughts, and later in my behavior and slowly in my character and personality.

This made me strong women, a person who knew that we can fight for our rights, we can speak up, and we can always take a stand and freely hold on to our beliefs.

I took part in the rallies (marches) dharna, Bandh (close down/ban), protest on collectorate, group meeting with city collector, public gatherings and addresses and road shows. This was the foundation stone which shaped my personality and the awareness to fight for right and truth prevails. I learnt the strength of slogans, anti-incumbency, educating the uniformed and power of reading.

This was the time when I read Karl Marks, Lenin, Confucius, Indian constitution, Bohra youth documents and silently observed people around and their behavior. I saw and watched and learnt from the behavior of many unsung heroes and heroines. There heroines were ladies of age between 15 to 70 years.

My Association with Student Welfare Society (SWS):

My first entry to the student welfare society was through the student library, to borrow books for Class IX commerce. I was amazed by the collection of books and facilities for the students and society's emphasis on education, which I thought never existed because of the regular fights amongst Youth-Shabab. Every year cultural programs like debates, mine, solo acts, general knowledge quiz, Quran recital etc. are organized. This platform gave me chance to portray myself. I was an active participant and took part in competition and also won many medals. Every year Student welfare society also gave prizes for the toppers in all fields of education, now the range of these prizes have broadened and is celebrated as big function on ALI DAY, but the onus of starting this intellectual academic activity goes to SWS only. I got gold medal for class X, IX commerce for securing highest marks in society.

These medals, certificate and honors empowered me with self-confidence, and boosted my morale. I was more happy and excited as I saw happiness and proud on my mothers' face. She was the only force behind my power. I was fighting on all fronts just to make her happy and proud of her upbringing, which she had molded with full perseverance and care. It was time for her to reap the crop. By this time I had become the role model for my younger sisters and cousins, it made me happy, confident and had already established me in the society. It made me fearless and bold. If it was not the reform movement, then who would have empowered me.? I did my graduation with good marks, did my masters and got married in between. But I completed my degree after marriage. I helped my in-laws family in business. I was a pure housewife. I had two children, but my books were never out of my shelf. I was a studious girl and still brushed my Accounting and Statistics. After my second baby, I joined a school, and then later shifted to college. I did my PhD after a break of almost 10 years. I started participating in conferences and seminars and started writing research papers. I am a good orator and a public speaker and so I found many platforms to speak. After that I did Faculty development program on entrepreneurship, my career rise was fast, from school senior teacher, I became Assistant professor, then Associate Professor and finally landed to the highest position in academics Professor. I became the Dean and Director of a Masters College. My Bohra Youth Association selected me to be member of Board of Directors for our own established and run, Cooperative Bank. Thereafter, I applied for the best institute of management for further studies in Management, Faculty development program at Indian Institute of Management, Ahmedabad (IIMA) and was fortunate enough to get admission. I applied worldwide, and I got selected in many institutes all over the world, I opted for Oman and till date I am serving there as Assistant Professor and Head of Accounting Department. I am recipient of highest honor National award from the government of Oman and I proudly dedicate these awards to my brave mother. It is not one thing that shapes you, it is the outcome of several forces that make you or break you. In my case, the world together conspired to make me. I am grateful to my beloved society BohraYouth and my family who believed in me and supported me in every path of life.

MalekaFaizee: migrated from Pakistan after marriage to an Indian boy

The consequence of social boycott imposed by our religious leader had an adverse effect on scores of lives, including mine.

I am Maleka Faizee, a Dawoodi Bohra born and brought up in Karachi, Pakistan. I from a respectable (elite) family in Udaipur, India but my father and one my paternal uncle settled in Pakistan as my grandfather had some property there too.Like any other Bohra family our household also observed all the customs and rituals with a lot of zeal and enthusiasm, like attending *majalis* during Moharram and going for prayer (*namaz*) during Ramadan.

The 70's turbulence in the Bohra Jamaat of Udaipur had affected us too, since my grandfather Janab Ghulam Ali Kathawala active participant of the reform movement that wanted a social transformation in Bohra society.

I was very young at that time when my father and uncle were called to the office of the Amil- Bhai Saheb of Karachi and asked to pledge their obedience and beg for *Mafinama* (forgiveness), just because their family in Udaipur was guilty in the eyes of *kothar*.

Initially the matter was resolved but then it became repetitive, every time something happened in Udaipur our part of the family had to bear the burns. The Amil Saheb's demand to curse(saying *la'nat*) upon their father proved to be last straw. My father and we all refused to do so and hence we were excommunicated. Consequently the doors of Bohra mosque, *jamaatkhana* and graveyards were closed for us. We are debarred from participating in any of the rituals or activities of the community.

The deepest wound was the separation from my childhood friends and close relatives who also made distance from us to follow the command of Amil. It was extremely painful for me to witness my mother breaking down several times. The climax was the day when she was forbidden to participate in the funeral ceremony of her father, my *nanaji*. She was totally shattered down.

The atrocities continued and we had to spend our growing up years outside the fold of Bohra community. Islam strictly forbids severing of the family ties but our so called spiritual head Syedna Saheb used social boycott to make his followers dance according his tools and maintained power over them. The biggest impact of *'baraat'* or social boycott on my life was that I had to be married with a reformist Indian boy and left my home country and settle in India, far away from my kith and kin. Luckily my marital family welcomed me warmly and proved to be very loving and caring.

I was shocked when some of family members from my father-in-laws family side left the reform movement and took *misaq* of Syedna Mohammed Burhanuddin who after 30 years came to Udaipur in 1998. They were the leaders of the reform movements in Udaipur. What motivated them towards Syedna's fold, God knows better. But it hurt the emotions of the common people very deeply. They did not understand the trap of Syedna. Thank God soon the reformist got rid of it. New leaders emerged and 'show goes on'.

I am Indian now and an active member of BohraYouth Girls' Wing. My elder son had graduate in Medicine and now searching for M.S. from foreign University. My younger son is doing MBBS too from All India Institute of Medical Sciences. I am enjoying life freely without any restrictions on my civil liberties.

Banu Bai Attarwala

I am a proud daughter of Sheikh Ahmad Ali Raj one among the four Sheikhs (Teacher) who were debarred from Jamia Saifiya, Surat and after that settled in Udaipur and led the reformists in religious sphere.

My childhood spent in scarcity as my father's salary was Rupees 20 only as a teacher of Jamia. We were four sisters and two brothers. Hence my parents could not afford me to send school. I was admitted in the school of Jamia Deeni School. At the age of 18 I was married with an Amil of RatangarhKheri(Madhya Pradesh) and lived a joyful life with husband and his family.

After the death of Syedna Tahir Saifuddin in 1966, Sheikh Hasan Ali Saharanpur Wala went to Haj pilgrimage and met with an Arab sheikh there. He disclosed before him that the present *Da'i* is not *Dai-ul-mutlaq* (Spiritual representative of Imam who is in seclusion) but *'Da'i-ul-nazim'*

(Managerial *Da'i*). This news reached to Syedna Burhanuddin. His whole and soul brother Yusuf Najmuddin called the four eminent Sheikhs- Hasan Ali Sarahanpur Wala, Sheikh Sajjad Hussain, Sheikh Ali Ahmad and Sheikh Ahmad Ali Raj to clarify the matter. All of them confirmed that the statements is correct and based on facts as the 46th *Da'i* Syedna Burhanuddin died without declaring *nass* (appointment of successor). Hence it was a matter of *katehnass* (breakdown of declaration) the continuity of *Da'i* as Naib-e-Imam (Deputy of Imam) had broken down. From 47th*Dai-uz-zamaan*all *Da'i*'s are '*Da'i*-e-nazim' only. Since that day the four eminent Sheikhs were expelled from Jamia Saifiya and their social boycott was declared. They were beaten by the mob of students and their houses were looted.

On hearing this news, I went to Surat from my husbands' house to console my father. This became a bone of contention between me and my husbands' family. They were provoked by Syedna's henchmen to divorce me. I begged pardon and promised not to meet my parents in future. But my voice was unheard like a cry in the wilderness. I was sixth months pregnant that time and due to anguish it aborted and I had to leave my husbands' house in this misery. My sister Nafisa too was divorced and she also came to Surat. We all worked day and night to earn bread. No one came to see us. We lived in isolation in a small rented house of a Sunni Muslim.

In 1974 we came to Udaipur on the invitation of reformists of Udaipur and settled there. I got married but it remained unsuccessful and within four months we separated by the procedure of divorce. It hurt my father deeply.

My father Sheikh Ahmad Ali was placed on a leadership post in the sphere of religion. He was who performed first *namaz-e-Imamat* without *raza* in Bohra mosque Rasulpura. He guided people on religious issues. Sometimes he differed with reformists' *jamaat's* liberal attitude towards *Shariat* law – like *iddah* after husband's death, the role of *vali* in *nikah*. Present of two witness of divorce be mandatory in the *nikah* of a divorcee woman, spread *Masallah* (prayer cloth) be compulsory on carpeted floor of the mosque etc. He translated Quran Shareef in Dawat's Zaban (Gujrati-Urdu-Arabic). He Wrote dozens of books in different issues of day to day life. In *Sansanikhez Haqaiq* (Vibrant truth) he disclosed the inner layers of Dawat's history. He also criticized reformists on the same religious view towards Da'i like orthodox Bohras. He established a publishing institution 'Tanzeem-e-Ishate-Islami Taleem" which published his works. He died in 2012.

My father insisted me to remarriage and I had to marry third time in Mumbai in 1978. This husband was a widower having three sons below 10 years of age. I with motherly love and affection brought them up. After grown up they left our house one by one to begin their career. My husband spent money on them to make them self-reliant. Ten years back my husband had died and again I left Mumbai and settled in Udaipur.

Today I am all alone in the big house, ground floor is on rent, the money earned from rent is sufficient me to lead honorable life. However after struggling with the implications of social boycott now, I empowered enough to look after myself with honour and dignity. I do some crochet work (lace making) and *Zari* work also which adds some money to my income. My two sisters are in orthodox group. Though we have telephonic relationship but do not physically meet with each other openly. Yet I remember my first husband and his love, if there was no social boycott I would have been spending life with him and my own children. Who is to look after me now at the age of 72? "Allaha Ki Marzee" (God's Wish).

Amina Naath-Ex-President of Bohra Youth Girls' Wing, Udaipur

I was born and brought up in Mumbai. I did M.A. from Mumbai University in Persian. Urdu and English were my optional subjects at B.A. level. I did B.Ed. also. We were three sisters and one brother. My elder sister Mehfuza Bai was a stalwart of Bohra Reform Movement in Mumbai. She was elected as first women Vice President of CBDBC in 1977. My father was an old reformist. He was active participant of 'Rafai-ul-Mumeen' (a reformist group of his time). This family background generated a sense of reform in me.

After marriage I had to settle in Udaipur in 1969. I was appointed as school lecturer in Saint Mary's Senior Secondary School. But after some months I had resigned to join Tayabia Senior Secondary School (A Syedna's establishment). Because the Secretary of Tayabia School, Nana Bhai Kurawarwala promised me to elevate me on the post of Principal as soon as the Acting Principal will retire. I trusted on his promise. But he betrayed and I remained in first grade only. In the beginning the school gave me so many responsibilities as extracurricular activities, so I became a very popular teacher among the student community, but when reformist movement started in Udaipur and my involvement in that, annoyed the school committee and they seized all these extra responsibilities from me. They tried to harass me so that I would resign. I did not resign, and then they terminated me without any valid cause. I filed an application to Rajasthan Teacher's Association and requested themto plead my case to the directorate of school education.

Thank God, within two months the Director of School Education advised Tayabia School to restore my services without break. Hence I continued with my reformist zeal and ideology and never knelt down on this issue. When I retired the school did not oblige me by granting gratuity. I filed a case in the Civil Court of Udaipur and won the case and school had to pay me two lacs of rupees. All this happened because I was the President of Bohra Youth Girls' Wing Udaipur and my husband and his family was hardcore reformists as well. My husband was elected President Local *Jamaat* of Udaipur two twice.

I joined Bohra Youth Girls' Wing in the year 1988. That was the period when reform movement was at the peak in Udaipur as well as in other places like, Mumbai, Hyderabad, Aurangabad, Pune, Ahmadabad, Patna, Neemach, Surat, Godhra and many more places. The Girls wing was an extension of BYA, Udaipur. Among women it was quite popular and women of Udaipur identified themselves with it. We organised Healthy Baby show, Women's health camp, funfair and women's indoor sports competitions. All these made women vibrant. Besides these many academic and awareness programmes were also organised such as Women Study Camp, International Women's Day, Quiz in 'Qur 'anic Rights of Women' and foundation day celebration.

For economic up liftment of women initially we started classes of stitching, needle work and crochet then we supplied sewing machines to the needy women free of cost to earn something out of it. Girls' Wing was also instrumental to membership campaign of Udaipur Urban Co-operative Bank. In the year 1991 a women primary co-operative store was established under the Rajasthan Co-operative Society Act. The objective of this primary co-operative store was to provide grocery and other house hold items on a fair price to its members and also motivated women for entrepreneurship. To increase the share capital we members of Girls' Wing executive Committee of Girls' Wing had purchased the maximum share of Rs.2000/- per member so the store might run without financial shortage. This effort remained successful and after an interval of two years its second branch was opened in Syedi Lukmanji Saheb Dargah compound. Women entrepreneurship also sparked and in short span of time. Bohra Women's shops have been seen in Bohra mohallas (locality).

When we were outcasted due to *baraat* and could not enter any Bohra MusafirKhana it caused a lot of difficulties particularly in the city like Ahmadabad. Ahmadabad is a medical hub and not far from Udaipur. Therefore, generally patients used to go to Ahmadabad for medical consultancy and stayed at Bohra Musafirkhana. But they were compelled to stay in hotel after boycott. So a patient had to spend more on lodging and boarding. To solve this problem we the members of Girls' Wing went door to door to the reformists Bohras and collected an amount of Rs.4 lacs for the purchase of a guest house there so the patient and his/her attendants could stay there with minimal cost. A three B.H.K. flat was purchased by the help of Ibrahim Engineer the then Director of Hindustan Zinc Ltd.

In my leadership Girls' Wing remained instrumental in making Galiakot a burning issue and successfully prevented Syedna's entry in Udaipur city for a long period of 25 years (1973 to 1978).

I am still active in the age of 77 in reformist activities. I wrote many poems on the movement and women's role in it. I hope the reform movement will continue.

Fatima from Doha – Middle East

I Fatima (changed name) grown up in a liberal family in Udaipur (Raj.) where son and daughter were sent to best English medium school. There was no discrimination between girl and boy. I used to wear pants, drive cycles, fly kites and play cricket.

I often heard stories from my parents and relatives about how a rift has emerged in well knitted Bohra community and how both groups have maintained a distance with each other. When I was in 12th standard I personally came across with this *baraat* experience. I and my mother were pulled out from the marriage hall by some volunteers and they shouted "You are *munafiq* and how you dare to enter in this hall, go, and never show your face again." We were so humiliated that we could not utter a word and came back home. Then I asked my mother, where was your sister who invited us to join the marriage ceremony of her daughter "She replied aguishly in low voice." She might be, so frightened that she hid herself behind the curtains, as the priest had refused to perform *nikah* in our presence." "Oh! Now I got the point that we are outcastes", I cried. Life is going on. I remained more serious about my academic career during student life and now I am more serious about service career than anything else. Though I got married before cleared my C.A. My husband is kind enough to care my career all the time. So, with his co-operation and encouragement I have cleared C.A.

Now I work at Entrepreneurship in Doha.

Thing started to change when my sister-in-laws family for some vested interest decided to give *misaq* (apology) to Syedna Saheb and left reformists group. They tried to influence my parents-in-law too to change the group. My parents-in-law so pressurized by them that they went to orthodox group and then forced us to do the same. Out rightly me and husband resisted to give *misaq*. This became a bone of contention between us and my parents-in-law. They were displeased with us. We have great respect of them and did not want to hurt them anymore. So we went to priest house at night and took *misaq*. But we had not changed our life style, not wear *rida*, *saya, topi,* not grew beard etc. and never went to attend any community functions.

Ultimately to escape this mental distress we decided to go abroad for work. Soon I got job opportunity in UAE. I joined, there later on my husband also got job there.

My husband is a doctor in medicine. We both are doing fine and happily living with our teenager children. We are successful in inculcating the best values to our children which is far beyond the sectarian mind set.

Rubiqa liyaqat – Delhi (News Anchor, ABP News Channel)

I am a journalist and working as a TV anchor for ABP News Channel. I have been performing here the 'Prime Time Show' namely 'Master Stroke' at 9.00 p.m. along with 'Seedhee Baat' at 5.00 p.m. Previously I was engaged with Zee News and for a long period I had worked on the show, 'Taal Thok Ke' which was very popular and its TRP was also high. Before that I have worked with 'Live India', 'News 24' and 'Channel 24' as well.

I achieved all this on the basis of my qualification and my parents' blessing. I have done graduation in mass communication from Bombay University and Diploma in FMCA from Delhi University in 2003. I have perfection in Hindi, Urdu and English languages. My schooling was from St. Mary's Senior Secondary School, Udaipur. The credit of success goes to my parents especially to my father who inspired me thoroughly to prefer journalism as a career.

I belong to Dawoodi Bohra reformists group. My father has sacrificed his whole life as a 'tireless soldier' of Bohra Youth Movement. It was he and his commando group which spread a feeling of fear among the orthodox Bohra as well as among *Kothar's* goons and henchmen after Galiakot incident in 1973. Hence they left the establishment in Udaipur and went underground for some time. Consequently all the mosques, *Jammat Khana, Qabrastan,* maternity home etc. were deserted. Slowly Bohra Youth taken over the charge of it and till date all above properties are under the possession of Bohra Youth Association. The possession of Bohra Youth on community properties remained a strong cause to deep-rooted the reformists' movement in Udaipur.

The orthodox group filed a number of criminal cases more than 50 against my father alone. Totally 200 cases were filed against Bohra Youth activists. These cases maligned the career of my father and his friends. From 1973 to till March 2018 (45 years) my father had to attend the court on hearing of this and that case. Any other person in place of him could not bear such type of difficulties.

My father was elder son of the family consisting nine members, parents, four sisters and three brothers. The family looked to him for financial support being eldest son so he began a job in Hindustan Zincs' Acid Roster Plant as charge hand (7th level in job hierarchy) and tried to support the family. He has passion of cricket. He was good player and he was about to be selected in 'Ranji Trophy' but due to his diversion for reform movement he missed the chance in 1973. His fondness for cricket remained alive and when he got opportunity as a General Secretary of Bohra Youth, Udaipur in 2002 to 2012, he established Bohra Youth Cricket Academy at Khanjipeer Compound and utilizes the waste land of Bohra community there.

My mother was higher educated (M.Sc. Chemistry) woman at the time of marriage. But my father never took it otherwise; instead he encouraged my mother for pursuing Ph.D. degree. My mother completed it in service in Hindustan Zinc Ltd. My mother too was supportive to my father's ambition to liberate the Bohras from religious dictatorship. This family background made me brave and fearless in life. I too participated in many agitations against religious orthodoxy. I feel proud that I was born in a reformist family and can enjoy freedom in life as a citizen of free India. I was awarded 'Humanity International Women Achiever Award' by former President, Pratibha Patil at Mumbai in June 2018. I wish to be instrumental to fulfill my parent's dream as freedom fighter of Bohra community.

Dr. ZainabPoonawala (Pune)

I am Dr. ZainabPoonawala. I did M.Sc. in Zoology from Pune University and Ph. D. in Entomology from Delhi University. I was the most educated sibling in my family.

I married with Tahir Punewala a rich businessman. He was born reformist. He was a close friend of Nauman Contractor and was an active member of Pragati Mandal. Hence he along with family was boycotted by Bohra priesthood. But we lived in cosmopolitan locality. Hence we could survive with the wounds of *baraat*.

I taught in a local college for some time. Later I started my career as a social activist. I took membership of many voluntary agencies. I was President of Poona Women's Council. I was an office-bearer in the Family Planning Association of India, Pune Branch. I remained central executive member of CBDBC two times. I along with my husband actively participated in Bohra reformist activities in Mumbai, Pune, Aurangabad and Udaipur. We attended so many All World Bohra Conferences in different cities and different States of India.

We organised Fourth All World Dawoodi Bohra Conference in Pune in 1983. The conference addressed the core demands of Bohra social reform movement. National press covered the event on front page.

I was also co-convener of the first All World Bohra Women Conference held in Udaipur in 1989. It was attended by 600 delegates. Needless to say the support of the women is of great importance for the Bohra reform movement. It was also heartening to note that the Bohra women were quite critical of certain age-old practices like undue restrictions on the widows during *iddah* period; Girls *Khatna* (FGM) and deprivation of women from inheritance in father's property etc. Resolutions were passed to ban these un-Islamic practices. The conference ended with the hope that the Bohra women would give lead to other women, especially the Muslim women, in emancipating them from male domination, and also from tyranny of the priesthood.

I made efforts to seek an appointment with the Prime Minister Rajeev Gandhi and I succeeded. Under my leadership a deputation of Bohra ladies met the Prime Minister on 22nd May 1986; three months after the delegation of CBDBC met him. Six ladies from Mumbai and 10 ladies from Udaipur joined the delegation. We while demanding enactment of 'Anti-Social Boycott Bill' threatened to go on indefinite fast in front of the Prime Minister's house if the bill was not introduced. Our meeting with Prime Minister was publicised in the press. A press conference was also held in Delhi after meeting the Prime Minister.

Our struggle is going on. Now I am crossed 80 years of age, I have a daughter. She is a thorough professional and doing a lot of social work. She is a multifaceted personality. She has a daughter studying in a college. My daughter is member of *Sahiyo*-a Bohra Women Group asserting for a ban on FGC/FGM in India. Though I saved her from this cruel injury as, I am against it.

My husband has passed away in July 2017. He was so annoyed with the high priest's farman that "no reformists be allowed to bury in Dawoodi

Bohra graveyard", he declared long before that his dead body be donated to Medical College for students use. So we have donated his body.

I and my daughter have written the same declaration. I did not set in *iddah* as well per Bohra practice. But I abided with the Quranic injunction that no *nikah* before 4 months and ten days after husband's death. To me Bohra practice of *iddah* is a weapon to control women, it is exploitative why should woman suffer in isolation? Women should have freedom to move. I hope my stand on *iddah* would pave way to other women.

Rehana Germanwala- Councilor, Municipal Co-operation Udaipur and President of Bohra Youth Association

I belong to a middle class family. My father was a government employee, mother belongs to rural area and had passed middle class but still our family was thorough reformists. My father always remained against the Bohra system of *raza* and *misaq* though it was very difficult for him to live surrounding the people of small township Vallabhnagar (*nanihal* mother's kin), Fatehnagar (*dadihal*father's kin) and Bhinder (*Sasural* wife's kin). My mother was his real power she supported him everywhere.

Therefore my upbringing was in reformist family and in early age I joined Bohra Youth activities. I contested first election at the age of 15 as a class IX student for the post of Executive Member of Student Welfare Society (a branch of BYA). As soon as I passed B.Com, I got married with a business person in Udaipur. My higher education was discontinued but my social activism continued. I contested election for the member of Dawoodi Bohra Jamaat two times and got elected. I was the first woman to be elected as Vice President of Dawoodi Bohra Jamaat Udaipur. I am member of the Central Executive Committee of CBDBC from last 30 years.

I came in lime light when I filed nomination for the post of Municipal Councilor from ward 48. The opportunity came when the ward was declared women ward as after 74th Constitutional Amendment, 1/3rd of seats are reserved for women by lottery system. As Ward No.48 has a majority of Dawoodi Bohra population, hence, Congress party contacted Bohra youth leaders to select a woman for this post. Being resident of this ward, they choose me. I took membership of Congress party and filed the nomination on Congress ticket. Interesting enough the entire Dawoodi Bohra community both progressive and orthodox groups came together and supported the Bohra candidates.Two other Bohra candidates from orthodox *Jamaat* won in this election, Muslim Ali BandookWala from Ward 47 and Nafisa Saif from women Ward 55. It was heartening to notice that the community which was divided on the issue of Municipal elections again got united on the same issue. We three won the election but this unity during election time could not be sustained as orthodox maintained distance with reformists as earlier.

My political career started from here. I used to attend the Congress party functions and meetings and remained loyal to them. But party refused to give me ticket in 2015 Municipal election from the women ward 47 it was also Bohra populated ward, while BJP was ready to grant me ticket. I accepted it and strived hard to convince community members to vote for me. They voted for me and again I took oath of Municipal Councilor Udaipur (single Bohra candidate). This time I became the Chairperson of water supply committee. At present I am in BJP party and a core committee member of 'Beti Padhao Beti Bachao' and 'Mahila Morcha Udaipur'. I give the credit of my social and political activism to Bohra reform movement from where I develop openness in thought and action.

Masooma Ranalwi

I was born in Mumbai in a reformist family. My father Shoeb Ranalwi was an outright reformist. He worked with Nauman Contractor and other Bohra reformists of that time. He worked on various posts of CBDBC in eighties and nineties. That time I was in school and did not know much about Bohra reform movement. My family was boycotted. Hence my mother lived in isolation. She did not go to my *dadi's* and *nani's* house. No relatives talked with her. She spent her maximum time in house hold job or playing with us. When my *dadi* (grandmother) died, my father was prevented to attend her funeral. He was even not allowed to see her mother's face.

It shocked me a lot and after that I joined the reform activities in Mumbai along my father. I did attend the meetings, conference and workshop of reformists Bohras and actively participated in the deliberations of reformists issues. I was elected executive member of CBDBC many times.

When my father died some years ago, he was buried in a Sunni Muslim's *Qabrastan* according to his will. He knew that in Bohra *Qabrastan* no place will be given to his dead body to be buried as he was an excommunicated person.

I currently work as trainer on issues of gender and sexual harassment and as a social activist as I am a Law Graduate from Mumbai, India, and a Chivalric Scholar, with a Diploma on Women in Leadership and Management, University of Bradford, UK in 2015. I took the bold step to be vocal about my views on the practice on FGM, and how having been a victim of the practice when I was young, it impacted me deeply and I mobilised support to start debate and discussion over the taboo issue in my community.

Since then I have been at the forefront of a wide survivor led campaign in India to end FGM in the community. I have inspired women and young girls across the country for openly speaking about their experiences with regard to FGM and to actively engage in a campaign against the practice.

I have founded an organisation called We Speak Out which is the largest survivor led platform working against FGM in India and the world.

I spearheaded a signature campaign asking the Government of India to ban FGM in India and the petition has mobilised over 200000 signatures so far. I am actively involved in exploring and researching the legal and policy level changes and options that would work in India to effectively end FGM here.

I have built a movement of women by actively using social media and technology to let the voices of girls and women be heard across the nation. The Face book Group: Speak Out on FGM has over 3000 followers and the WhatsApp group of over 50 women engaged in daily conversations on FGM.

I have actively mobilised national and international media to support the end FGM campaign with hundreds of articles being published regularly on FGM in India in various languages, and more importantly calling for members to question and be critical of the blindly followed tradition.

I have taken the issue of FGM in India to the UNHRC and presented the details of the practice and called for action.

I am an intervening petitioner in a matter before the Supreme Court of India which is challenging the practice of FGM and calling for its ban.

I believe 'where there is a will, there is a way' soon Supreme Court of India will ban the practice of FGM in India. During interviews and formal talks I observed that the orthodox women have realised that FGM is a taboo and it should be stopped but remained tight lipped due to the fear of excommunication. Though Maharashtra government has already passed the Ex-communication Act in 2017 but in Bohras the practice of excommunication is still prevalent.

Conclusion

The above case studies are only the reflections of a few Bhora women's uprise and empowerment. In Udaipur every Women has her own story to tell.

The Dawoodi Bohra women's main concern is that their human and democratic rights which are being violated by the priesthood through imposition of social boycott. The reformists are demanding that the government of India, in order to uphold constitutional values, declare such coercively imposed boycotts illegal. The reformist women are struggling to free the community from the slavery of the priesthood by putting their own inspiring examples how they redressed Syedna's hegemony from their life and are enjoying empowered and self-respected life.

Future of reform movement depends on the good education and awareness of the next generation. Generally women as mothers have greater influence on the children. Therefore reformists must try to reach out to Shabab women to enlighten them, to make them aware of their rights, to remove their ignorance of the basic principles of Islam.

Notes and References

Following is the list of articles, published on FGM:

http://www.ndtv.com/opinion/i/was-circumcised-when-i-was-a-girl-of- 7-1238068

http://www.hindustantimes.com/static/fgm-indias-dark-secret/

http://www.vagabomb.com/In-Historic-Protest-Women-Fight-against-Female-Genital-Mutilation-in-India/

http://theladiesfinger.com/lets-talk-female-genital-mutilation/

http://www.idiva.com/news-work-life/the-most-inspiring-indian-women-of-2015/15121824

http://www.bbc.com/news/world-asia-india-35129466

http://www.muimbaimirror.com/mumbai/others/Chucking-the-anonymity-veil-17-women-call-for-ban-on-genital-mutilation/articleshow/50036285.cms

http://www.dnaindia.com/mumbai/report-bohra-women-campagin-for-outlawing-female-genital-muitilation-2153937

http://www.thequint.com/women/2015/12/30/silence-nomore-dowoodi-bohra-women-crusade-against-fgm

http://www.thequint.com/india/2015/12/05/i-suffered-genital-mutilation-support-me-to-stop-it

http://cj.ibnlive.in,.com/stop-female-genital-mutilation/45584/

http://www.msn.com/en-in/news/watch/stop-female-genital-mutilation/vp-AAgo9cO

http://www.elespectador.com/noticias/elmundo/blkoguera-puso-pie-una-minoria-tumbar-ablacion/india-articulo-606104

http://www.huffingtonpost.com/entry/indian-women-ban-fgm us 56993990e 4b0b4 eb 759 e3 efd?section=india.

http://news.trust.org//item/20160112150723-xkmft/?source=leadCarousel

http://www.themalaysianinsider.com/world/article/indian-women-speak-out-againt-female-genital-mutilation.

http://news.yahoo.com/india-urged-ban-fgm-women-break-silence-secret-153700977.html.

http://www.allgov.com/india/news/top-stories/womens-group-calls-for-ban-on-genital-mutilation-in-india-so-can-you-1191974.html

http://www.asianetnews.tv/web-story/opffbeat/India-urged-to-ban-FGM-as-women-break-silence-on-secret-rutual-42650

http://nofgm.oprg/2016/01/10/petition-to-end-female-genital-mutilation-in-india/

http://www.ndtv.com/health/month-long-campaign-on-female-genital-mutilation-launched-1274532

http://www.business-standard.com/article/pti-stories/online-petition-against-female-genital-mutilation-lauynched-116020401300 1. html

http://www.thenewsminute.com/article/female-genital-mutilation-survivors-launch-month-long-campaign-38640

http://indiatoday.intoday.in/story/mnonth-long-campaign-on-female-genitasl-mutilation-lalunched/1/589361.html

http://indiatoday.intoday.in/story/rptng-after-change-in-para-5/1/588025.html

http://www.deccanherald.com./content/527358/month-long-campaign-female-genital.html

http://www.mid-day.com/articles/online-petition/against-female-genital-mutilation-launched/16929172

http://punjabstarnews.com/online-petition-against-female-genital-mutilation-launched/

http://www.thehindu.com/news/cities/mumbai/news/online-petition-against-female-genital-mutilation-article8196598.ece?css=print

http://www.freepressjournal.in/online-plea-against=-fecmale-genital-mutilation-launched/ 773068.

http://www.business-standard.kcom/article/pti-stolries/month-long-campaign-onfemale-genital-mutilation-launched-116020600764 1.html.

http://www.thequint.com/videos/2016/02/05/female-genital-mutilation-must-be-stopped-and-thisd-could-be-a-start.

http://indiatoday.intoday.in/video/women-ruise=against-female-genital-mutilation/1/587469. html.

http://weww.firstpost.com/livingh/many-stay-silent-to-avoid-backlash-this-female-genital-mutilation-victim-is-speaking-out-and-you-should-listen-2615284.html

http://timesofindia.indiatimes.com/city/mangaluru/Bohra-women-strenghten-campaign-to-end-FGM-in-India/articleshow/50868268.cms.

http://www.dnaindia.com/health/report-international-day-for-zero-tolerance-of-fgm-ngo-sahiyo-s-petition-to-end-female-genital-mutilation-in-india-2174354.

http://www.thecitizen.in/index.php/OldNewsPage/?Id=6502&Against/Cutting/Up/Women.

http://netzfrauen.org/2016/02/056/38112/.

http://www.scoopwhoop.com/Barbaric-Female-Genital-Mutilation-Is-Very-Much-A-Reality-In-India-But-These-Women-Want-To-Eng-It/.

http://www.thehealthsite.com/news/shocking-80-of-bohra-women-have-been-subjected-to-female-genital-mutilation-survey-v0216/.

http://www.catchnes.com/social-sector/30-female-genital-mutilation-survivors-push-to-end-barbaric-practice-1454655949.html.

http://www.catchnews.com/life-society-news/the-horror-of-fgm-bohra-community-shames-women-by-kcutting-genitals-1454749683.html.

http://m.dailyhunt.in/news/india/english/catch-news-epaper-catchnew/the-horror-of-fgm-bohra-community-shames-women-by-cutting-genitals-newsid-49366231.

hjhtp://www.governancenow./com/news/regular-story/dawoodi-bohra-women-practice-female-genital-mutilation.

Chapter - 8

Bohra Reform Movement: Challenges and Weaknesses

Bohra reform movement is an ongoing movement. It has passed through various ups and downs. Until Udaipur's mass movement, the reform movement had not been alive at all times. Occasionally it withered away and then again resurfaced. But after the success of Udaipur's mass movement, the Bohra reform movement took an institutional shape under the auspices of CBDBC and initiated an alternative system of community management.

The Bohra priesthood and their orthodox followers often allege that the reformists have gone astray and in some extreme cases they even allege that reformists have abandoned their religion. Is it really so? Certainly not, if one goes with what the reformist's themselves believe (mentioned in chapter IV). Some reformists themselves have certain doubts about their beliefs and practices when anyone erroneously describes the orthodox Bohra as constituting the main stream.,[1] What is the logic behind describing the orthodox Bohras as mainstream? It is their beliefs and practices or is it their numbers? If it is belief and practices, there is hardly any difference between the two. Both are followers of Fatimi Da'wah, both accept the chain of *Da'is*, including the present *Da'i*.

Is it then numbers? No quite so. If this logic of numbers is accepted, then only Shiah Ithna Asharis among all Shia sects[1]would be accepted as mainstream Shiah and among all the Muslims the world over, only Sunni Muslims will constitute the mainstream of Islam. So this argument of mainstream is quite misleading to say the least.

Most people call any larger group as "main stream," even though it may have deviated from the original main course of morality and basic principles. This is quite misleading because the smaller group may be following the original "main stream" right path.

Another important question is in what way the orthodox and reformists differ from each other? Do they differ in fundamentals of faith or in subsidiary matters? Are then differences based on '*Usul*' (principles) or in *furu'al* (secondary matters) as pointed out earlier there in is no question of differing in fundamentals or 'Usul'. Asghar Ali Engineer[2] explained "All of us orthodox or reformists subscribe to same fundamentals of faith and even accept the office of *Da'i* too. There is much misunderstanding on this question among our orthodox friends. They think that we reject the office of *Da'i.* It is far from true. The reformists give as much importance to the office of a *Da'i* as the orthodox Bohras. The office of *Da'i* is an integral part of Fatimi Da'wah. There is a lot of misinformation campaign against the reformists by the vested interest. We also do not differ from each other even on the question of *nass.* The doctrine of *nass* has been quite fundamental to all the Shi'ah sects. It is fundamental to the reformists as to orthodox Bohras."

The real difference between the two is not on the question of the office of the *Da'i* but on obedience to *Da'i.* The orthodox have been made to believe that unquestioning and absolute obedience to *Da'i* has been almost elevated to the position of divinity through clever maneuvering of the *Kothar*. The reformists oppose this and consider it as deviation from the basic Ismaili doctrines. The reformists asserting that obedience to truth is more fundamentals than obedience to authority. Allah has made it individual responsibility in the Qur'an to follow the truth rather than authorities. The Qur'an requires every individual to use his intellect (*aql*), to reason out and accept the truth.

The orthodox Bohars violate the doctrine of the Qur'an and fall for authority based guidance. For them the present *Da'i* is authority is far more important than the Qur'anic truth. This is very crucial difference between orthodox and the reformists.

Authoritarianism of Religious head

Authoritarianism, as is quite natural, refuses to accept doctrine of accountability in any form or any field. A true religious spirit never leads to Authoritarianism in any form, not even in religious form.

The holy Prophet Mohammed (PBUH) was extremely gentle and polite and never showed any trace of Authoritarianism. No one could accuse him of authoritarianism even in religious matters. It should also be remembered that- Islam categorically rejects Authoritarianism and absolutism even in religious matters. It was not for nothing that the holy Qur'an says, "Call to the way of the lord with wisdom and goodly exhortation and argue with them in the best manner," (16:126) Also the Qur'an has reasonably proclaimed, "There is no compulsion in religion." (2:257).

The Bohra priestly establishments conduct, on the other hand, represents total negation of open, democratic conscientious and humane religious-cultural model represented by Islam and early Islamic society, the Bohra priestly model is authoritarians to the core. It has no place for democratic openness, let alone conscientious dissent. It is most intolerant and absolutist. It is highly coercive and far from persuasive.

However the Bohras have not only been governed, under absolutists rule, they have faced certain adverse historical situations as well. They were, until 19th century a persecuted community[2] considered as heretical by other Muslims. Persecution leads to sense of insecurity which in turn results in dependence syndrome on some or the other authority and if this authority happens to be religious, this dependence gets further reinforced. Thus persecution complex breeds dependence-complex and creates fertile ground for development of authoritarianism.

51st Syedna Taher Saifuddin was intelligent, cunning, over-ambitious, scheming and ruthless. Immediately after assuming the office of *Da'i* (24th Jan, 1915, 10th Rabiul Awwal 1333 Hijri) he left the dilapidated old devri, in Zapa Bazzar, surat and came down to Bombay, the commercial capital of India. On one side he projected his image as exclusively great religious and divine personality by stage managing meetings with world dignitaries and by acquiring honorary titles and degrees, on the other side he parted with traditional simplicity, god-fearing and honest life. In order to establish his supremacy, Tahir Saifuddin who was called Mullaji Saheb in the initial period of his Dai ship soon started addressing himself[3] as '*Da'i-ul-Mutlaq', 'Sultan-e-Bawahir', 'Shamsu-Duatul-Mutlaqeen', 'Naib-e-Imam', 'Illahul-Ard'* (God on earth),'owner of soul, body mind and properties' of his followers, divine and spiritual personality and 'all-knowing', infallible and above all supreme authority to allot choicest accommodation in the heaven to loyalists.

Before him the *Da'i's* were poor and indebted[4] and local Jamat's were quite independent. But Tahir Saifuddin concentrated both wealth and power in his hands and began to exercise strict control over the religious as well as secular life of his followers. Consequently he raised himself to the god and, lowered his followers down to the level of bonded slaves.

He established that Syedna is the representative of God. Whatever he does; he does with the permission of God. So if there is faith it has to be in totality, because he has the powers[5] of God on behalf of God.

He introduced the practice of excommunication social boycott for the first time in the Bohra history, as a weapon to silence the conscientious objectors to un-Islamic, unethical and illegal activities with which he had started to amass wealth and property. Anyone against whom social boycott is declared becomes a social pariah and gets completely isolated even among his own family and friends. He cannot even attend the marriage or funeral function of his near and dear ones. There have been instances of marriages breaking even after years of staying together, especially if the husband or wife develops[6] reformist sympathies, mothers break off relations with their children as do sisters and brothers.

***Misaq*:**

Fear in the form of *misaq* was incorporated in Bohra community by Syedna Taher Saifuddin. *Misaq* is a bond of slavery and very fundamental in Dawoodi Bohra community.[7] Misaq (oath of allegiance) means everything that the believer possess as personal property including wife and children, all belong to the Syedna (Bawa Saab/*Da'i*). Here the *misaq* taker does not know that he/she is making the *Da'i* an absolute dictator controlling all aspects of his/her life. If ever he or she disobeys any dictate or order of the *Da'i* his *misaq* is considered broken. However *misaq* has become an instrument of slavery. It is important to note that misaq was an instrument of quasi-religious and quasi political instrument. In the early days of the Isma'ili movement, *misaq* was an instrument of acceptance of religious as well as the political authority of the Fatimi Imams. Syedna Hamiduddin Kirmani has rightly described it in one of his *risalas* as both religious and political in nature. It was for this reason that the text of *misaq* was not incorporated in any work of Isma'ili. *Da'i's Misaq* is no more necessary to enforce political authority of Imam. It is its religious component which is important in the present circumstances. And it is also important to note that since the real religious authority lay with the Imam- and not with the *Da'i* the misaq can be given or taken only for imam, not for the *Da'i*. Syedna Hatim (3rd *Da'i* after Imam Taiyab) makes this abundantly clear in his classical work *Tuhfat-al-Qulub*. The most fundamental aspect of *misaq* is acceptance of the Qura'nic teachings on one hand, and *walayat* (i.e. love) of *ahl-al-bayt*, on the other. Every Bohra, orthodox or reformist accept both without any reservation anyway. All Bohras swear allegiance to Quranic teachings and the Holy Prophet and his family. This is what *misaq* is all about. But today *misaq* has become more fundamental than the faith itself. It is so because for *Kothar* it is a powerful instrument of promoting authoritarian culture. The reformists reject all forms of authoritarian culture.

***Raza*:**

In order to implement above, condition of 'Misaq'*Raza*(prior permission) for all religious and social matters was introduced by Syedna Taher Saifuddin and made compulsory. For example before performing *nikah*, burial *Namaz*, *Namaz-e-imamat* (congregational prayer), Haj and other religious activities vis-à-vis in all social and welfare activities like establishing school, college hospital, library, bank, musafir khana etc. He made any act done without his prior permission a sin and punishable.

To maintain the record of once allegiance towards *Da'i*, every member of the Bohra community has to carry what are known as 'e-*Jamaat* cards'.[8]the cards were issued nearly two decade ago, but recently the documents were upgraded as '*smartcards* 'with GPS features. GPS features raise privacy concerns just like India's UIDAI (Aadhar Card) which continues to face logistical and legal hurdles.

These smart cards are used to gain access to community mosques, mausoleums and graveyards.

One important trend of authoritarian rule of Syedna reflects that large sum of money are extracted from Bohras right from birth to death by way of religious taxes. This is extortion. For every ceremony one has to pay up.As for every ritual Bohras are dependent on priesthood and for everything they demand money even to bury the dead. So they have a total control over Bohras' lives. They levied seven-eight types of taxes, namely. '*Zakat'*, '*Sabeel' Sila-Fitra'*, '*Khamus'*, '*Huq-un-Nafs'*, '*Nazrul Muqam'* and '*Salaam'*all these categorized in *wajebat.* On an average even from poorest of the poor they have been taking a minimum of Rs. 5000 per annum. The general principle is that if, money is being collected then they are entitled to its accounting. Actually what is happening is that the money goes to a single family and their annual income runs into thousands of crore.

The Syedna confers titles of 'Sheikhs', 'Mullas', NKDS, MKDS which is referred to as *Hadiyats* and *mafsusiyats* and which have been cunningly made to look as an academic qualifications and status symbols. There could be no less than 50,000 Bohras adorning such titles, the selling price of which also widely ranges from Rs.2.52 lakhs to Rs.1.52 crore. It was said in an interview that "during the recent visit of 53rd *Da'i* Muffadal Saifuddin to Dahod, he managed to sell this title to gullible *abde* for Rs.1.05 crores."

Grave price: No dead body is allowed to be buried in Bohra *Qabrastan* unless money is paid for burial place though the government provides land for burial and cremation free of charge. In Mumbai, the Narialwadi

Qabrastan is like the Manhattan in USA where property prices are the highest. One of the respondents told her relative had paid Rs. 2.52 lakh for getting his mother buried 12 years back.

Masjid Wakaf: No Bohra mosque gets its religious sanctity unless the property is transferred to the *Da'i* and for which he charges an amount equivalent to the cost of Masjid from the local *Jamaat*.

Gallas-collections at various *Darghas* count crore in a month that goes to Syedna's pocket only. Hence there are innumerable ways in which money is taken. Syedna's wealth at present is roughly estimated to be over Rs. 2 lakh crores. In this context, the reformists demand a proper auditing of accounts including offerings made by devotees as *Nazrana*. While the orthodox term these offerings as "their love for Syedna", without whose intercession they would not be allowed to enter *Jannat* (paradise) by Allah.

The authoritarian and dictatorial attitude poses a great challenge to the reformists. They do not understand how to pull out the community from the clutches of Syedna's tyranny. The reformists observe that Bohra community crawls where it only needs to submit and it prostrates where it has only to bow. In a way the problem of this community is probably shade worse as it is not only tightly knit but also under the tight grip of priesthood used to govern the community with an iron hand.

The reformists appealed to the Bohra sisters and brother to understand that a true religious spirit never leads to authoritarianism in any form, not even in religious form. Islam, let us remember, is not a religion of blind faith. It calls upon mankind to follow rational faith – synthesis of faith, and reason. Even Imam *bil-ghayb* (faith on unseen) cannot be construed as irrational though it may at the most be described a supra-rational. It is in fact faith in future and its various potentialities as they unfold and whom we have no knowledge and hence it is described as *ghayb* (unseen).

The Bohra should not only be justly proud of this intellectual heritage but should do everything to disseminate it and elevate it to heights in this age of explosion of knowledge. However it is very sad, indeed very tragic, that the Syedna's establishment does everything to negate this proud intellectual heritage and instead inculcates slavish mentality and blind faith. Syedna has vested interest in keeping Bohras ignorant about the actual fundamental and basic principles of Islam.

"Ilm" is the only foundation stone of Dawat-e-Hadiya. Today those opposing Khuzema Qutubuddin and his successor Tahir Fakhruddin, do not possess knowledge not understand compassion, nor good character and therefore depend on force, intimidation and persecution to achieve the worldly agenda." Said,Tahir Fakhuddin. (In *Sijiil Articles*, 21 Oct, 2017 www. fatemidawat. com).

All the ills Bohras are suffering today is on account of centralized control in the hands of the priesthood. In fact it has become virtual owner of all that which rightfully and legitimately belongs to the community. Bohra people have made the priesthood so powerful that they themselves have become so powerless and are hence being treated as utter slaves and nothing but blind submission is demanded from them. The reformists paved the way of liberation from the clutches of exploiters but the fact still remains that Syedna has more following then opposition.

Most people in orthodox group are not really followers of Syedna, they are there because of the fear of social boycott, family and business compulsions. It requires moral courage and readiness to suffer the consequence of social boycott to be reformists.

Culture of Violence

The Bohras, like the other smaller sects, maintain their respective identity and guard it almost jealously. As far as there sectarian identity is concerned they distance themselves from the Sunnis and the Ishna Ashari Shi'as. Bohras have a hierarchical priestly structure bearing close resemblance to the Catholic Church both structurally and functionally. Among Muslims only Agakhani come closest to them.

Such a wall of structured religious hierarchy can prove both an asset and a liability depending on who controls it and with what intensions. The Bohra hierarchy came to be controlled by those who developed insatiable lust for power and money and every Bohra feel crushed under its weight. The suffocation in the community is to be felt to be believed. The reformists Bohras have challenged the powerful hierarchy and succeeded in at least exposing its machinations and its political linkage.

This continuous exposure well over four decades has highly embarrassed the priesthood and it has adopted various strategies to strengthen its iron grip over the community. When any person raise question or oppose any instruction of Syedna, he/she has to face the wrath of the *Kothar* in the forms of mob violence and persecution. Generally followers' spit on the family members of the accused (who raised question) throw stones, pull them back and beat up. Almost every reformist has such mob violence experiences of his/her own. Sometimes this type of violence turns into riot between the two groups of the community and it becomes a 'law and order issue' which requires police intervention.

Udaipur revolt began with the violent attack on women at Galiakot shrine itself. After that Udaipur remained violent prone city for decades. About 200 criminal cases were filed against reformists youth workers. These cases ruined their careers as they could not get their passports to go abroad. Some faced difficulties in getting admission in reputed institutions or in getting jobs. There was tension in the city during the first ten world conferences and during Nathwani commission hearing. Shezada Taha Bhai's stay in Udaipur for more than a month made Bohra Mohallas unsafe for both the groups as anything could occur at any time. The following are the unforgettable violent incidents.

Galiakot Outrage and Subsequent Events

We have mentioned Galiakot outrage in Chapter-6. After that on 23rd June 1973some youth leaders and supporters went to the residence of the local *Amil* to complain against the violent attacks being made by the Shababis (orthodox). While the Youths were standing near the *amil's* residence, there started a shower of stones from inside the *amil's* house. The youth retaliated in self-defense. The police were then summoned and they started ruthlessly attacking the Youths. The police went into the Bohrawadi areas and started beating the women, children and old people without any provocations from them.

The police also made arbitrary arrests of helpless people going to hospital or returning from work were rounded up and 70 persons were arrested.[9] They were hand cuffed, and paraded through the streets of Udaipur. Prof. M.S. Agwani wrote a letter to the times of India[10] about this happening, he wrote. "As one hailing from Udaipur the epicenter of the Bohra reform movement, I wish to invite the attention of your readers to the ruthless manner in which the local administration has sought to crush the morale of the partisans of reform by parading them hand cuffed along with the main stream of the city, even though most of the persons thus humiliated are from the cream of Udaipur society in terms of education, professional skill and public service. The question that all thinking people, more particularly the legislatures in Jaipur and at the Centre must ask themselves, "are we reconciled to permitting a religious pontiff to flout the fundamental rights of a section of our citizenry?" The role of administration, it is very clear from Agwani's letter, smacked of partisanship.

Violent protests against Shashi Bhushan

Shashi Bhushan, an M.P. of the then ruling Congress, addressed a meeting of the Bohra Youth in the Nagpada Neighborhoods House on

22 November 1974. Among other things he said, "Those who renounce worldly temptations are worshipped like gods in this country whereas those who run after power and pelf are denounced as devils."

Next day a large number of orthodox Bohras, as ordered by *Kothar*, surrounded Shashi Bhushan and demanded an apology for allegedly calling the High Priest a devil. Shashi Bhushan maintained that he did not say anything derogatory about the Syedna. However if any word of his had hurt the feelings of Syedna's followers, he is sorry. The mob was satisfied with the apology and dispersed.

The revolt in Udaipur not only inspired the old reformists to be active again, it gave Bohras everywhere courage to start raising their voices against *Kothars* oppression and injustices. In order to reinforce their control on Bohras, Priesthood decided to make full use of this opportunity to launch[11] an offensive against the reformists, their supporters and suspected sympathizers within his own apparently blind followers.

Shashi Bhushan was to visit Surat the next day. *Kothar* ordered Bohras to close their shops come out in large numbers to not allow him to enter city. They went on a rampage and blocked the Bombay-Surat highway. Shashi Bhushan had to cancel his surat visit in view of grave situation there[11]. The situation was so serious that police officials imposed section 144 in Surat. For two days there were violent incidents in Surat. A large crowed, allegedly instigated by Dr. Yusuf Najmuddin, the Rector of the Jamia Saifiya, went to Shaikh Sajjad Husain's (who had reformist sympathies) house and beat him up. His house was ransacked and his wife and daughter-in-law were molested. The old man died next day in the hospital as a result of severe beating. He lost his life at the altar of Bohra High Priest.

A procession was taken out led by some notorious elements of the Bohra Muhallaha in the Bhindi Bazar area of Bombay on 25th November 1974.The procession soon turned into unruly mob and started looting the shops and offices of those suspected to have reformist sympathies. The office of a cooperative society belonging to the Bohras of Udaipur was also looted and its record was burnt. Later the police made several arrests and raided a room by the side of the Qutbi mosque to recover some documents and goods looted from the shops. Among the paper seized there were placards and documents clearly showing a conspiracy to murder some key reformists leaders before 27 Nov1974, the day of the protests. The leaders named for liquidation were Asghar Ali Engineer, Noman Contractor, Yahya Bhai Lokhandwala and Ismail Attarwala. These heads should roll; it was said in the conspiracy papers, if the reform movement is to be liquidated.[12]

A big protest march was planned for 27 Nov. 1974 All the Bohras were required to close their shops on that day in order to join the protest morcha. Anyone who did not join ran the risk of having his shop looted in addition to being socially boycotted. As a result of this threat a large number of Bohras in Bombay joined the procession which went up to Sachivalaya. It is said there were around 12000 to 15000 Bohras in the procession. On the same day similar processions were organized throughout India and memoranda protesting against the alleged remarks of Shashi Bhushan were given to the perspective district authorities.

In every town a meeting was organized in the mosque the day after the procession to boycott those "erratic soul" who dared to keep out of the procession. In every town a few persons were chosen for this punishment. Invariably the following procedure was followed to tighten the iron grip on the community. The chosen persons would be asked to sign a very humiliating apology which amounted not only to self-debasement but also negation of basic democratic rights. If a person happened to be a firm supporter of the reformist cause he would not be pardoned on the basis of mere written apology. The priest in charge would first treat him with the choicest of abuses. He would then be taken to the high priest where host of his followers would hit him or kick him while calling him *Munafiq* (hypocrite), *Kafir* (unbeliever), *Shaitan* and so on. After being subjected to such indignities the person would be granted pardon by the high priest, the so called embodiment of mercy. Even then the person concerned would remain on the blacklist and could be hauled up at any time on the pettiest of excuses. In that period of priestly terror thousands of Bohras had to undergo this agonizing experience in order to make their peace with the community.

Assault on Moyyedpura Masjid

In Udaipur, on 18th January 1975 (6th of Moharram) when a large number of the supporters of the Bohra Youth were busy listening to religious sermons inside the Moyyedpura mosque, about 400 followers of the Bohra high priest stormed into the mosque armed with knives, cycle chains and lathis and attacked them. A large number of men, women and children were injured in this bloody attack. The walls of the mosque were splattered with blood. The blood stains on the walls of the mosque were visible till it was white washed. These blood thirsty followers of the high priest made women and young girls special targets of their attack, molested many of them and hurled them down from the first floor gallery of the mosque. Later one person Rajab Ali Chaurasi Wala succumbed to his injuries.

Godhra Incident

Noman Contractor was struggling for reform in Bohra community for a long time. Syedna's men made several attempts to eliminate him. A most determined attempt took place on 12June 1977. Noman Contractor had gone to Godhra, his native place along with his daughter Yasmin and son-in-law Rahim to visit a reformist friend Saifee Pawgadwala who was residing close to Bohra locality. A 3000-4000 strong mob surrounded Pawgadwala's house in no time which clearly indicated prior planning. The mob carried kerosene tins and rags to set fire to the house. But the fact that a few more families stayed in the same building restrained the action.

The mob then tried to break open the door and lynch Contractor along with Pawgadwala's family. The police who had arrived on the scene was watching without taking any steps to disperse the mob. However the time the mob succeeded in breaking open the door, the Collector arrived on the scene along with more police. He rescued Noman Contractor and Pawgadwala families and they were escorted away in the police van. After the collector departed Pawgadwala's house was looted and Contractor's car along with the furniture from Pawgadwala's house was burnt down. Later police made 52 arrests some of whom were committed to the session court for attempted murder. The incidence was so violent and had created such provocation that the entire town remained under curfew for three days.

Brutal attacks on reformists in Udaipur

There was blood shed once again after two decades in Moyyedpura Mosque Udaipur on 25 June 1997 on the holy night of *Chehlum* (40thnight after the martyrdom of Imam Husain).The main culprit behind the episode was Taha Saifuddin; the grandson of Syedna Burhanuddin who was sent to Udaipur in the last week of May 1997 for breaking the reform movement. He started his dirty game by provoking hatred against the Bohra Youth. He changed the venue of his Chehlum waaz from Ajanta Hall to Moyyedpura Mosque to provoke the Bohra Youth members. Since 1973 the orthodox (Shabab group) Bohras in Udaipur were performing all their religious rituals at Ajanta Hall. The Bohra Youth opposed this act of Taha and made an appeal to the local administration to prevent Syedna's grandson to hold his *waaz* in Moyyedpura mosque in order to maintain the status quo and peace and order among the local Bohras. But it seemed that Taha had already taken care of the local authorities. They rather than taking any action against him gave him full protection and support.

Then as planned by Taha, the reformist members' were attacked inside and outside of the mosque and then their houses were also attacked unwarranted by his goons. Next day these goons ransacked the offices of the Dawoodi Bohra *Jamaat* and Janta dispensary. I and Dr. Abbas Alwi were present in the *Jamaat* office. We hid ourselves behind the cupboard and saved ourselves. While windows, doors and furniture were smashed, medicines and other medical equipment were damaged. Three office persons who tried to stop them were mercilessly beaten up. They were badly injured. A murderous attempt was made on the life of Shafee Sabunwala, social worker who was on his routine medical aid services. He was hospitalized. Dozens of reformist's house, including that of Mr. Abid Adeeb (Secretary of Bohra Youth) were also attacked and damaged. Many Bohra women who went for usual morning prayers to Moyyedpura were arrested.

Attacks on Dr. Asghar Ali Engineer

Dr. Asghar Ali Engineer was a scholar and one of the prominent visionary reformist leaders who gave a dynamic direction to the Bohra reform movement by making it a fight against injustice, persecution and for human rights and social changes. Due to his tireless efforts, two Dawoodi Bohra enquiry commissions[13] were appointed by the Citizens for Democracy to enquire the atrocities committed by *Kothar*. The reports of these commissions brought out into the open the inhuman atrocities committed by the priesthood on its Bohra followers. Hence in sheer desperation *Kothar* made several attempts to eliminate Asghar Ali Engineer. The first violent attack on the life of Asghar Ali Engineer was made at the venue of the press conference at Calcutta in November; 1977 a similar assault by knife was made on him at Hyderabad in December 1977. The attacker succeeded in slitting his cheek. He was assaulted again in Cairo in March 1984, when he was there to attend a seminar. He was again assaulted at Bombay airport in the security area when he was returning from Bhopal after conducting a workshop on communal harmony for Madhya Pradesh police on 13th Feb 2000.

Blind hatred of Asghar Ali Engineer by *Kothar* was evident once again in 2000 when Maharana Mewar Foundation Udaipur announced "Hakim Khan Sur National Integration Award "for Dr Asghar Ali Engineer for his work of permanent value for the cause of national integration. *Kothar* ordered Bohras to send lacs of Post Cards, Emails and other threatening messages to the Maharana of Udaipur for cancelling this award to Asghar Ali Engineer. But Maharana remained firm on the decision.

Then with the instruction of Central Government Asghar Ali Engineer was provided 'Z' category of security during his stay in Udaipur on 9 & 10 April 2000. He stayed at Lake Palace as Maharana's guest and brought to the function venue amid tight security following a threat to his life from certain quarters. Maharana Arvind Singh in his welcome address noted, "We are continuing with the awards against all odds and pressures as Mewar does not have the tradition of turning back."[14]Speaking on the occasion, Asghar Ali cautioned against mixing religion with politics.

The list of the victims of the *Kothar*'s violent attacks is endless. Zehra Cyclewala (in Surat), Tahir Bhai and Zainab Poonawala (Pune), Zainuddin Wali (Godhra), Tayyabi Zamidar (Ahmedabad), Mohammed Husain Bhopali (Indore), Mulla Tahir Ali, Ismail Attarwala and Saifuddin Insaf (Bombay).

Renewed unwarranted attacks on reformists in Udaipur

With the arrival of *new Amil Sheikh Mustafa*, Udaipur became a center of hatred and atrocities again in 2007.Sheikh Mustafa used the weapon of *Baraat* (Social boycott) most ruthlessly in order to create panic among the reformists. The *Amil* instigated Shababs (Orthodox Bohras) to harass and humiliate the reformists.

A group of his fanatic followers went on rampage and attacked residences of the several office bearers of the Bohra Youth at Kharol colony. The residences of Liaqat Amar, Abbas Ali Nath and Hibtullah Attari were also damaged. One of the attackers was caught and handed over to Ambamata Police Station and a case was filed against him. Zonal Secretary of CBDBC was assaulted by two persons on motorcycle when he was on the way to home near Sehelio ki Bari. The orthodox group also tried to encroach the land of Bohra Youth Public School, Khanjipeer and damaged the two office of Bohra Welfare Society at Syedi Lukmanji Dargah campus.[15]

The next day on 29 July, 2007 the reformists in a rally marched from *Jamaat Khana* to Collector's office and gave him a memorandum against the unprovoked sudden attacks on the residence of reformists and demanded security for reformists in the city.

All the above incidences created an atmosphere of unrest among both the Bohra groups when the holy month of Ramadan began; there seemed a battle like situation in Moyyedpura mosque for getting space for Namaz. The fanatics were ordered by the *Amil* not to pray with reformists, hence on 15th Sep, 2007 in a planned way the reformists were not only denied entry into mosque but also beaten up and thrown out of the mosque which soon turned in a riot situation. Local police and administrative machinery strived hard to control but failed. Even lathi charged could not disperse the mob. Therefore looking to the uncontrolled situation curfew was imposed in Bohrawadi area of Udaipur.

Many persons were injured including five counselors who were witnessing the situation there. Police arrested a number of women and men of both the groups and sent to the central jail. First time in the Bohra history some women had to spend night in jail in the month of Ramadan. On 16th September2007 at 9.00 p.m. after compromise between the two parties, curfew was lifted but Article 144 remained in force for two days. Both the groups prayed *namaz* together in the Moyyedpura mosque but within their allotted space (permanently barricaded area for reformists According to Islamic teachings all are equal in *namaz*, king and slave all must pray together standing side by side, as rightly said:

"Ek hi saff mein khade ho gaye mehudo-ayaz
Na koi banda raha na koi banda-nawaz.

On August 6, 2012 i.e. 19th th of holy month of Ramadan a small group of reformists men and women were violently attacked by orthodox Shabab Bohras inside the Moiyedpura masjid at Zuhar time. Syedna's grandson Alikadar Mufadal Bhai Sahab was presiding over the majlis there on occasion of Hazrat Ali ibne – Abitalib's shahadat. The entire space was occupied by Shabab members and doors of Masjid were closed. The police were keeping the vigil outside (according to court orders the - police will have open and shut the door of the Masjid at scheduled namaz times). As it was namaz time, therefore, reformists urged to enter the masjid for zahur namaz but police stopped them and asked them to wait. The reformists peacefully waited till police made arrangement to vacate the allotted space for their prayer. The reformists brutally attacked while they were praying by shabab fanatics. Out of which many women and men injured, two were hospitalized in intensive care unit .Next day nine members of the shabab group were arrested along with their leader Shabbir Mustafa. The city magistrate refused to bail as attempt to murder was one of the charges laid against them.

Death of Syedna Mohammed Burhanuddin

After the death of 52nd *Da'i* Mohammed Burhanuddin a stampede occurred when the gates leading to the Syenda's Palace Saifee Mahal were closed forward, many people got crushed near the gates, 18 persons were killed and 40 were injured. The Police Commissioner of Bombay Satya Pal Singh attributed this to poor crowd management.[17]

When Khuzema Qutubddin died two years after the death of Mohammed Burhanuddin, his death was celebrated by Muffadal Saifuddin group by displays of fireworks, distributing sweets and by burning his effigy. His dead body was not allowed to be buried in *Raudat-Tahira* where 51st and 52nd *Da'i* are buried. The sons of Khuzema Qutbuddin then took seven rounds of the *Raudat-Tahira* with Khuzema Bhai's dead body via helicopter and buried him at Thane, Bombay where he resided to avoid the violence and dishonor of the dead body.

"In the holy month of Ramadan 2017, private security personnel, namely Burhani Guards 'Jihadi group' assaulted the three sons of Syedna Khuzema Qutubddin, when they were offering prayer at Raudat Tahera mausoleum in south Mumbai. The three Shehzadas (Abde Ali, Hussain and Aziz) registered police complains about the incident and police then detained three personnel of Burhani Guard." This was reported by Business Standard on July 4, 2017.

Syedna's establishment is resorting to violence in order to keep their iron grip over the community as more and more people are attracted to the positive activities of reformist. The culture of violence by power hungry materialistic, ruthless Kothar is not only destroying the reputation of the simple, dignified, peaceful Bohra community but also hindering prospects for its orderly progress by making them their ignorant slaves by forbidding them from reading a translation of the Quran and other religious books. Bohras today know little about their religion, Islamic history, Isma'ili renaissance, Fatimid traditions, its great thinkers and their very own Bohra heritage. *Da'i*'s main duty is calling unbelievers to Bohra faith by discussions, reasoning, knowledge, wisdom and goodly exhortation by removing all their doubts but they are punishing their already believing pious Bohra followers for merely asking questions!

Da'i must be symbol of mercy and love, according to the qualifications laid down for a *Da'i* in the time of 18th Imam, Mustansir Billah, in Risala (IXV-14) (C). However present and previous *Da'i* have been violating the above requirement while stirring up violence among Bohra community. The forever peace-loving orthodox (Shabab) Bohras are today looked down upon as either intolerant fanatics or lifeless robots. This has become a great challenge for reformists, how to address it and restore the original character? *Kothar* has succeeded in brainwashing and manipulating them, so they become violent against reformists without realizing that reformists are in fact struggling to liberate them from the mental slavery of *Kothar*.

Leadership Crisis

Social movements must have effective organization and strong charismatic leader in order to succeed. The members or supporters must be recruited in greater number, financial support must be procured and various tasks connected with the movement must be properly allocated. There must also be proper coordination among personnel assigned to more or less specific roles. In social movements the role of the leader is very important.

Many a movement failed due to lack of leadership. The leader is the spokesman of the group. He is the coordinator and the important participator in the decisions as to the goals and methods. He is an example to others. He enjoys greater authority and power. He also enjoys great prestige. He excels others in personal qualities. The leader has great responsibilities. He is expected to fulfill them.

He is expected to keep his word, to stick by the members and to uphold the group norms and values. If he does not live up to the level expected he suffers a loss of prestige and even of position in the group. He can be thrown out of leadership. If he betrays the confidence reposed in him by the supporters, he may even be killed. Thus, the leader plays a crucial role in a social movement. The success or failure of the movement depends largely on him.

The leader has the basic responsibility for seeing that the social movement achieves its goals. The followers follow the leader because they recognize that he can lead them to the goal. The leader should select his technique with great forethought. It should be "reality-oriented". The leader should know that in case of failure of the movement he may have to suffer rebuffs, loss of status and blame. He should, therefore, be very cautious in assuming the leadership, and having assumed it he should be careful in handling it successfully. A leader cans channalise the mass enthusiasm into constructive social reforms or he can eventually destroy the social system.

The history of the reformist's movement is more than a century old. It started with turn of the 20thcentury and we are in the end of second decade of 21st century. The well-wishers of the Bohras who spearhead the struggle for modern education in the community much against the opposition of Bohra priesthood were Headmaster Hasanali Chakera, Hassan Ali Gulzar, Mohammed Ali Bulbul Khan Bahadur, Fakhruddin Mota Bhai, Mohammed Bhai M, Khan Saheb, Habibullaha Vakil and Imran Ali Vakil. They were the founder leaders of Hakimia High School, Burhanpur in 1901.

Abdul Tayab Maskati, Seth Amiruddin Saleh Bhai Tayabi, Taher Ali Kazi, Abde Ali Qazi (the first Bohra judge of Bombay High Court), Qamruddin Isabhai Hakimi and others deposed before the Wakaf Committee urging it withdraw exemption from the Wakaf Act, 1923, because the community required most of the protection of the Act.

After independence Mohammed Ali Allahbaksh, Tayyab Bhai Zarif, Fazle Abbas Zamindar, Ishaq Bhai Bandook Wala, Noman Contractor, Hussain Bhai Sanchawala, Abbas Ali Kazi, Mohsin Nora and others were on the forefront to organize conferences to chalk out further programs of action for realizing their longstanding demand for democratization of the *Jamaat's* management.

After mass revolt in Udaipur and institutionalization of movement and formation of CBDBC as central organization of reformists Dawoodi Bohras, Noman Contractor, Dr. Asghar Ali Engineer, Ismail Bhai Attarwala, Saifuddin Insaf, Nazim Sahib, Shoeb Ranalwi at the central level and Tahir Bhai Poonawala, Tayyabi Zamindar, Zainuddin Vali, Hussain Bhai Sanchawala, Idrees Kinkhabwala, Ghulam Husain and Abid Adeeb were regional level leaders, they all were stalwart of their time. They worked in team spirit with due respect to each other in the early era of reform movement in independent India. Zulfiquar Husain Bhai from Aurangabad, Dr. Yusuf Arastu, Prof. Akhtar Husain and Iftikhar Husain Bhai from Hyderabad and Shabbir Bhai Madras Wala had joined the movement in late eighties. Shabbir Bhai a leading industrialist infused a new spirit in the movement through his multifaceted intellectual personality. He wrote many articles which were published by leading national dailies including the Times of India, Indian Express, The Hindu, The Telegraph and The Statesman. These articles shook the priesthood. He also used the modern management techniques to accelerate the pace of the movement. He had also taken responsibility to coordinate the activities of various centers. Match the city, 'to reach out' etc. were his flagship schemes to spread the movement in all over India. During his leadership as Chairman CBDBC the movement emerged vibrant. Unfortunately he did not remain active long enough due to illness and he died in 2017.

With the passage of time, some[29]misunderstanding emerged among the central as well as regional and local leaders. One of the trustee of *Ikhwan-us-safa trust* became hostile to Asghar Ali Engineer (Gen Sec., CBDBC) and he refused to sign the cheques of Ikhwan-us-Safa Trust - A corpus of Rs.16,00,000 was deposited to charity commission Mumbai. Hence a time came when it was frozen by charity commissioner. The trust is defunct till date after the death of original trustees (Ismail Attarwala, Shoeb Bhai Ranalwi, Tahir Bhai Poonawala, Asghar Ali Engineer, Saifuddin Insaf, Qamruddin Bhai Palanawala).The Ikhwan-us-Safa Trust was established by visionary reformist leader Noman Contractor to meet the requirement of funds for the reform movement for very long time. The previous movements could not be sustained due to lack of fund.

The reform movement became less visible due to internal differences among leaders. Many centers like, Aurangabad, Patna, Hyderabad, Neemuch, Surat and even Mumbai (head office) became passive. The death of many stalwarts within 8-10 years also affected the movement as no second line of leadership was trained for future leadership roles. The new generation has not seen the difficult time, sacrifices, pains suffered by their parents and family due to oppression and atrocities of *Kothar*. They are born free and are ignorant of the aims and objectives of reform movement so they are indifferent and not so enthusiastic towards reform movement. Asghar Ali Engineer tried to reach out to the younger generation by holding Youth Camps from time to time. His suggestion to start "Chhupi Tehreek" among Shabab around Udaipur was not taken seriously; otherwise Bohras of all towns around Udaipur would have been with the reformists. Most leaders in Udaipur did not make any effort to publicize widely the aims and objectives of the reform movement among the younger generation of orthodox Shababs as well as reformist Youths. Reformists' leaders react if *Kothar* does any mischief; otherwise they remain dormant and inactive. Key to success of reform movement is to remain proactive all the time.

Though there are a lot of qualified and capable women who played very important role in sustaining the reform movement for such a long time in Udaipur, they are not represented adequately in the Central Board of Dawoodi Bohra Community and in local *Jamaat* committees. Victims of *Kothar* all over the world look to Udaipur with hope and expectations as it still remains the vibrant center of reformist activities. But could not spread its influence beyond Udaipur even to its neighborhood, Wagad region of Rajasthan.

From the beginning Ghulam Husain Manager and his team Abid Adeeb, Mohammed Husain Haidary, Yahya Ali Vakil, Saifuddin Taj and others were very popular among the masses. People had faith and full trust in them. One of the top leaders Ghulam Husain who was in the forefront of the reform movement betrayed the confidence of people as he defected to Syedna's group and took *misaq* unexpectedly. Majority of people did not follow him; they took this setback in their stride. The remaining reformist leaders accepted the status quoi.

Shaikh Ahmad Ali Raj, former Professor of Jamea Saifiyah, Surat was a respected religious leader with the reformists at Udaipur. His orthodox views often clashed with the progressive views of well-known scholar Dr. Asghar Ali Engineer. These differences in opinion used to create disagreements and confusion among their respective followers.

On the occasion of Golden Jubilee Year of reform movement in Udaipur, absence of many stalwarts of reform movement is being felt acutely. It is wishful thinking of some people that visionary leaders like Noman Contractor and Asghar Ali Engineer would have succeeded in liberating the orthodox Shabab from the two claimant of *Da'i*'s title. The Mumbai High Court will decide succession issue.

Strong liberal and forwarding looking visionary proactive leadership is the need of the hour. At present Abid Adeeb- the senior most leaders is the patron who has devoted his full life for Udaipur reform movement, Irfan Engineer son of Asghar Ali Engineer is the Chairman of CBDBC after the death of Saifuddin Insaf. He is very active in academic and secular society in Mumbai and other places and he ably manages reformist's conferences and seminars. Further he writes well on reformist's issues regularly. Mansoor Ali Commander is the Secretary General; he has in-depth study of religion and law and is an able administrator. It is hoped that these trio together will be able to induct more young enthusiasts and mentor them to take the reform movement to at least its former glory of 1970-1990 period.

Women Empowerment

Women have been a strong backbone of the reform movement. There is no reformists function or agitation in which women's participation remained less than men. It is the women who had to bear the brunt of the atrocities of social boycott in everyday life. It is the women who stood up against the oppressive social boycott of *Kothar* and gave a taste of their own medicine by banning Syedna's entry in Udaipur from 1973-1998 (25 years). It may be noted that Syedna used to visit Udaipur every 2-3 years for prolonged stay to collect all the savings made by Bohras during this period. This prevented Bohras from becoming industrialists like other communities like Jains etc. and to remain petty traders forever. Bohras of Udaipur were so much loyal to him that he used to call them people of Madina.

In spite of their huge contribution to reform movement, women could not get the rank, position and space in the decision making process as much as they deserved. As a result women's issues are stone-walled as soon as someone dares to raise them. It appears as if reformists are waiting for Syedna's *Raz*a even for non-religious social issues and customs before providing any relief to suffering women. The originators of reform movement, Bohra Youth Association and its Girls Wing, both have no plans for any future reforms. Dawoodi Bohra Jamat is satisfied with managing day-to-day affairs and maintaining status quoi. No one seems to have thought about the necessity of vision document, think tank etc. Some of the issues which are troubling the orthodox Shabab as well as reformist women are as follows:

Khatna/ Khafz (FGM)

The Dawoodi Bohra community practices FGM in the form of *Khafz* (female circumcision), which involves the total or partial removal of the clitoral hood. In the name of tradition, young girls aged seven are cut up regularly by midwives or doctors. The clitoris hood is often referred to '*haram ki boti'* or immoral lump of flesh which is removed in order to suppress sexual urges in a woman, which is simply continuation of Pre-Islamic practice prevalent in some Arab and North African tribes, when women were considered property of men.

The Bohra priestly class-*Kothar* of Syedna Mufaddal Saifuddin supports the practice in India; claim that it is not mutilation and simply a 'nick of the skin' where the clitoris hood is removed with no real harm done to the body. However the clitoral hood plays a very important role in the protection of a woman's clitoris. It is anything but useless. It is an erogenous tissue with a protective function akin to the eyelids.

Bohra are not the only community to practice FGM in India. It is also practiced among different sects in Muslims in various parts of Kerela, where it is called 'Sunnath Balyanam'.

Delhi based advocate Sunita Tiwari has filed a Public Interest Litigation (PIL) seeking a ban on *Khafz*. The PIL has stated that *Khafz* does not have any religious context and is carried out without any specific medical requirement. According to the PIL, the practice should be made a non-bail able offence since it includes "unhygienic and illegal surgeries performed on their (Bohra minor girls) person for non-medical reasons.

A group of claiming the support of 69000 Dawoodi Bohras women under the banner of "Dawoodi Bohra Women's Association for Religious

Freedom" (DBWRF) has approached the Supreme Court, seeking its intervention in the matter. This group of Rida wearing orthodox Shabab women is formed with the blessings and *Raza* of Syedna. This group believes that the practice of *khafaz* does not involve genital mutilation but is simply circumcision.

During the hearing, senior advocate Abhishekh Manu Singhvi appearing for the DBWRF contended that "the practice of *Khafz* is an essential part of the religion as practiced by Dawoodi Bohra community and their right to practice and propagate religion is protected under Article 25 and 26 of the Constitution of India."[19]

However, such a position contradicts international definitions According to the world health organization (WHO), FGM refers to all procedures that involve partial or total removal of the external female genital organs for non-medical reasons. By this definition, *Khafz* constitutes type 1 FGM/ FGC and is universally recognized as violation of human rights. Since this practice is mostly conducted on minor girls, it is also in violation of UN convention of rights of a child, of which India is one of the signatories. In the year 2012 for the first time, the UN included India in the list of countries which practice FGM.

The government's position on *Khafz* in India has been riddled with contradictions in the past. Menaka Gandhi, minister for women and child development in 2017 said," we will write to respective state governments and Syedna, to issue an edict to community members to give up FGM voluntarily as it is a crime under the Indian penal code (IPC) and the protection of children from sexual offenses (POSCO) Act, 2012. If the Syedna does not respond, then we will bring in a law to ban the practice in India. However in response to the perception poll by Reuters, which called, India the most dangerous country for women, the ministry released the following statement of June 27, 2018. The cases of acid attack are only incident in the country and as mentioned earlier; practices of stoning, female genital multination etc. are not seen here[20].The National Crime Records Bureau (NCRB) provides no data for FGM in India. However "we speak out" a survivor led movement to end FGM, has released a data based report to highlight the extent to which *Khafz* prevails in India.[21]

Khafz at multiple levels causes physical harm to women, including severe pain, excessive bleeding, fever, infections, urinary tract infections (UTIs), and pain during sexual pleasures and difficulties in child birth. 'Sahiyo' one of the leading organsation working in FGM activism conducted a study according to which 86% Bohra women rely on traditional practitioners. Dr. Sujaat Vali, Obstetrician and Gynecologist said, "The clitoris is very small and there is a very small region between the skin and the clitoris. Only a specialist with a lot of experience can cut only the hood. So in most cases the clitoris does get affected." The case is currently referred to constitution bench.

The reformists have yet not officially taken up the issue decisively, though the matter was first discussed in all India Bohra Women Conference in 1989 at Udaipur. Many women dared to speak against it and finally a resolution was passed to end the practice for the protection of women's human rights of bodily integrity.

But after the conference, within a week time a hand bill (mentioned elsewhere) was published, condemning the resolution and organizers of the conference. The hand bill reflected a sick patriarchal mindset which demanded to restrain it with iron hand. Hence the follow up went in dark zone.

Some reformists had been raising the issue in personal capacity from time to time. For instance, Saifuddin Insaf in 'Bohra Chronicle, Zainuddin Wali in 'Mumbai Samachar'(in Bohra Vartman Column) Asghar Ali Engineer in 'Islam and Modern Age.' Rehana Gadgili, Prof. Ismail Poonawala, and Prof. Zenab Banu have written research paper on it.[22]

Unfortunately dozens of resolutions (average six-seven) have been passed in All World Bohra Conferences, but not a single resolution was passed on women related issues. Masooma Ranalwi an active Bombay based Bohra reformist and now founders of "wespeakout" tried to pass a resolution against *Khafz* in the last 15th World Dawoodi Bohra Conference but failed. Only a few minutes discussion was allowed on *Khafz* under the pressure of women delegates.

Field study data report supports the ban on FGM. I have conducted online survey and done semi structured interviews to collect in depth qualitative data on Bohra reform movement related issues of Bohra persons residing in Rajasthan, Maharashtra, Andhra Pradesh, Madhya Pradesh and Gujarat. The Non-Resident Indian Bohras living in Canada, USA, UK, UAE and Kuwait were also included. Most of the respondents were leaning towards reformist side, were in favour of reforms.

In response to the question 'What is your stand about *Khafz*? 86% of the respondents expressed that *Khafz* is an outdated un-Islamic practice which must be stopped with a heavy hand. Some wrote, "It is a hidden practice which is done in a hush-hush manner. Even the father of the girl and other family members are kept in the dark which itself proves that some wrong is going on ." Eight percent respondents were undecided (male-female both) and 6 percent were supportive of *Khafz* as a symbol of Bohra religious identity and purity (*Taharat*).

Orthodox Shabab Bohra authorities around the world where FGM is banned (with Syedna's prior permission of course) have issued letters stating,"All parents/guardians are here by directed in the strictest term not to carry out *khafz* under any circumstances. Abide by the law of the land." The same Syedna is opposing the ban on FGM in Indian Supreme court indirectly through DBWRF.

Since 2012 the Bohra community has been involved in at last two major legal cases in connection with FGM/C. One in Australia where three people were charged with performing FGC on two young girls in 2012. Second in 2017 the first federal prosecution for FGC in USA occurred in Detroit Michigan under a 1997 Federal Law (18.USC.116) an emergency room doctor and seven others were arrested for performing FGC on two young girls. Soon it was revealed that the defendants may have performed *khatna* in at least 100 girls in the USA in the last 12 years. On 20 November, 2018 a Michigan judge dismissed FGM charges in historic case on technicalities of the State v/s Federal Law. Though the judge has called the practice despicable yet upheld State law over Federal law. There was no specific law against FGM in Michigan at the time of assignment. On Jumana Nagarwala meanwhile is still facing a conspiracy charge and an obstruction count that could send her to prison for 20 years along with others.

Further Syedna Taher Fakhruddin, who claimed to be 54th*Da'i* has condemned FGM as operated on 6-7 years girl without her permission.[23]He supports ban on FGM based on his interpretation of Dawoodi Bohra religious literature.

Twenty seven countries world-wide including Egypt- the country Bohras trace their ancestry to have already banned this practice. What is preventing the reformists to declare the practice inhuman and violation of human rights of bodily integrity of girl child?

Virasat - inheritance

In pre-Islamic Arabia, property passed down the male line primarily to male heirs. The Qur'an, while sanctioning the rights of these heirs, added twelve more categories of heirs, eight of which are for women. These are known as 'Quranic heirs'. Let us consider first the verse on inheritance which fixes various shares in the property of a deceased person. It says:

Allah enjoins concerning your children for the male is the equal of the portion of two females; but if there be more than two females, two-thirds of what the deceased leaves is theirs; and if there be one, for her is the half. And as for his parents, for each of them is the sixth of what he leaves, if he has a child; but if he has no child and (only) his two parents inherit him, for his mother is the third, but if he has brothers, for his mother is the sixth, after (payment of) a bequest he may have bequeathed or a debt, Your parents and your children, you know not which of them is the nearer to you in benefit. This is an ordinance from Allah.[24]

A careful reading of this verse shows that the *Qur'an* has taken care to give women a share in property of the deceased not only as a daughter but also as a mother similarly; they also inherit as a wife according to the *Qur'an*[25] and "their wives is the fourth of what you leave if you have no child, but if you have a child, their share is the eight of what you leave". In the pre-Islamic period there was no regular law in this respect. Sometimes women inherited property, sometimes they did not. According to al-Razi, a great commentator, during *jahiliyyah* (pre Islamic period) there were two criteria for inheritance: 1) relationship, and 2) oath. According to the former criterion male relatives who took part in raids and captured loot were generally entitled to inherit property, while female relatives were excluded. In the latter category, two persons would say "Your blood is my blood and your garment is my garment, you inherit me and I inherit you" and thus a mutual relationship on oath would be established. Also an adopted child would inherit similarly.[26]

Razi also tells us about the context of revelation of this verse, i.e. verse 4:11 According to him, when S'ad bin Rabi was martyred he left behind his wife, two daughters and brother. The brother took away the entire wealth of his deceased brother leaving the wife and daughters high and dry. The wife went to the Prophet and complained about her husband's brother appropriating all his wealth. The Prophet sent her away saying Allah would decide the matter. After some time she again went to complain about it. It was then that this verse (4:11) was revealed. The Prophet ordered S'ad's brother to pay two-thirds of the property to the daughters and one –eighth to the mother. He could keep the rest.[27]

Thus, seen in this context too, it becomes clear that whereas women were not regularly, as a rule, given any share in inheritance. The *Qur'an* ensured that they got it in their capacity as a daughter, wife and mother. The fact that they were given half of the share of male heirs is to be seen in its sociological and economic context. It is a well –known principle of

Islamic *Shari'ah* derived from the *Qur'an*[28] that a wife is to be looked after by her husband even if she possess a great deal of wealth. She is not obliged to spend any of her wealth and it is her right to claim maintenance from her husband. Not only that: at the time of marriage she gets *mahr* which is hers and hers alone. Whatever the amount, and she can demand whatever she wants which husbands are obliged to pay with good grace [29] thus as a wife she adds to whatever she got by way of inheritance as a daughter, and that too without any obligation either to maintain herself or her children.

A daughter among Dawoodi Bohras is generally deprived of inheritance in her father's property in complete disregard of *Qur'anic* law. She is usually given only a few thousand Rupees. One respondent, who happens to be a father said, 'I have performed my duty by giving fifty thousand rupees to each of my daughters.' On enquiring whether his daughters have accepted this as their share he replied, 'why not, after all it is the will of their father and a daughter is born to obey her father or her brother in the absence of her father. 'It shows that a woman has no option but to obey and respect the feelings of elders in the family. One old woman explained that as sons, rather than daughter support and look after parents in their old age, (daughters leave after marriage for their husbands' homes). Sons should inherit the parents' property.

In a few cases daughters exhibited courage in questioning their fathers' decisions and consequently they got a little more. But by getting a little more the fathers' affection turned to hostility. It has been found that when a man has more than one daughter the men in the family often adopt 'divide and rule' tactics in drawing up a will or dismiss the daughters' significance altogether.

If the division takes place in the lifetime of the father, the daughters seldom object. But if the matter is decided after his death then a sister may contest the will. Objections are usually confined to verbal discussions alone. It is on rare occasions that a daughter/sister dares to take the matter to a civil court. One case study is sufficient to highlight the point.

A man, who had six daughters and four sons; left behind a handsome property worth millions, during the division of his property a dispute arose among his heirs. One of the daughters filed a 'partition suit' in the District court of Udaipur. The petitioner was a widow who resided in her father's home. Subsequently the other sisters also field similar suits independently, the case is still pending. When we probed more deeply into the case we found that one of the brothers himself instigated his sisters to file the suit against the others. Later on, it was learnt that, he turned tables and sided with his brothers. This caused a rift amongst the brothers and sisters who are no longer on talking terms.

The above case study throws some light on why women are often reluctant to file court cases. They are aware that these cases invariably breed animosity and lead to never-ending litigation. All this destroys the harmonious brother-sister relationship which is such a vital element of the Bohra social structure.

All immovable and movable property, cash, gold, silver, heavy copper and brass utensils, etc. is distributed among the sons. In past mother's ornaments were given to her daughters after her death. But nowadays gold ornaments are also equally distributed among sons and daughters equally. One respondent said that her father had categorically stated that whatever property had been registered in a daughter's name or in the name of a son, mother or wife would go to him or her irrespective of its market value. But she revealed that it was all preplanned according to the prevailing Bohra practice. 'I did not receive what I was entitled to receive according to *Qur'anic* law. My share was about ten times less than that of my brothers' share.' I often told my father that it was a violation of the *shari'a* and the *firman* (commandment) of Prophet Mohammed (S.A.) but he'd conveniently change the subject.

An irate thirty-four year old woman was highly dissatisfied with the discrimination she faced on the basis of sex. 'My sisters and I were equal partners in our father's firm. We signed every legal document, tax returns, cheques and other relevant papers. After my marriage I took up a government job. However I was apprehensive about my services being terminated, or a charge of irregularities being instituted against me, if the authorities found out about my involvement in the family business. Therefore, on several occasions I requested my father and brothers to free me from the partnership deed but, this was to no avail, after my father's death, it become necessary to redraft the deed, it was only then that I was relieved from the "dummy' partnership. Although my sisters and I were original partners we were never given our share of the profits. We had every right to claim what was due to us but never did because we knew the entire arrangement was 'formulated to avoid payment of taxes.'

The Bohras are very particular about *roza, namaz, zakat, Haj* and all other *Daims* (Pillars) of Islam. They claim that they are the true followers of Islam. However, in reality it is quite the contrary where a daughter's inheritance is concerned. They feel no sense of guilt or accountability to

God and the Prophet for violating the laws of inheritance. They do not feel guilty because most Bohras, particularly the orthodox Shababs are completely ignorant about Allah's commandments because Syedna has forbidden them to read the translation, and explanation of the Quran. Besides, they are borne and brought up in such a patriarchal atmosphere where the violation of women's rights are not considered as sin.

Reformists can inform and educate all Bohras about what *Qur'anic* law of inheritance is and that it is applicable to all Muslims including Bohras as it is directly from Allah.

The reformist must also demand that the Indian law of equal inheritance should be applicable to all including Bohras.

Iddah (iddat) After Husband's Death

The manner in which *iddah* (period of 4 month and 10 days) after the death of husband is practiced among Bohras makes life of a woman worse than hell. She is virtually isolated from all things as to wear white dress from top to bottom. She is confined in a room where door and windows either remain closed every time or covered with thick white curtains so she cannot peep out of window. She has to sit in a corner of the room and keep herself busy in reading Qur'an Shareef. She cannot see her face in mirror so every mirror in the room is covered with newspapers or any cloth. She cannot talk to any (*gair mehram*) male members who is not within prohibited category of matrimonial relation even a child, she cannot read newspapers, talk on telephone, watch television. If she gets ill then only a lady doctor may check her in her room only. She cannot go to any hospital for treatment. If by chance she fails to observe anyone of the above restrictions, then her *iddah* is assumed to be broken or void and she has to restart 4 month and ten days of isolation and confinement in her room. She is not allowed to go to court or complete any necessary government formalities, or work for living. If the woman is working (having a job), she has to remain on leave and if leave is not granted then she has to face the consequences of disciplinary action including termination. When I was working as UGC Emeritus Fellow (2014-2016) on 'Violation of woman's human rights in South Rajasthan' during the field work, I had interviewed 27 widows who had experienced *iddah*, 25 of them admitted that the period was like a night mare. Only 2 of them said that they faced no problem. 16 women told aguishly that during this period, they became patients of arthritis, hypertension, tuberculosis and blood pressure.

The *Qur'an* says, "And those of you who die and have wives behind them, they (the wives) shall wait (as regards their marriage) for four month and ten days, then have just filled their term, there is no sin on you if they (the wives) dispose of themselves in a just and honorable manner (i.e. they can marry). And Allah is well acquainted with what you do." (2: 234).

The above verse clearly depicts that wives shall wait for four month and ten days with regards to remarriage after the death of her husband. The main purpose of undergoing *iddah* is only to confirm the non-pregnancy of widow from her dead husband. Medically, pregnancy gets confirmed within 18 weeks, so that the Qur'an mention that the widow has to wait for remarriage till 4 month and 10 days is over. The Quran does not require women to be isolated and confined in a room.

But, according to Bohra custom the widow cannot enjoy freedom of life during period of *iddah* whereas in other Muslim sects, women observe *iddah* but in a normal way without any of the unnecessary restrictions stated above. They do not marry till *iddah* period is over. Otherwise they feel free to go out to meet the basic necessities of life.

Da'im-ulIslam' of Al-Qazi-al-N'uman is very important religious book of guidance of Bohras, next in importance only to *Qur'an.* AA Fayzee translated it in English and completely revised and annotated by Ismail Husain Poonawala "*The Pillars of Islam: laws Pertaining to Human Intercourse*" (first published in 2004 by Oxford University).

In this book in subtitle 'Waiting Period (AL'IDDA) on a page 276 a woman asked Mohammed Saheb (PBUH),"the husband of so and so has died can she go out of the house to attend some urgent business"? The messenger of God said, "She should go out after the night has vanished and return by evening so that she does not pass the night out of the house." The lady asked can she go on pilgrimage (Haj)? The Messengers of god replied, 'yes'.[31]

The above dialogue proves that during *iddah* a widow can go out of the house during day time. But in Bohra Community it is a not allowed. The Girls wing of the Bohra Youth Association has been demanding since a very long time that woman in *iddah* be allowed to walk on the open corridor or lawn of her house to breath in fresh air and consume sunlight on her body. Similarly 82 percent of the respondents of the above mentioned survey of widows demanded that the widow should be allowed to go out at day time either for necessary work or livelihood and to return home to spend the night at her house only. Even the reformists who advocate changes in society show very little interest in addressing this issue. Indeed some of them strive hard to suppress the voice of change. For instance, about four year ago iddah issue was raised by then Secretary of Dawoodi Bohra *Jamaat*, Udaipur against me. He was angry because during an interview to *Dainik Bhaksar* (Hindi Daily), I pointed out that 'the Bohra practice of *iddah* is not in conformity, to Allah's commands in the Qur'an and the Sunna of the prophet'. 'The presiding Mullah Peer Bhai went to the extent of demanding a declaration of social boycott against the women who were propagating (allegedly) anti-Sharia laws." I and some women present there got up immediately in protest. This resulted in pandemonium in *Majalis* for half an hour. This shows Syedna has succeeded in keeping Bohras so much ignorant that even some leaders of the so called reformists are very ignorant of true Islam and as a result their views and thinking are as orthodox as the Syedna's blind follower Shababs. Unfortunately a few persons with rigid views and closed minds among reformists have effectively silenced majority of liberals, even the women victims hesitate to speak out. Except the elections of *Jamaat* etc. no other reformist activities are visible to an objective observer among the reformists. It is very easy to silence someone by calling him enemy of Islam.

Low Representation of women in Decision Making Bodies

The Bohra women are generally more empowered compared with women in other communities. They have relatively higher decision making power at the house hold level and they are also more likely to have control over the relationship with two rival groups of the Bohra community but the reformist women have not yet gotten the space they deserve in decision making bodies from top CBDBC and at bottom local *Jamaat*. They have never been elected for the post of Secretary, President or Treasurer. They have to be satisfied with being only Executive Members of the CBCBC's governing body. Recently in March, 2017 during 15th Conference one woman was elected as one of the three Vice Presidents. Zehra Cyclewala was elected as Zonal Secretary as she alone represents Surat. Similarly in Udaipur local *Jamaat* women did not reach beyond Executive Members of the *Jamaat*. Unlike rural and urban self-bodies, where at least one third are women, they were always in very small percentage of total representatives. During the *Jamaat* election in 2015, women nomination was zero. No one motivated or encouraged women to contest and file nomination. After election only two women were co-opted among 11 co-opted members. The situation did not improve in 2018 elections. Mumbai local *Jamaat* is an exception where a woman is working as President since the democratic formation of the *Jamaat*.

When respondents were asked why women have not taken leadership role in the Bohra reform movement at the central and local level as well? 68 percent respondents expressed that in patriarchal society, women's capabilities are generally underestimated. 45 percent revealed that women should come forward form a pressure group and contest.73 percent were of the opinion that to begin with certain posts should be reserved for women in the central leadership so that they may stand at par with men.47 percent women respondents expressed their anguish that the meeting of the *Jamaat* and other bodies are held in night (8:00 to 10:00 p.m.) which is inconvenient time for ladies Their request for changing the night time to more convenient time was completely ignored.

In short women are effectively marginalized by giving them under representation in decision making activities. This is at par with the status of general women in India, they are neither opinion maker nor the decision maker. Generally they are treated as mere voters only.

Lack of coordination Between Various organs of Reform Movement

With the growth and consolidation of any social movement many new institutions may come into existence. But the success of the movement depends on how much interlinked the institution are with each other and the co-ordination between them. Dozens of institutions were setup in Udaipur Bohra reform movement in different fields like health, education, social welfare, women, charity and religious rituals. All these are working independently without interference of central and local leadership. Consequently repetition and overlapping in work is visible. They are neither responsible nor accountable to *Jamaat* Committee.Few of them publish annual audited account statements.

Reformist movements at various times in the past floundered, could not be sustained due to lack of funds. 'Ikhwwan-us-SafaTrust' was established to provide long term support to reformist movement. This was visionary Noman Contractor's brainchild.

The reformists had set up '*The Institute of Islamic studies'* in Mumbai to promote equal respect to all religions and democratic rights of religious - cultural groups guaranteed in the Constitution of India. In addition this institute also promoted field studies and empirical studies of Indian Muslims and problems related to them.

The Institute of Islamic Studies was established by scholar Asghar Ali Engineer. This institution organized number of camps and workshops on communal harmony in Bombay, Ahmadabad, Udaipur and other places.

The institution also carried out detailed investigation on major communal riots in the country and circulated its reports as far as possible. The Institute of Islamic Studies also organized in collaboration with Centre for Social Sciences, St. Xavier College, Bombay, a series of lectures on 'Religion and concept of man covering Islam, Hinduism, Christianity, Jainism, Buddhism, Sikkim's and Zoroastrianism.' These lectures were primarily meant to enhance understanding of true spirits of these religions and to promote inter-faith dialogue and inter-communal harmony. A joint dialogue between these major faiths of India was also organised.

The Institute of Islamic Studies also organized many seminars in various cities of India in collaboration with university department of religion, philosophy, social sciences and comparative religion, on the minority issues, problem of Muslim women, common civil code and other subject related to Muslim in India.

The Institute also published a bi-annual Journal called *'Islamic Perspective'*. A fortnightly paper, entitle '*Islam and Modern Age*'was being published regularly till the passing away of Asghar Ali Engineer (Honorary Director of the Institute) on any current issue related to Islam. The Institute had also done field research on '*Memons*' Bohras and '*Khojas*'the three business communities of Gujarat, on the attitude of Muslim women in Bombay belonging to Konkani, Deccans, Ansari, Qureshi, Khoja Bohra and Memon Communities. It had also conducted a survey in 18 top industries in private sectors on employment of Muslim and other minorities. The reports of all these surveys were published.

Unfortunately both the institutions are defunct now. Ikhwan-us-Safa became in operational due to misunderstanding among the trustees with the passage of time most of the trustees have passed away for heavenly abode. Hence it needs to be reactivated, reorganized and strengthened .for giving a boost to reform movement.

Institute of Islamic Studies is lying idle after Asghar Ali Engineer's death in May 2013. The Institute of Islamic Studies may be revived again by appointing a reputed scholar of Islamic knowledge as director to continue the work of the institution.

The reformists also need to maintain and improve the existing institutions- Jamaat Khana, mosques, cooperative bank, schools, dispensary and library.

Myths and Superstitions

Syedna Taher Saifuddin (51st *Da'i*) and his successors have systematically spread myths and superstitions in the community in the guise of religious beliefs. Moreover he banned reading translations and explanations of the Quran. Bohras are encouraged to recite and memorize Quran without understanding it. Authentic Bohra literature of Imams and previous Dais, which does not suit them, has been withdrawn from circulation. *Raza* (Syedna's prior permission) for every activity, religious or otherwise, has been made the most essential part of the Bohras belief and religion. Raza did not exist before 51st *Da'i*. The orthodox Shabab Bohras now believe that Allah will not accept Haj, Namaz etc. if done without Syedna's Raza. It implies that only Bohras will go to Jannat (Paradise) because billions of pious Muslims, who understand Quran and follow its instructions, do not take Syedna's Raza.

Another belief of orthodox Shabab Bohras is that their prosperity is due to Syedna's blessings only, and that they will be ruined if they dare to question him. This fear is instilled in Bohras mind by Syedna himself and all his Amils during sermons year after year by describing false stories about present and past reformists. The fear of losing Jannat (Paradise) and the fear of getting ruined are used by Syedna to exploit his followers and keep them under his tight control.

Orthodox Bohras are made to believe that Syedna has supernatural as has supernatural power. And various *mojezas (miracle)* performed by him is proof of it. But the big question is why do Syedna run Saifee Hospital in Mumbai when he has such supernatural power? Can he not cure patients by his miracles? A strong campaigning mechanism needs to be developed to remove these superstitions from public minds.

Ailing Publications

Propaganda is information that is not objective and used primarily to influence an audience, often by presenting facts selectively to encourage a particular synthesis of perception. Richard Alan Nelson observed "propaganda as a form of persuasion with intention with the aid of controlled transmission of single sided information through mass madia."[32] Modern propaganda includes using a variety of media in order to spread messages. Conventional media could include using press, radio, television, film, computers, fax machine, postures, meeting, door to door canvassing, handbills, poetry etc. Social media include Face book, Twitter, Website, WhatsApp, Instagram Messenger, etc.

Initially CBDBC and Ikhwan-us-Safa trustees have done their best within their means on this front Mouthpiece The Bohra Chronicle is being published regularly without missing a single issue despite financial constraints. Malegaon reformists also have been publishing 'Jurrat' quite regularly with limited financial resources.

'Khabarnama' an Urdu newspaper pertaining to reformists activities was published by Saiffudin Insaf. It had been greatly appreciated and many Urdu papers carried extracts from it thus giving much wider publicity to reformists cause and activities. But its publication could not be continued. 'All Worlds Bohra Journal' – Hindi Weekly paper published from Udaipur was popular. Its editor Saleh Mohammed Nayab was very efficient in gathering and publishing in the paper all information related to reformists from local to global This is also not being published at present. Mr. A.H. Nazim had been doing very useful work by circulating extracts from newspapers to reformist's friends abroad to keep them well informed about the reform movement. This continued until his death.

'Bombay Samachar' included a column exclusively for Bohra issues, entitled "*Bohra Vartman*" (Bohra present) which regularly provided opportunity to all the Bohras and other leaders to air their views freely has been discontinued.

Many pamphlets, handbills, booklets were also published from time to time to reach out to the people. Asghar Ali Engineer, Gen. Sec. of CBDBC wrote *'The Bohras'* an authentic and encyclopedic work on Bohras in 1980.

At present reformists are not spending much on propaganda due to limited financial resources. The situation is so pathetic that even the young generation of reformists is ignorant about the history, aims and objectives of Bohra reform movement.

Social media have become a powerful and cost-effective tool of propaganda as the internet is unprecedentedly accessible for each individual and interactive social networking sites provide a strong platform for debates and sharing opinions. Propaganda in forms of a video uploads to YouTube, a post on face book or twitter or even a piece of comment has far reaching effectiveness to disseminate certain values and beliefs. But it is on a very low key because there is neither any dedicated team nor budget for this very important activity. The need of the hour is to reach out to all orthodox Shababs as well as reformists all over the world to counter the misinformation of *Kothar* and increase understanding of the Quran, *Daim-ul-Islam* etc. increase awareness about their rights etc.

Good Governance

Governance is the process of decision making and the process by which decisions are implemented it is essential for a company or organization to achieve its objectives and drive improvement, as well as maintain legal and ethical standing in the eyes of the wider community.

Good governess has major characteristics it is participatory, consensus effective and efficient, equitable and inclusive, and follows the rule of law, it assures that corruption is minimised, the views of minorities are taken into account and that the voices of the most vulnerable in society are heard in decision making. It is also responsive to the present and future needs of society.

Bohra reform movement is based on democratic good governance set up where every adult of 18 years old has a right to vote, right to contest and right to hold highest official position. They have right to participate in reform activities. The voice of dissent is respected to extreme end and at the time of dispute rule of law prevails. But the ground reality manifests different picture where democratic spirit is confined to vote without applying one's own discretion and will. Women constitute the half population but are marginalized, given insignificant responsibilities and they have to rely on rumors as they are not kept well informed. Voice of dissent is presumed as voice of enemy and crushed. Consequently enthusiastic volunteers get discouraged and stop volunteering for the reform movement. A stage of idleness and inaction prevails. The so called elected office bearers come and go without leaving any foot print of their service period. The questions of accountability transparency, responsibility, inclusiveness rule of law and corruption free administration remain unanswered. It is a common stage of any social movement's life cycle. Such a movement grows, it often tends to become bureaucratized and paid leaders and paid staff replaces the volunteers that began the movement .Gradually, failure to accommodate new members and mentor them for future leadership roles, gaps between members' and leaders' goals and misdirection of energy and resources towards internal disputes rather than external opponents made the reform movement run out of steam.

Youth Alienation

Majority of the modern Indian youth are not interested to be bound by the traditional norms and values. They are interested to adopt the secular life style and rational outlook. These causes conflict which leads to alienation from the established social and cultural norms.

The Bohra reform movement speeded up in Udaipur and elsewhere, because young energetic people from all walks of life were the primemovers. Their struggle succeeded in liberating reformists from under the yoke of *Misaq*, *Raza* and *Baraat* of Syedna's authoritarian rule.

But this enthusiasm among today's youth is eloping somewhere leading to frustration and lack of zeal. The reason may be excessive burden in the form of competition, facing acute pressure in every field from getting job to performance at the job.

Young women to prove themselves and become independent are pursuing higher studies and doing jobs at various cities away from their families. Majority of youth are settled either in Metro cities in India or abroad for their livelihood in corporate sectors. Thus the transformation of joint families to nuclear family, and from nuclear family to empty nest did not result in automatic transfer of the enthusiasm, the spirit and the ethos of the Bohra reform movement to the younger generation contrary to old generation's expectations.

In all institutions and committees under Bohra Youth Association, the median age is 25 years whereas the average age of office bearers is 60 plus this generation gap in age leads to wide differences. Our online survey shows minimum participation of youth in All World Bohra Conference. Only 4 percent of the youth attended two or three conference out of 15 conferences. Neither, they subscribe The Bohra Chronicle nor other papers. They have little bit participation through social media only.

The first two generation of Bohra reform movement were active and dedicated to the cause of reforms. Sadly, most among third generation men and women are conspicuous by their absence in reform movement's activities None of senior leaders who were in charge of various institutions for decades never thought of mentoring the talented juniors for future leadership roles at all causing vacuum at top and discontentment in followers in general. It is absolutely necessary to have forward looking visionary leaders to sustain and give momentum to the reform movement.

Mr Asghar Ali Engineer used to take leading part in organizing study camps, youth camps, women camps, to generate greater awareness and thinking about future action plan. All these activities stopped after his death.

Greater participation of the younger generation is a must for reinvigorating the reform movement and attracting the orthodox Shabab Reaching out to younger generation of orthodox Shabab could ignite sparks of reform movement from within the Shabab. Dwindling numbers of reformists should be a cause of concern for all.

Victim of Political Disparity

Politics, Nehru thought will be an effective instrument of social change and secularization of society. But over the years what has happened is just the opposite because of growth of communalism. Secularism unites the people, whereas communalism divides the people along religious lines. Conservatives and the vested interests now enter politics to serve their own narrow interests these forces manipulate democratic process to sabotage all progressive measures and liberal movements. The success of Ramjanam bhoomi movement and Shah Bano are proof of this, if any proof is needed. The fact that these issues remained at the centre of our politics is a matter of great concern. Our political democracy is being used to throttle all liberal and progressive social movements with hardly any exception. Religious, cultural and social intolerance is growing, and needless to say this intolerance is either being promoted or supported by the politicians with certain honourable exceptions.

Now unprincipled politicians give top priority to getting themselves elected to legislatures by making false promises. One does not get state support for reform movements as it is these politicians who make decisions. Raja Ram Mohan Roy succeeded in abolishing 'sati' as he was supported by the British Government of the time. The 'Sarda Act' could be passed in 1929 against child marriage due to government support. Also it had the support of political leaders like Jawaharlal Nehru. The Hindu code bill could be passed due to the unqualified support of Nehru though it was much watered down due to the stiff opposition of the communal leaders.

It is unfortunate that in the independent India no worthwhile reform movement has been launched and those which were launched faced unprecedented difficulties and died down for lack of support. Initially judicial support was also lacking and even if some group succeeded in pressuring the government into enacting a law the then conservative judiciary came in the way and government threw it away under pressure from society.

Here are some examples from the Bohra reform movement which have seen many ups and downs since independence. As the Bohra reform movement was nationalist to the core, they had built up a good support with the Indian National Congress leadership of the then Bombay State for legislation against ex-communication which was the main weapon of coercion in the hands of the Head Priest. Morarji Desai who was the Home Minister took special interest in the matter and a bill titled "The Prevention of Ex-communication Act" was passed with an overwhelming support for the first time that the reformists got government support. But their hard-won gain was short-lived as the Bohra high priest challenged the legislation in Bombay High Court. The High Court upheld the enactment. The high priest then filed an appeal in the Supreme Court. The Apex Court struck down the Act in 1963 by a majority decision.

The reformists have repeatedly drawn the notice of successive Prime Ministers and Chief Ministers but nothing has happened because the dishonest politicians are easily influenced by the High Priest's enormous wealth and captive vote bank of his blind followers.

Dishonest politicians, be they of Congress, BJP, Janta Dal or Shiv Sena or other parties, all prefer to extend their full support to the priesthood blindly and uncritically without ever verifying the issue involved. All this is done for fear of losing votes and lure of money. During Galiakot agitation, Congress Government in Rajasthan did not support the reformist's entry into Galiakot Dargah. Chief Minister Barkatullaha Khan favored Syedna by exempting Bohra Waqaf property from the Rajasthan Waqaf Property Act in 1972. When Syedna visits any city, the State Government grants him State guest 'status. On his request sometimes the Chief Minister of the State or Union Minister even receives him on his arrival.

State Government even sends its government plane for bringing the High Priest. For example Gujarat Chief Minister Amar Singh Chaudhary sent an aeroplane for bringing the High Priest from Bombay to Surat for his private visit; Madhya Pradesh Government had also sent an aero plane to take the High Priest from Bombay to Indore and he was received at the Indore airport by the Chief Minister Motilal Vora and Arjun Singh, the then Vice President of the ruling Congress Party. Man Mohan Singh had inaugurated Saifee Hospital in Bombay in 2005. Recently during 'Moharram Waaz' (Sept 2018) Prime Minister Narendra Modi along with Chief Minister of M.P. Shiv Raj Singh Chauhan attended Syedna's Moharram sermon at Saifee Mosque Indore and accepted a shawl from the Syedna while he had famously refused to wear a skull cap offered by a Maulana during his 2011 fast for harmony and peace in Ahmedabad. Mr. Modi walked the premises of Saifee mosque bare feet. He gave a speech in the mosque in which he said that his fond association and community's support had drawn him to Indore. Describing the Bohras as 'family', he said he was using the live telecast of the occasion to tell the world of "the contribution of Bohras to peace, development and amity". All these are enough to prove that unscrupulous politicians can hardly resist the temptation of money and votes. It is not a secret that the Bohra High Priest Syedna dangles the carrot of money and votes before the ruling party politicians.

Spirit of Democracy Derailed

Liberal democracy is an ideal one where every citizen has equal rights and access to the law, there is strong freedom of expression; good institutions systems to deliver justice, freedom of association, participatory elections etc. Only 39 nations met this standard in 2017. Similarly semi-governmental and non-governmental organisations do have the same record.

The Bohra reform movement also sails on the same boat. The Bohra reform movement started with one of the major objective to establish a true democratic set up where every member of the community - man and woman would possess equal rights and equal power to administer reform machinery, where the voice of dessent would be most respected and decision would be taken after deliberations. The system worked in the said spirit for quite some time. Slowly this democratic spirit degenerated in one man show or manipulation by a group of persons (oligarchy). The criticism and dissent were so much suppressed that some erstwhile very active enthusiastic young workers felt suffocated and were compelled to leave reformists and join orthodox Shabab! Many potential reform leaders became inactive. The common people remained mute spectators.

Elections take place on time without democratic zeal. The contesters do not contest for having new ideas and programme for giving momentum to reform movement, they just file their nomination papers for the sake of election only. Sometimes the group in power patronage the list of members to be elected and if some persons out of the list file their nomination then they are considered as rebels. Every effort is made to defeat the rebels. Constructive criticism and dissent are not tolerated. Anyone who suggests Some needed reforms or improvement is silenced by personal criticism. Some leaders who remained in power and control of various reformist institutions for very long time developed vested interests. During the field work many senior members complained that they were not heard by the establishment so they keep mum now. One of the respondent complained that during discussion in 15th conference in delegates session when she was speaking the mike was turned off so that anti establishment voice could not reach to the audience. Six respondents expressed that generally pro establishment group disrespect the voice of dessent in executive or general body meeting. They are either not allowed to speak or their Speech is drowned out by making noise. It is not an ideal democracy but it is still much better than being in orthodox Shabab under Syedna's tyranny.

Fund raising is another challenge as well. Lack of funds discourage the social activists to go ahead. Obviously there is an unequal battle between - *Kothar* at one end who is loaded with money power, on the other end is the reformists - not having any kind of power except the power of truth and power of peoples' assertion.

To sum up reform movement has reached at the middle age (48 years). Everyone knows that the reformists have worked consistently, unflinchingly and with unshakeable determination for last so many decades to liberate the Bohra community from the shackles of Kothar. The *Kothar* has failed in terrorising the reformists with most violent attacks. So reformists have to continue their struggle till they completely over throw the repressive and authoritative *Kothar* they must have facing. They should remain united specially now when the orthodox *Kothar* is on the verge of crumbling on the question of successor of 52nd Dai.

Notes and References

1. Asghar Ali Engineer, 'the reformists and their religious beliefs, (booklet by CBDBC) p. 1.
2. Ibid.
3. Saifuddin Insaf, *Bohra Chronicle*, Nov,2014 p. 9.
4. The author of *Mausam-e-Bahar* tells that 47th Da'i also faced considerable financial difficulties which in fact, had begun from his predecessor's time. The financial troubles continued and were even further aggravated. The 49th *Da'i* was heavily indebted. Two Hindu Mahajan and one of his own Amil filed suits in the courts of the first class Magistrate of Surat, the Amil Sheikh Abdul Tayyab claimed Rs 56,650 including interest.The case was settled and Syedna Burhanuddin agreed to pay Rs. 54000 along with interest in 12 installments from his personal income as well as from Dawat's account (see special issue of the Dawoodi Bohra Bulletin,Surat, March 1965).
5. Kumkum Chaddha, 'Divinity under dispute', *Hindustan Times*, Sunday Magazine, Oct 3, 1993, p. 9.
6. Shabbir Hussain Madraswala, 'Bohras: The Scourge of Social Boycott', *Souvenir,* to commemorate the 10th All World Dawoodi Bohra Conference, Udaipur, 1999.
7. It is said, "No one is born a Dawoodi Bohra. On reaching puberty every person who so desires can voluntarily give the *Misaq,* which one is enjoined to according to the tenets of the faith and so become a member of the Dawoodi Bohra sect." In actual practice, Misaq is compulsory for every Bohra. Reformists contest the present form of Misaq altered by Syedna Taher Saifuddin. It is oppressive as it binds the follower to a total surrender not to God but personally to *Da'i*. The text of *Misaq* is in the Arabic language so that the Dawoodi Bohra who gives *Misaq* does not know what he is committing. He remains unaware of the implications of his *Misaq* for rest of his/her life.
8. Manoj R. Nair, 'Bohra ejumaat cards raise privacy concerns', *Hindustan Times (Mumbai)*, 9 Oct, 2015.The article is based on the findings from an annual worldwide survey for Dawoodi Bohra, that tracks opinion about community issue after the death of 52nd *Da'i* Mohammad Burhanuddin.
9. Narrated by Abid Adeeb during interview.
10. *Time of India,* 15th Sept., 1974.
11. Shashi Bhushan was then a member of parliament (MP) belonging to the ruling Congress Party and was known for supporting the cause of minorities in India.

He was to visit Surat(a city of Gujarat which has large Bohra population) to address a meeting of Youth Congress.

12. A A Engineer, The Bohras, Op. Cit., P. 236.
13. Justice Nathwani Commission: Dawoodi Bohra Commission, May 1979, NP Nathwani, Chairman, V.M. Tarkunde, Dr. Moin Shakir, Dr. Miss Aloo Dastur were members and late CT Duru was member secretary. The report was submitted to Citizen for Democracy (CFD).

    AG Noorani's comment on the above report is "the practice which the report expresses are totally opposed to Islam and it would be suicidal of Muslims to show any sympathy for the Bohra priesthood. It would serve only to discredit the Muslim's plea for the redress of their legitimate grievances bring the religion into disrepute and betray the Bohra community…..

    Second Report on 'Violation of Human Rights of Dawoodi Bohras' by D.S.Tewatia (Retd.) Chief Justice of Calcutta High Court and Kuldeep Nayyar-President of the 'Citizen for Democracy', submitted to the Human Rights Commission of India and Citizens for Democracy, Aug. 1993.
14. *The Hindu*, 10th April, 2000.
15. *Rajasthan Patrika,* 29 July 2007, p. 18.
16. *Pratakal* (Hindi daily newspaper) 17 Sept 2017, P. 1; Rajasthan Patrika, 18 Sept 2007, P. 1.
17. The Associated Press, Saturday Jan 18, 2014.
18. Vartika Neeraj 'Genital mutilation plagues thousands of Bohra women in India', https://*thewire.*in/worn, 27 July2018
19. www.timesofindia.com, July 9, 2018.
20. Indian Express, 9th November, 2018.
21. The report is considered to be the most comprehensive study yet on India's female genital mutilation tradition. The study shows that 75% of the respondents comprising mainly Bohra women, have been subjected to FGM.As many as 97% of the respondents describes it as painful and traumatizing.
22. Rehana Ghadially, 'All for Izzat': the practice of female circumcision among Bohra Muslims', *Manushi*, No.66, 1991.

    Zenab Banu, *Deprivation of Women's Human Rights and the Strategies for Resolution*, Kanishka, New Delhi, 2014, PP133-35.
23. www.fatimidawat.com/syednatahirfakhruddin-tus-statement on *Khafz* (*Khatna*-CHR), www.google.com/thewire.in /culturer/fakhruddin.com.
24. The Qur'an, 4.11
25. Ibid, 4, 12
26. Fakhruddin Al-Razi, *Tafsir Kabir* (Beirut h.d.), Vol.5, P.210
27. Ibid.,
28. The Qur'an, 65: 67.
29. Ibid, 4: 4.
30. *Iddah* from *adda* to count (days of menstruation). It is technical term in Islamic law for legally prescribe period of waiting during which women may not marry after being divorced or widowed. It was unknown in pre-Islamic Arabia and was

instructed by the Qur'an. The three men objectives of observing the *iddah* are (1) to ascertain whether the wife is pregnant and if so, the paternity of the child, (2) to provide the husband with an opportunity to reconsider and return to the wife (if the divorce is revocable), (3) to mourn the deceased husband, in the case of widow EI[2] S. V. Edda, Nasir, *status of women* 99-106. For foot note No. 1399 of *the Pillars of Islam,* Oxford University Press, 2004, New Delhi p. 275.

31. It is implicit that she should go out early morning so that she might finish all her work and return to house by evening. Kafi, VI, 121-3; Kulyani reports another tradition which states that she can go out after mid night. Several other tradition which states that she can move from her residence from one house to another every few weeks and go out for important business (*The Pillars of Islam* see foot notes 148, P. 277).
32. Snow Nancy, *Handbook of Public Diplomacy,* Rutledge, 2008, P. 338.

Chapter - 9

Major Achievements of Bohra Reform Movement

The Bohra reform movement in Udaipur will be completing its **golden jubilee in 2020.** Fifty years is a long time for any movement to have sustained. In itself, this is an unprecedented achievement because all previous reform movements petered out in relatively very short time due to lack of resources and because Kothar succeeded in isolating reformist leaders from the Bohra masses. During the struggle to liberate Bohra community from the tyranny of *Kothar,* there were some achievements and failures. The reformists succeeded in overcoming the odds to some extent.

Liberation from *Raza*

Reformists stopped seeking Syedna's *Raza* (prior permission) for everything from 16th March 1975; the day mass marriages of 106 couples took place in Udaipur. This liberated the reformists from the tyranny of Syedna's weapon of mental slavery. *Raza* is used by Kothar to extract money from the followers before they think of doing any religious or temporal activity and also to punish the dissidents by denying it. Reformists now feel free to read translations and explanations of Quran and other religious books from the time of Imams and previous pious spiritual Dais. They are now relatively less ignorant about the true religion compared to orthodox Shababs whose knowledge is limited to what they hear in the sermons of Syedna and his Amils, because orthodox Shababs have *Raza* to memorize and recite Quran in Arabic without understanding it but do not have *Raza* to read its translation or *tafseer* (explanations).

Elected Local Jamaat

Reformists main demand that all Bohras of each city must have right to elect Local amaat members of their choice instead of being nominated by Syedna has not been accepted by Syedna. The nominated members do Syedna's bidding ignoring the interests of local Bohras as they are answerable to Syedna and not the local Bohras. Syedna never nominates women in Jamaat or other committees.

In several cities where the reformist Bohras are in sizeable numbers have formed local Jamaats by free and fair elections, after liberation from the scourge of Raza from 1975 onwards. The free and fair elections are held every three years. The elected members are answerable to local Bohras only. Women also take part in the elections enthusiastically and some get elected. Women are underrepresented and are now encouraged to demand 30 % reservation for them.

All local Jamaats of all cities are members of Central Board of Dawoodi Bohra Community, whose members are also democratically elected. This is an umbrella organization uniting reformists worldwide. This is a democratic alternative to Kothar to manage secular affair of the community in fair and transparent manner. It organizes World Conferences every three years of the democratically elected representatives of Bohras worldwide to discuss reform and other issues.

Accountability and transparency

Accountability and transparency are the characteristics of responsible administration. The functionaries of the reformist's Jamaats and other Institutions from top to bottom are answerable to the Bohra people. They maintain account of every single penny and publish if after it is duly audited by recognised chartered accountant. Most of the amount is collected voluntarily and without any coercion and it is spent locally. People have freedom to ask questions and criticize if they wish without any fear of persecution.

Reformists are also demanding accountability and transparency from Syedna and his administration Kothar. He has over the years, accumulated thousands of crores through coercion and he refuses to give account of this huge wealth. He and his large extended family live in luxury ignoring the plight of the suffering Bohras in slums of Mumbai and other metros.

Non-interference in Secular affairs of individuals

The reformists are upholders of principles of human rights, civil liberties and respect for human dignity. They stand for non-interference in secular affairs of individuals. Reformist Bohras enjoy all human right, civil liberties without any interference in their personal secular affairs because unlike orthodox Shababs, they do not have to seek *Raza* from Syedna. This give them freedom to publish newspapers, start new business, read translation and understand Quran, acquire religious or any other knowledge, form associations, express their opinion freely etc. This is real freedom.

The priesthood rejects these principles outright. The two commissions of inquiry headed by retired high court judges inquired into the allegations of serious violations of human rights in the Bohra Community at the hands of the priesthood. The Nathwani Commission and Tewatia Commission upheld the allegations of violations of human rights. The Nathwani Commission observed in the concluding chapter of its report, "Our inquiry has shown that there is large scale infringement of civil liberties and human rights of reformists Bohras at the hands of the priestly class and that those who fail to obey the orders of Syedna and his Amils, even in purely secular matters, are subjected to *baraat* resulting in complete social boycott and frequent physical assaults."

Democratic Formation of CBDBC

In 1974the reformists formed a central organization namely Central Board of Dawoodi Bohra Community (CBDBC) to provide a democratic alternative for the secular affairs of the community. It was not a religious alternative. For this reason the Central Board made it very clear that it had no reservations about accepting the religious leadership of the High Priest. It was only opposed to his total domination over the secular affairs and personal lives of the Bohras.

An adhoc body was formed with Noman Contractor as Chairman and Ismail Attarwala as General Secretary. A sub-committee was appointed subsequently to draw up a Constitution on a democratic pattern which was ratified in the All World Dawoodi Bohra Conference. It was decided to hold the All World Dawoodi Bohra Conference on 17 to 19 February 1977 in Udaipur. The priesthood started their machinations to sabotage the conference at any cost. They wanted to take advantage of the emergency in the country to get it banned under the pretext of hurting the religious sentiments of the Bohra community. However, the conference was held under police protection though it had to be curtailed by a day.

According to the Constitution any Bohra above 18 years of age is entitled to vote irrespective of sex in the *Jamaat* elections. The Constitution accords complete autonomy to local *Jamaats*. Another unique feature of this Constitution is that anyone who declares himself to be a Dawoodi

Bohra (believing in the *Shia's Ismaili-Mustalian faith*) will be treated as such. The High Priest, on the other hand, insists that it is his personal prerogative to accept or reject a person as a Dawoodi Bohra.

The Constitution provides for a central executive committee comprising 60 members elected from different zones in India as well as abroad. The Executive Committee is elected once in two years. This Committee is the central policy making body and oversees the administrative affairs of the community. The members, the Chairman and the Secretary-General are directly elected. The Member of Council are elected from Udaipur (Rajasthan), Gujarat, Madhya Pradesh and Maharashtra in India and Canada, Kuwait, Yamen, Pakistan, U.K. and Ceylon from abroad.

The CBDBC has been working satisfactorily and has established its identity as a representative body of reformists all over the world. Syedna is not at all interested in the reforms, enlightenment and welfare of the Bohra community. Therefore instead of contacting CBDBC, he instigates his blind followers to pressurize their relatives and friends to leave reformists and submit to his authority to avoid social boycott.

Report of Two Investigation Commission

The repressive policies of *Kothar* have been brought on record by two commissions of inquiry appointed by the 'Citizen for Democracy' (CFD). The first Justice Nathwani Commission was appointed when some leaders of the reformists approached the Citizens for Democracy with a complaint that the members of the community did not enjoy the civil liberties and that the priestly class and its associates were harassing the reformists members in a variety of ways which amounted to infringement of human rights. They requested the CFD[1] to look into these allegations and make a proper investigation. The National Executive Committee of the institution accepted the request of the reformists Bohras and appointed a committee under the chairmanship of Justice Nathwani with five other members – V.M. Tarkundi, Dr. Alam Khundgiri, Dr. Moin Shakir, C.R. Daru and Dr. Miss Aloo Dastur in 1978.

Soon after the commission was appointed, a hue and cry was raised by the priestly class against the commission. A cry of 'religion in danger' and 'hand off religion' was raised to mislead the members of the community. State Governments were urged to ban the activities of the commission. Processions of the members of the community were organised in various centers where there was some concentration of the Dawoodi Bohra Community to demonstrate against the commission. The priestly class tried to enlist the support of other Muslims in their campaign against the commission but did not have a significant success.

The commission had prepared a questionnaire for this investigation and sent to those Bohras who wanted to support the commission to find out the truth. The respondent's replies were considered by the Commission.

The Commission published a brochure giving the facts about the commission and explaining the scope of its inquiry. It was made clear that the commission will not probe into the merits of the religious beliefs of the community. It was solely concerned to find out whether or not the allegations of the infringement of human rights of the members of the community were true.

The Commission held its meeting in Bombay, New Delhi and Gandhinagar (Gujarat) to examine the witnesses in order to elicit information and to verify the answers given by those who had replied the questionnaire. The number of persons who answered the questionnaire was 1075.

The Nathwani Commission submitted its report on the 8th April 1979. It found widespread violation of human rights of Bohra community members. It was expected that the report would bring change in the behavior of *Kothar* towards common people but there was no change in their methods to bend or break the opponents. Their attitude, in fact, became more inhuman and authoritarian to further tighten the grip on the Bohra community.

Tewatia Commission

Having failed to persuade the High Priest to see reasons, the Bohra reformists again approached the Indian Human Rights Commission and the CFD to appoint another Commission to enquire into the excesses committed by the High Priest and his mode and manner of functioning.

The Human Rights Commission and the CFD appointed the Second Commission in 1992 comprising of Justice Debi Singh Tewatia, former Chief Justice of Calcutta High Court, Mr. Kuldeep Nayar, the CFD President and former High Commissioner of India in United Kingdom and a renowned journalist. The Commission started its work on the same pattern of the Nathwani Commission.

The Second Commission too received no cooperation from the High Priest and none appeared on his behalf before the Commission at Udaipur and Bombay. But this time no obstruction was created by them before, during or after the sittings of the Commission neither in Bombay nor in Udaipur.

In all 232 individual representations were submitted to this Commission. At Udaipur, Bohra Youth Girls' Wing which has on its role about 700 women members submitted a joint petition. The Commission submitted its report on 25th August 1993. The findings of both the Commission can be summarized in the following points.

- There is large scale infringement at the hands of the priestly class and that those who fail to obey the orders of the Syedna and his Amils, even in purely secular matters are subjected to *baraat* resulting in complete social boycott, mental torture and frequent physical assaults.
- The root cause of the reformists' grievances can be attributed to the fact that instead of acting as a spiritual leader, the Syedna is acting as an oppressive materialistic despot extorting money and forcing Bohras in his stranglehold.
- It is this deadly combination of religious and economic power which creates huge problems not merely for the reformists but for all members of the Bohra community and for the State as well. Problems of such magnitude may require drastic remedies consistent with the principle of democracy and fundamental rights guaranteed by Art. 25 and 26 of the Constitution of India.

Excellent Intellectual Resources

The reformist movement produced many intellectuals, visionary and charismatic leaders at various times. They succeeded in exposing Syedna's atrocities and violation of human rights to the people outside the Bohra community and made it concern of all human beings. People remember with nostalgia many modern leaders including Noman Contractor, Husainee Sanchawala, Asghar Ali Engineer, Professor Ismail K Poonawala, Professor Abbas H Hamdani, Saifuddin Insaf, Shabbir Bhai Madraswala, Ghulam Husain Manager, AbidAdeeb, ZainuddinWali, Mansoor Ali Bohra, Saleh Mohammad Naib, Dr Zenab Banu, Husain Udaipuri, Sheikh Ahmed Ali Raj, Irfan Engineer etc. who reached out to outer world by their power of writings and oratory.

Asghar Ali Engineer was Director of Indian Institute of Islamic Studies (a unit of CBDBC) and regularly published a fortnightly 'Islam and Modern Age'. Since he believed with conviction that we must respect other people's faith, he worked to promote pluralisms and an interfaith dialogue through his research, speeches and books. As a result he enjoyed the support of liberal minded people of all faiths who helped in spreading the reformist's aims and objectives to everyone whether they may be of English or Hindi or Urdu or Gujarati or Marathi speaking. Asghar Ali conveyed reformist's main concern to all major universities of India and abroad with his academic excellence and convincing arguments.

Asghar Ali Engineer highlighted origin, history, belief, reform movements and the status of *Da'i* in Bohra community in his monumental book "The Bohras" (1980). Many editions have come out which show its popularity among academic world.[2] Thus the reform movement won over a sizeable sections of the academic community.

Asghar Ali believed that women should be treated as equal to men and said that people who support an unjust order, or remain silent in view of gross injustice were not religious people. Women's inequality topped his priority list of injustices.

Professor Ismail Kurban Hussain Poonawala has published many research papers and books including the Pillars of Islam (Da'aaim al Islam translated from Arabic). Professor Emeritus Ismail K. Poonawala, University of California, Los Angeles, USA along with Professor Emeritus Abbas H. Hamdani had prepared a Manifesto on behalf of the Dawoodi Bohra Community in January 2014. The salient points of this manifesto are that for the future prosperity and progress of the Bohra community, the Syedna must pledge publicly the following shortlisted overdue reforms in social and religious spheres-

- that he is only a *Nazim Da'i* (administrator) and not a *Da'i Mutlaq* (with full powers);
- that he is prepared to accept all past and future charities as *waqf* properties of the community with an independent authority and financial transparency, and that he should not claim to be the sole trustee as claimed by Syedna Taher Saifuddin and his successors;
- that he would accept democratic constitution of all the local Jamaats and for the Central Jamaat Board to be elected directly by the community, and that this body should be consulted by him in all matters affecting the welfare of the community;
- that he will abolish all non-Islamic collection of taxes called *wajeba*t and several other taxes at the time of death, such as *ruku' chiththi* (recommendation letter that the deceased has paid all his dues and should be welcomed to paradise), etc;
- that there should be no *baraat* (excommunication) of an individual member or a family of the community, which is a form of

religious tyranny. Membership of a community is a voluntary thing;

- that he will put an end to conferring honorary titles based solely on payment of large sums of money;
- that he should abolish restrictions on dress, both for men and women;
- that there should be no payment of so-called deposits for men to grow beards;
- that the crude rules of *iddat* be reformed bringing it in accordance with the Islamic principles;
- that there should be an end to feminine *khatna* (circumcision) which is a form of female genital mutilation is therefore un-Islamic;
- that a council of scholars and a database of *da'wa* literature be established; the community scholars should have easy access to *da'wa* collection of manuscripts both in Surat and Mumbai and that it is a community property; acquisition of religious knowledge is not a monopoly of the clergy or a specific group; all the manuscripts need to be properly catalogued and special steps be taken for their preservation;
- that a fund / trust be setup to support future generation of young Bohras pursuing the study of Tayyibi Ismailism and related fields; or to pursue legal advocacy and revision of detrimental statues and laws that serve as justification for the *Da'i's* hold on power;
- that the reform in the educational institutions (madrasas, and the seminary at Surat) should be carried out and for that purpose a committee of highly qualified scholars be established;
- that the custom imposed by Syedna Taher Saifuddin to obtain *raza* (permission) for each and every petty matter is against the teachings of Islam and should be abolished;
- that he should declare his predecessor's claim to have authority over the *jaan* (soul) or *maal* (property) of a member of the community as totally against the basic Islamic teachings and bring it to an end;
- that he should be easily accessible to any member of the community and listen to his/her complaint and access should not be controlled by a coterie of henchmen around him, in short there should not be either an iron or bamboo curtain around him;

- that effort should be directed towards building a civil society that not only includes the admirable charitable, educational, and social welfare organizations, but also an alternative religious or scholarly elite to prevent the attrition of Bohras to other branches of Islam, and provide the progressive spiritual guidance that is sorely needed.

All the above are basic human rights and supported by the long tradition or *sunna* and many precedents of the Dawoodi Tayyibi Ismaili *da'wa.*

Sheikh Ahmad Ali Raj compiled 'Ismaili Tafseer of Quran' in four volumes. *Nahjul Balaga* and *Kitab-as-Shihab-ub-Nabavi* under the title of '*Majm-ul-Bahrem'* in two volumes and *Daimil-Islam* (both parts) in *Lisanu ddawat* style of reading. In addition he compiled around hundred other epistles essay and books penned by eminent *Ismaili* scholars[3]. He also trained little young man in Bohra rituals.

Saleh Mohammed Naib started a '*Deeni Taleem School'* for children, translated *Saheefatus Salaat* in English, Hindi and Urdu. He also started an Islamic Study Group for elders where interested persons had an opportunity to understand Quranic exegesis (*tafseer*) by eminent Islamic scholars. This study circle was a debating group where anyone could participate. The classes in this study circle were undertaken by late Dr. Abbas Alavi who used to address Moharram *vaaz* in Udaipur and other places in India as well as in Kuwait, UAE, London, etc. Both the above institutions are working till date.

The sharing of knowledge by intellectuals encouraged independent and critical thinking among the reformists. The orthodox Shabab- blind followers of Syedna are deprived of all these activities. Blind submission is the negation of true religiosity.

All World Bohra Conferences

Since 1977 till date 15 such conferences have been held by Mumbai, Pune, Aurangabad, Indore, Bhopal, Ahmadabad, Surat and Udaipur. The reformists hold the conference every three year at a strategic location to strengthen their struggle for reform and to weaken the stranglehold of *Kothar.*

These conferences succeeded in exposing the barbaric practices of human rights violations of Bohra religious establishment tothe world. This brought support of many eminent citizens from different walks of life.

The conferences provide opportunity to the reformists to periodically get together and evaluate their achievements, discuss their strong and weak points and prepare action plan for future.

Lobbying for Legislative Efforts to Prevent Excommunication

The question whether the *Da'i* had power of excommunication, in a case that ultimately reached to the Privy Council. The Privy Council held that he had, but it also held that normally the members could be expelled only at a meeting of the *Jamaat* after being given due warning of the fault complained of and opportunity of amendment and after a public statement of the grounds of expulsion.[4] The Privy Council further said that excommunication, if justified, necessarily involved exclusion from the exercise of religious rites in places under the trusteeship of the head of the community in which religious exercise are performed.[5] However, the above decision recognized the rights of the Syedna to excommunication the Bohra community members subject to the procedural safeguard mentioned above.

When it came to the notice of the Bombay Government that the practice of excommunication was prevailing in certain communities, the government felt that in keeping with the spirit of changing times it was necessary to stop that practice by law. It, therefore, introduced a Bill in 1948 in the Bombay Legislative Assembly called 'a Bill to prohibit excommunication in the province of Bombay', being L.A. Bill No.49 of 1948. There were lively debates on the Bill in the Assembly. Mr. Morarji Desai, the then Home Minister of Bombay Government introduced the Bill and said, "the monstrous things in the name of excommunication cannot be allowed by a government in which all of us consider that rights and liberties of even humblest and weakest may be protected. Therefore, the Bill has been brought forward in such a careful manner that even public opinion was invited for six months. I do not see how anybody can object to it."[6]

Shri Babu Bhai Patel, former Chief Minister of the State and then member of the Assembly had participated in the debate and said, "They argue that the religious rights of certain class of people are encroached upon and they feel that government is putting its hand on religion. The old cry of religion in danger is put forth. They say "Do not touch what we describe as our religion. It is they alone who are to decide what religion is. But in all humility, it may be asked what this religion is. Is it that you have a right to say that a man shall not grow this size of beard or that size of beard? Is that a man shall not hold any progressive view in matter of social reform. Is it that to open an educational institution or aiding the spread of education is an encroachment on religion? If these are the rights that are being encroached upon, and if any person takes a risk in doing any of these things and thereby suffer excommunication, then I humbly submit that it is not an encroachment on any religious rights but it is only an attempt to secure civil liberty of the citizens of this province" (See Bombay Legislative Assembly Debates, Vol.14 Part II, March 1949).

The Bill then became the Act called the Bombay Prevention of Excommunication Act, 1949 (Bombay Act 4[2] of 1949). The Act in substance provided that no excommunication of a member of any community shall be valid and shall be of any effect. And it was also provided that doing of any act which amounted to or was in furtherance of excommunication of any member of a community would be a criminal offence punishable, on conviction with fine which may extend to one thousand rupees.

It will be seen that the Act applied to all communities in the Province of Bombay. It prohibited excommunication altogether. It had a special significance for the Dawoodi Bohra Community in view of the power of the High Priest to expel any person on ground which he considered proper and sufficient for expulsion. This right was recognized by the Privy Council as seen earlier. It is true that this could be done only by the *Jamaat* and not by the High Priest alone. But this safeguard was practically ineffective if it is remembered that the *Misaq* required the whole *Jamaat* to obey the commands of high priest. If, therefore, the proposal of expulsion emanated from him or with his consent, the *Jamaat* have to vote in favour of the proposal. Therefore, consent of the claim asserted by the Syedna that whoever broke the *Misaq* was a *Satan* whose property could be looted and whose wife stood automatically divorced. Thus the safeguard provided for by the Privy Council was illusory in case of the Dawoodi Bohra community. The notices of expulsion of Members issued on behalf of the Syedna reproduced elsewhere clearly go to show that disobedience of any command by him in any manner, secular or religious is treated by him as breach of the *Misaq* which is sufficient ground for expulsion. In these circumstances to hold, as the Privy Council did that the decision be best left to the religious sense of the community amounted to holding that the High Priest was the sole judge of what would or would not warrant expulsion. The safeguard it should be done only at the *Jamaat* meeting was meaningless. It therefore had the effect of vesting absolute and uncontrolled power into his hands. He was not bound by any fair norms in judging the conduct of any member. The *Jamaat* which considered his proposal was not a free agent, in reality, the fate of any proposal which had the support of the high priest would be a foregone conclusion. Anyone who opposed the proposal was himself liable to expulsion for the only reason that he opposed it. In our considered opinion the view taken by the Privy Council in the said decision is incorrect because it omitted to consider this vital aspect of the matter, namely the effect of *Misaq*. It is required to be reconsidered by the Supreme Court or made ineffective by proper legislation.[7]

The Bombay Act referred to above was a step in the right direction. It did give some relief to the members of the community. But the then Syedna finding his authority shaken, challenged the constitutional validity of the Act on the ground that it violated religious freedom guaranteed by Articles 25 and 26 of the Constitution of India. The challenge arose in this way. The then Head Priest Syedna Taher Saifuddin had made orders of excommunication against one Tyebji Moosaji Koicha who was a Dawoodi Bohra. The latter filed a suit against the Syedna for among other things, a declaration that the said orders passed on February 28, 1934 and April 28, 1948 were illegal and void. He said that these orders had become ineffective after the coming into operation of the Bombay Prevention of Excommunication Act, 1949. The defendant Syedna in his defense urged that the Act was unconstitutional and void. The suit came up for hearing before Mr. Justice J.C. Shah (he was then a judge of the Bombay High Court) who held that the Act was a piece of legislation and rejected the contention of Syedna.

This decision was taken in appeal by Syedna to a division bench of the Bombay High Court. Chagla C.J. and Bhagwan J. who heard the appeal dismissed the same holding that the Act does not contravene Articles 25 and 26 of the Constitution of India and is not ultra virus the Constitution.

Having lost in Bombay High Court, the Syedna carried the matter to the Supreme Court. There his appeal was allowed and the Court held by a majority of four to one, that the Bombay Act in so far as it destroys the right of the *Dai-ul-mutlaq* of excommunicating any member of the Dawoodi Bohra Community on religious grounds is void being in violation of Article 26(b) of the Constitution of India and is not saved by Article 25(2) of the Constitution (A.I.R., 1962 S.C. 853) Chief Justice B.P. Sinha dissented from the majority view and held the Act valid. He was of the view that:

> "The right of excommunication is not a purely religious matter. The effect of excommunication or expulsion from the community is that the expelled person is excluded from the exercise of the rights not only in connection with places of worship but also from burying the dead in the community which are all disputes of a civil nature and are not purely religious matters."

The Act is intended to do away with all that mischief of treating a human being as a pariah and depriving him of his human dignity and of his right to follow the dictates of his own conscience. The Act is thus aimed a fulfillment of the individual liberty of conscience guaranteed by Art. 25(1) of the Constitution and is not in derogation thereof.

"The position of an excommunicated person becomes that of an untouchable in his community, and if that is so, the Act in declaring such practices to be void has only carried out the strict injunction of Art. 17 of the Constitution, by which; untouchability has been abolishedand its practice in any form is forbidden. The Article further provides that the enforcement of any disability arising out of untouchability shall be an offence punishable in accordance with law. The Act, in this sense, is its logical corollary and must therefore be upheld."[8]

Three out of four judges who struck down the Act, however made it clear that the Act was bad because it invalidated excommunications on any ground whatsoever including religious grounds. This view necessarily implies that if the Act had forbidden excommunication on any ground other than religious grounds it would not have been vulnerable to attack on the ground of violation of Art. 26 (b).

The position taken by the Supreme Court is open to criticism. It appears that the Court's attention was not drawn to the actual contents of the *Misaq* and the manner in which it is enforced by the high priest. The Court was also not aware that the matter of excommunication the high priest makes no distinction between the religious and the secular. The Syedna's commands in whatever field are expected to be implicitly obeyed without question on pain of expulsion. Moreover, the court's attention does not appear to have been drawn to the fact that *baraat* is much more than a mere exclusion from the places of religious worship. It involved breaking up of marriages, separation of family members one from another closing down of institutions formed for the welfare of the community and above all expulsion of all those who maintain intercourse with an expelled members.

The Commission's findings were ignored by successive governments, but a group of reformists, led by the Late Asghar Ali Engineer, went to court with the judge's findings.

The case has still not been disposed of and the three decade old petition may come up for hearing in near future. Though Asghar Ali Engineer has passed away, the CBDBC will continue to fight the case as families continue to complain of excommunication.

Excommunication is not only unconstitutional but also un-Islamic as there are no doctrinal provisions for excommunication or social boycott. In fact it was unbelievers of Mecca who had declared social boycott of the Prophet (PBUH) and his family and companions.

Maharashtra recently passed what has been called the country's first law against social boycott. The Maharashtra Prohibition of Social Boycott (Prevention, Prohibition and Redressal) Act, 2016 makes social boycott a crime.

The offence is cognizable and bailable as per the Act. The enactment of the Act leads to the repealing of the Bombay Regulation II of 1827; The Caste Disabilities Removal Act, 1850 and The Bombay Prevention of Excommunication Act, 1949. The Act provides for prohibition of social boycott of a person or group of persons by an individual or a group like caste panchayats. Social boycott has been made a criminal offence punishable with imprisonment up to three years or a fine of Rs 1 lakh or both. It even makes it an offence to create cultural obstacles by forcing people to wear a particular type of clothing or use a particular language.

Reformists Gain Deep Respect for Their Progressive and Liberal Outlook:

> The new phase in the Bohra reformists movement actually commenced in 1973 with a massive revolt against the high priest in Udaipur. Personality like Dr. Asghar Ali Engineer joined the movement and tried to broaden its base by involving democratic, secular, liberal and rational minded people from other communities in the Bohra reformist movement. It was with this philosophy and outlook and sound social basis that reformists are wedded to the cause of secularism, communal harmony and national integration. It has become reformists' main objective to make Bohras an integral part of the Indian community. If there is conservatism, religious fanaticism and fundamentalism in the society the reformists cannot reform the Bohra community alone. The whole society has to change and the change can come about only by strengthening secular, liberal and rational forces.

Convinced about the justness of the struggle of the reformists the members of the reception committee of the 8th AWDBC (held in Bombay) declared in a press release that "as far as our knowledge goes, they are not opposing religion but want to promote its true spirit. They are opposed to authoritarianism and coercive imposition of religious rituals. They also oppose mixing of religion in politics and its exploitation for personal or political ends."

"We are convinced that strengthening reformists' hands will strengthen forces of liberalism, secularism and democracy in our country. It would also lead to promotion of personal liberty and human dignity which are intertwined. The reformists struggle is not directed against any individual but against coercive system. We, therefore, appeal most earnestly to the Bohra priesthood to enter into dialogue with reformists listen to their grievances and resolve them in a spirit of dialogue and reconciliation. We also appeal to the government at the Centre to consider the demands voiced by the reformists sympathetically as a secular and democratic country cannot tolerate coercive imposition of religious authority and persecution of the citizenry in its name."[9]

Medha Patkar a social activist working for social justice in India and Narmada Bachao Aandolan saw the Bohra reform movement in the perspective of people's struggle for liberation. She urged the reformists Bohras to be part of struggle by weaker sections of society and express their solidarity with them.

Many prominent non-Bohra politicians, intellectuals, social workers and others not only stood by reformists but wrote to Prime Minister, Chief Ministers, etc. from time to time. A large number of journalists have stood by reformists.

Even high government officials and police authorities have deep respect for reformists and their progressive and liberal outlook. Everywhere their work for communal harmony and inter-religious unity is greatly admired. Bohra struggle was greatly appreciated and reported in the international journals also.

Underground Movements: Impact of "Reach Out" and "Chhupi Tehreek" on Orthodox Bohras:

> The whole Bohra community except a few appreciates the reformists cause, but due to fear of social ostracism they do not support them openly. Reformists have been able to bring tremendous consciousness through their struggle; it is not in hand to induce courage among people to take a stand, consciousness is not enough, courage is needed equally. Therefore reformists launched underground movements where there are some courageous people who can speak out in favour of reformists.

During early nineties of twentieth century underground movement worked successfully in Calcutta, Madras, Indore, Bhopal and some other places. At present many orthodox Shabab Bohras from Pune, Indore,

Ahmedabad, Jamnagar and some other cities are in touch with reformists secretly.

In this mission the reformists provide relevant literature to the underground supporters in the form of newspapers, pamphlets, booklets and Xeroxed material from various clippings to the Bohra friends in India and abroad. This updates the sympathizers and supporters. It also helps the movement to grow as it has taken the movement to many doorsteps. Social networking is now above all.

Success in Challenging Syedna's Sole Trusteeship of all Bohra Properties

Syedna's claim of 'Sole Trustee' was challenged in High Court of Rajasthan by the reformists of Udaipur during Udaipur mosque case and got victory. Now all the Bohra community properties in Udaipur except Taiyabiyah Senior Secondary School; are in the possession of reformists. They have been maintaining the six mosques, *Jamaat Khana,* Dispensary and Medical Care Centre, two School buildings, one cricket academy, community centre and few shops very well with the voluntary contributions of the members of the community.

Sine the value of the Bohra properties much exceeds the threshold fixed in Waqf Act[10], the Syedna's establishment wanted Syedna to be made Sole and unaccountable custodian of Bohra *Auqaf* by paying an annual lump sum of token money. The State Government of Rajasthan entered into an agreement with the late Syedna Saheb where the Syedna was made 'Sole Trustee' of all Bohra *Auqaf* properties in Rajasthan in the year 1970 clandestinely behind the back of Bohra population. In return the sole trustee would pay a sum of Rs. 5000/- per annum. The agreement was given the glamorous name of 'Aide Memoir' as per the terms; the agreement was to be reviewed by the Board every three years. Since the State government itself was one party of agreement the Board stood as onlooker. Taking Rajasthan's agreement as example the late Syedna Saheb became Sole Trustee in States where huge Bohra *Auqaf* properties were located and then to countries outside India. The reformists challenged the above agreements on following ground.

- There is no place of trustee in the Act because in waqf the property is vested in Allah. The waqf properties are only to be used for purpose religious in nature as defined in Islam. The *mutawalli* is only a manager of this property. After the agreement the sole trustee became the sole *mutawalli* of all *auqaf.* The

English concept of a trust is not applicable for a Muslim Waqf. A Waqf once made cannot be revoked.

- Each Waqf should have a separate *mutawalli* as per the Act. Here one person sitting miles away is sole *mutawalli* of every property spread in different cities, towns and villages throughout India.
- Each *mutawalli* is accountable to the board in management of waqf and is supposed to pay a percentage of earning from that waqf to the board along with annual budget and accounts. Here by paying a lump sum, the sole trustee is free from every burden of all the *auqaf.* No accounts no check and no Board supervision.
- As a beneficiary every Muslim is entitled to make use of waqf. Here even orthodox Shabab Bohras who fail to pay Syedna certain amount are denied entry.

The matter was taken up with board as well as State government. A protracted struggle finally culminated in the declarations that the agreement was illegal from 1978 onwards in following declarations:

1. To a written question in State Assembly, the minister concerned replied that it was illegal.
2. The minister concerned noted in the file on the subject that the agreement was illegal and be revoked. And the Syedna be asked to give accounts.
3. The Board itself passed a resolution to the effect that the agreement was 'null and void'.

Unfortunately, despite these declarations the agreement is very much in operation. Obviously there is something beyond the control of all the regulators.

In the meantime despite proper information to the Board, the sole trustee has ensured:

- Appropriation of a big chunk of land measuring 23.5 bigh as or 5.5 lakh square feet located in the heart of Udaipur city. This land was to be used by local Bohras for religious purpose as per the verdict given by the Supreme Court of Mewar State and thus by nature a Waqf and it was registered as Waqf by none other than Syedna's representative at Udaipur. The Board was even requested to intervene and the cost would be borne by the reformists.
- The aggrieved reformists have passed a resolution in their 15th All World Dawoodi Bohra Conference held at Udaipur in March 2017 and expressed as resentment to the stand of both the State

government and the Board and resolved to take the matter to these bodies again as well as with the Central government to forthwith nullify the said agreement and seek accounts.

In 1992, the reformists of Canada were successful in the Bill related to sole owner of all Bohra properties, both public and personal in Canada. Actually when the Bombay was burning in communal riot after demolishing of Babri Masjid, Syedna Saheb was busy using all his power and influence to get Bill S13 passed in the Canadian Parliament. If this Bill had gone through, it would have allowed him to be sole owner of all Bohra properties. But the active and dynamic members of the Association of Progressive Dawoodi Bohras of Ontario (APDBO) worked overtime to defeat the Bill. They acquired documents and affidavits from reformists worldwide, as well as by political action, and prevented the Bill from being passed. In the process they raised an awareness of the ploys of *Kothar* among those senators who were been lobbied by it. All the documentation is now in the Parliamentary library. The Association of Progressive Dawoodi Bohras deserves appreciation from all Bohra community for this great victory for the reformists against mighty and corrupt *Kothar.*

Mainstreaming of Bohra Women

Gender equality is granted in the Constitution of the CBDBC and Udaipur *Jamaat*. Women have equal rights to vote, to contest and to be elected President, Secretary, Treasurer and other responsible posts. They have voice in policy and other decision making. They remain present in all the activities of reformists including *dharna, pradarshan*, rally, *upwaas*, etc.

Needless to say the support of the women is of great importance for the Bohra reform movement. If the women accept the need for social reform, it would be much easier to bring about social change in the community. Though it would be certainly wrong to hold women fully responsible for what is happening in the community today.

The reformist movement not only paved the way for equal women participation in community affairs but also promote mainstreaming of Bohra women. When they came out from their houses onto road for battling against religious dictatorship, they came in contact with women NGOs, human rights' workers and organizations for the weaker sections of the society. These interactions brought impetus of awareness, courage, openness and fearlessness among them. They celebrate Women's Day on 8th March and take part in different activities related to women empowerment. This is a big achievement in itself.

From Fatima Bahen of Abde Fatima Nikah Case 1937 to present day women – Masooma Ranalwee and Zehra Patwa of 'WeSpeakOut'; Mariya Taher and Dr. Farzan of 'Sahio'; ZehraCyclewala of 'Surat Mahila Sangh' and Zenab Banu and others of 'People's Union for Civil Liberties',- all are actively participating in public life. Thousands of women from various parts of India have sacrificed a lot for the reform movement. Zehra Patwa and Mariya addressed[11] FGM in the United States – UN CSW 63rd session on 22nd March, 2019.

Various Reformist Institutions

Establishment of Deeni Talim and other such institutions (Anjuma-e-Luqmani, Anjuman-e-Fidayeen-e-Hussain and Hussaini Marriage Bureau) under the leadership of Late Janab Ahmed Ali Raj and Janab Saleh Mohammed Nayab have flourished to perform every ritualistic activities based on *Ismaili Mustali Tayyabi* traditions. These trained persons are surplus in number and are ready to carryout religious rituals anywhere in the world. They are leading prayers, making arrangements for burial, performing *nikah* and Muharram *waaz* and go abroad when called for these functions.

Udaipur Urban Cooperative Bank with thirteen branches in the district of Udaipur and Rajsamand is working successfully in the economic field.

Bohra Youth Medical Relief Society, works for the health and wellbeing of the community and suffering humanity at large has grown from one doctor to a full fledge polyclinic with facilities of two ambulance, a pathological laboratory, ultrasound sonography and services of specialized doctors. Organizing blood donation camps, health awareness camp and free checkup for diabetes, cardiology, and Hepatitis B vaccination are its regular activities.

The Bohra reform movement is a very long movement. The reformists of Udaipur have succeeded in sustaining the struggle for reforms continuously without break for the last fifty years. The reformists are busy in preparation for the golden jubilee functions which are going to be organized in 2020. The inaugural function was held on 29th April 2018. It is an ongoing movement and the active support of women is crucial to sustain it. Hope the future generations will take it to further heights.

Notes and References

1. CFD – The Citizens for Democracy was an organization formed for strengthening democratic values in all sphere of life, social, economic and cultural. It was

neither a political party nor It was committed to supporting any political party. It strived to guide public opinion by propagating rational and constructive views so as to counteract demagogic and sectarian appeals. In the past, the CFD had taken on hand important matter and appointed committees for that purpose. One committee is known as 'Tarkunde Committee' which was constituted to suggest electoral reforms in the country. Another committee also known as Tarkunde Committee, investigated into the killing in alleged 'encounters' of several Naxalites in Andhra Pradesh. One committee constituted to prepare a practical plan for education for our people. Thus CFD has been doing work for educating public opinion and inquiring into matter of public importance.

2. Asghar Ali Engineer was reformist writer and social activist. Internationally known for his work on liberation theology in Islam. He had more than 50 books on his credit: "The Rights of Women in Islam", "Islam women and Gender Justice", "The Problems of Muslim Women" etc. His autobiography "A Living Faith: My Quest for Peace, Harmony and Social Change" was released by Hamid Ansari, the then Vice President of India on 20th July, 2011 at New Delhi.
3. Mansoor Ali Bohra, "Coming of an age: Dawoodi Bohra *Jamaat* (reformists) Udaipur", ***The Bohra Chronicle,*** Feb.2019, P.15.
4. Report of the Justice Nathwani Commission, 1979. (Dawoodi Bohra Commission), 2nd Edition, page 115.
5. See Hasan Ali and Others V/s Mansoor Ali and Others; AIR 1948, PC 6.
6. See Bombay Legislative Assembly Debates, Vol. 14, Part II, March 1999
7. Report of Justice Nathwani Commission, Op. Cit., P. 119.
8. Ibid, P. 121.
9. Dr. Usha Mehta, Chairperson of the Reception Committee and Members – Narendra Nathwani, I.M. Kadri, Vijay Tendulkar, Govind Nihalani, A.K. Hangal, V. Kamath, KaifiAzmi, Prof. Dilip Singh and Others.
10. In order to protect and regulate an enormous properties worth billions of Rupees endowed/donated by erstwhile rulers, Nawabs and Jagirdars of princely States of India as well as philanthropic individuals the benign governments of independent India enacted first Waqf Act 1954 followed by Waqf Act 1995 which stands amended by Waqf (Amendment Act 2013). These Acts envisage establishment of a separate Board each for Sunni and Shia Muslims, if the Shia *auqa f*exceed a threshold of value of their *auqaf.*

    Under these Acts each State was to create its respective Boards of Muslim Auqaf. In addition a Central Waqf Council was also established or act as link between the Central government and the State units.

    Elaborate Rules and Regulations were framed by way of which the management and working of these Boards be regulated and monitored including their finances.

    The key aspect of the Act is that each property is to be registered with the Waqf Board along with a '*mutawalli*' (loosely translated as custodian and manager). This *mutawalli* is directly responsible and accountable to the respective Board and as such the Board is entrusted with the superintendence of respective *auqaf* of the State concerned through these *mutawallis.*

Accordingly all the properties belonging to Dawoodi Bohra within the definition of 'Waqf' in Rajasthan were registered separately along with their respective *mutawalli.*

11. MALA – Muslim American Leadership Alliance had hosted a parallel event on "Addressing FGM in the USA: Safeguarding Survivors and Potential Victims". This panel took place as part of the 63rd Annual Meeting of the UN Commission on the status of women. In January 2018, the World Health Organization reported that over 200 million women and girls alive today are survivors of FGM/FGC.

Chapter - 10

Miles to go for Social Reforms

The reformists among the Bohras have never tried to form a separate group, separate preaching or a separate theology. They have tried to reform their community from within, keeping themselves a part of it. So they have never tried to weaken their community by forming a separate group having a distinct sectarian view. Bohra reformists are only demanding some basic minimum rights for all Bohras which are part of universal human rights common to all human beings. Hence the Bohra reform movement is not exclusively a concern of the Bohras alone but also of all the social reform movements all over the country. When an entire community's values, ideas, identity and rights are at stake, the secrecy or privacy of religious autonomy should not be allowed to be used to suppress dissent or prevent changes in an ossified and repressive system controlled by a few.

Then who are the reformists? They are not outsiders; they are from among the Dawoodi Bohras. The conscientious followers of Bohra faith resented when *Kothar,* in its lust for power and wealth, started exploiting religion to enrich themselves at the cost of ordinary Bohras. The reformists came forward to stop this exploitation. Therefore, the entire struggle of reformist is for the protection of true religion and betterment of the whole community.

What is *Kothar*? *Kothar* is not a part of the original genuine *Dawat-e-Hadiyah.* It is Syedna's administration controlled by Syedna and his very large extended family, which is generally perceived by any Bohra as a gang of community's blood suckers, who in the name of Islam, Bohra religion, *Da'i* and *Dawat* is oppressing Bohras by imposing conditions of *Raza,* Green and Red cards and controlling the entries to mosques, *mazars* and graveyards and making the lives of Bohras miserable. They have even made Syedna their money making machine. It is alleged that *Kothar* compelled more than 100 years old Syedna Mohammed Burhanuddin run around the world to collect the money for them.

Syedna used to visit East Africa regularly where many wealthy Bohra families used to host him in their Bungalows and give him maximum possible money. When Idi Amin expelled Indians from Uganda after confiscating all their wealth and businesses, these wealthy Bohras became penniless. They pleaded for help from Syedna but he did not spare a penny for them. Syedna behaved with them as if they were complete strangers to him. It is the common Bohras, relatives and friends who helped them resettle. In contrast to this, Agha Khan, the Imam of Shia Khojas, extended all possible help to his followers and facilitated their resettlements in Canada and several European countries.

Any Bohra readily blames *Kothar* for any wrong doing, implying *Kothar* acts without Syedna's knowledge, although everyone knows that nothing happens in Bohra community without Syedna's *Raza*. This is also contrary to *Kothar's* assertion that Syedna is "*Ghaibnaa Sahib*" (i.e. Syedna is all knowing, knows all hidden, unseen, secret things including the future). Orthodox Shababs complain secretly among themselves about atrocities of *Kothar* or suffer silently. One of the major differences between orthodox Shabab and reformists is that the reformists complain openly and oppose injustices of *Kothar* without fearing the consequences.

The big Question- Why the reform movement is not much acknowled-ged in Bohra Community as a whole? The answers could be summarized as:-

A. Misinformation campaign by *Kothar*

(i) Anyone who dares to question *Kothar* is immediately declared apostate and enemy of Dawat-e-Hadiya and Dai. This is enough to arouse hatred among Bohras who do not bother to verify the truth. There is much misunderstanding on the office of Dai. The reformists give as much importance to the office of a Dai as orthodox Bohras. The office of Dai is an integral part of *Fatimi Da'wah.* Reformists also do not differ with them even on the question of *nass.* The doctrine of *nass* has been quite fundamental to all the Shia sects as well as reformists and orthodox Bohras. According to the doctrine of *nass,* the predecessor appoints his successor through divine inspiration. In other words he determines his successor, not through his desire but as per *ilham* (through divine intervention). Thus a succession is not an arbitrary one put properly determined. The Imam and *mansus* (divinely determined successor) are also believed to be *m'asum* i.e. infallible, but not the Da'i; Da'i can err, Dai is fallible.

(ii) Initially the *Kothar* had disseminated lot of misinformation about the reformists among the Muslims and portrayed the reformists as enemies of faith. They were also described as agents of Israel. The propaganda barrage by the *Kothar* was so strong that during early seventies no Muslim leader was prepared to listen sympathetically to the reformists' grievances. They invariably showed their sympathy with the *Kothar*. But the reformists were not dismayed and continued to contact Muslims leaders and explain their cause to them. The progressive Muslim intellectuals and writers greatly sympathised with the reformists and lent their moral support. In 1978 more than hundred professors of Aligarh Muslim University signed statement supporting the reformists and condemning the repressive policies of *Kothar*. The words of reformists on Islamic front also paid rich dividends. The Institute of Islamic studies published number of research papers on Islam and projected Islam in the light of modern developments. The clouds of misunderstanding and misinformation began to disperse.

(iii) Also, initially, the Bohra community had expressed solidarity with the Syedna sensing danger in reformist movement as a negative development ultimately harming the unity of the community. They prefer to compromise instead of resisting the oppression. The *Kothar* propaganda machinery was much more vigorous within the community projecting the reformists as enemies of *Da'wat*. But soon the truth became known to some interested orthodox Bohras through secret contacts on one hand and through sustained publication of the 'Bohra Chronicle'(Gujarati and English) and All World Bohra Journal(Hindi). The chronicle has played very crucial role in spreading the reformists cause throughout the world among the Bohras. It is read in several countries by the Bohras like Kenya, Tanzania, Mauritius, UK, USA, Canada, Sri Lanka, Malaysia, Thailand, etc. Syedna has forbidden reading of reformists' literature and publications. Thousands of orthodox Shabab Bohras from all over the world anonymously visit the website www.dawoodi-bohras.com read the literature and take part in discussions in the reader's forum.

However half of the energy of reformers is thus wasted in defending himself/herself rather than working for change and reform. Now a days dozens of groups are active on social media campaigning for reform but they have maintained a distance with CBDBC in fear of being labelled *Dai na dushman* (enemy of Syedna). To be effective, reformists must find ways and means to penetrate the minds of the blindest orthodox Shabab followers of Syedna. They are blind followers because of ignorance of true religion and the grip of myths and superstitions spread by *Kothar*. One of the ways is to somehow make these people read the translations and explanations of Quran, and genuine Bohra literature from the Imams and the first 45 Dais. They will be awakened and truth will dawn on them even if they can read relevant excerpts from these sources. This is not interference in religion. It is simply spreading awareness about the actual religion.

B. Political use of Religion

The Bohra priesthood's behaviour is much worse than the Sikh or any other priesthood. What happened on Dec 5, 1988 at Golden temple, Amritsar, shook the whole country. The former Chief Minister of Punjab, Mr. Surjit Singh Barnala, had to submit himself for pardon to Sikh high priests at "Akhal Takht" for committing the 'sin' of refusing to dissolve the 'Akali Dal (L)' in the interest of larger Sikh unity. The Sikh high priests ordered him to be tied to a post with a signboard around his neck reading "I am sinner seeking pardon". Not only that, he was also required to clean shoes at the Gurdwara for seven days. It is truly shocking that the former Chief Minister submitted himself to such humiliation not for religious but for political reasons.

One single high priest, Syedna controls, totally and unquestioningly, all the aspects of the life of the Bohra Community. As Mr. Barnanal's refusal to dissolve the political party became 'sin' in the eyes of the Sikh priest. The Bohras refusal to obey the Syedna's command to vote for particular political party is dubbed as unpardonable 'sin'. The punishment is, like the one in the Sikh Community (*Tankhia*), *baraat* (ex-communication).

It is not only political commands of the Syedna that are to be obeyed: one has to pay obeisance to all his commands; social or economic. If he wants all of your bank account closed, they must be. If he wants you to grow a beard, grow one you must. In his eyes the religious is the political and political is the religious. No Bohra dare defy these politico-religious dictates of the Syedna. As Barnala had to clean shoes, a Bohra religious teacher of *Jamia* (Surat) had to put his shoes on his head and presents himself before Syedna with folded hands for being pardoned for his sins. Before he was 'pardoned' his mouth was opened and spat into by his own students. His humiliation was complete.

One must be clear in one's mind that such ghastly happenings cannot take place without the tacit political support of the powers that be. The Sikh priests may or may not derive direct political support from the ruling party but the Syedna does. It is very simple: he has turned his economic clout into political clout. No wonder many Chief Ministers fall into his basket like ripe fruits. The Chief Minister of Madhya Pradesh, Mr. Motilal Vora, sent the State Government's plane for bring him from Bombay to Indore and he, along with Arjun Singh (then Congress Party's Vice President), was present to receive Syedna at the Indore airport. The Chief Minister of Gujarat Mr. Amar Singh Choudhary, with all the way to Surat in 1985, wore the cap given by the Syedna and had himself photographed proudly standing beside him and joined the procession organised by the Bohra high priest. The Chief Minister of Rajasthan, Mr. Harideo Joshi stood unflinchingly by the Syedna and publicly defended his interest when the reformists Bohras launched a struggle in Udaipur to visit the Galiakot shrine. The Sharad Pawar government in Maharashtra had come to the Syedna's rescue by filing a petition in Bombay High Court to quash the proceedings of a suit against him (i.e. Syedna) in a Bombay Court in December, 1988.

Prime Minister Man Mohan Singh had obliged Syedna by inaugurated Saifee Hospital in Bombay in 2005.Recently during Muharram (Sep. 2018) Prime Minister Narendra Modi along with Chief Minister of Madhya Pradesh, Shiv Raj Singh Chouhan joined Syedna's Sermon (*waaz*) at Saifee Mosque, Indore and accepted a shawl from the Syedna. While during his 2011 fast for harmony and peace in Ahmadabad where he had famously refused to wear the skull cap offered by a Maulana, Modi walked the premises of Saifee Mosque bare feet, declaring in his address that "his fond association and community's support had drawn him to Indore". On the question of FGM when a women delegation met Menaka Gandhi (Union Minister for Women and Child Development), she showed keen interest. But when Supreme Court asked the government about its data, her Ministry submitted an affidavit stating, "At present there is no official data or study (by NCRB, etc.) which supports the existence of FGM in India." Congress leader Manu Singhvi pleaded the case for the party in favour of FGM. Many more examples can be given to show that unscrupulous politicians belonging to various parties- BJP, Congress, Janata Dal, Shiv Sena or any other party can hardly resist the temptation of money and votes. They all prefer to extend their full support to the Syedna blindly and uncritically without ever verifying the issues involved.

It is not only in India that he has cultivated political relations with the powers that be : he has done so in a number of other countries including those in East Africa (where there are a large number of prosperous Bohras) and Pakistan which is another gold mine for him. He had cultivated special ties with Zia-ul-Haq and Nawaz Shareef, Imran Khan who used to grace his (Syedna's) function there.

However the voice of the reformists remained unheard in the orchestra of Syedna's political affiliation. Votes and notes get precedence over social reforms and political democracy is misused to negate social democracy. Bohras, a minority within the Shia Muslim minority, the reformists again a minority within Dawoodi Bohras have a little political impact or no ballot power impact as we all know, cornering vote-banks is the mainstay of parliamentary democracy. For example during Rajasthan Assembly election 2013, the Bohra reformists *Jamaat* of Udaipur decided to boycott the election and issued notice that no one would go to caste the vote. This protest was to draw attention to serious grievances regarding Bohra Waqf properties and they wanted to settle it before election. Sadly, neither the party in power nor opposition party came to console them. Obviously a handful of votes of reformists in one constituency have no value in comparison to lacs of votes of Syedna's followers in number of constituencies.

It is this political clout which has made the Bohra high priest so invincible in the eyes of Bohras who fall at his feet not so much out of respect but for fear of consequences. The Bohra high priest openly brags in his sermons that no one can touch him.

C. Iron Curtain

The term iron curtain symbolises the efforts by the Soviet Union to block itself and its satellite states from open contact with the West and its allied states during cold war period. Similarly on Syedna's instructions his followers block, themselves from open contact with the reformists. Interpersonal communication is not possible even in blood relations. For example, if someone's son is a blind follower of Syedna (orthodox Shabab) then he does not talk with his reformist father or mother. Written communications also do not work as either they burn it or throw it in dustbin without reading for the fear of social boycott. Those who dare to violate

Syedna's dictates are punished severely. Bohra masses are afraid of Syedna's henchmen who act like secret service agents and report the violations to *Kothar*.

The whiplash of social boycott is employed by the clergy to stifle all debate, dissent and disobedience of its dictates as these are perceived as threats to its authority and harmful to its interests. For the supposed Islamic clergy it is immaterial that social boycott is un-Islamic in origin (as it was practised by the Pagans against the Prophet) and uncivilised in practice. All that matters is that it is effective in subjugating the community and promotion of its interests.

It is difficult for a non-Bohras to comprehend the nature, totality and the consequences of the social boycott enforced by the Bohra clergy on the community. The community ethos and its milieu are quite different, perhaps outside the pale of normal human experience. *Kothar* has effectively converted Bohra Community as an exclusive club. A typical Bohra's, particularly Bohra women's most time is spent in Bohra religious or social activities, within the close circle of friends and relatives. Any person expelled from the exclusive club feels suddenly friendless, lonely and nowhere else to go. He also wrongly believes that his life hereafter is also ruined.

A Bohra lacks virtues like honour, valour, self esteem and courage to question or to resist the oppression. Blood ties and friendships are also inconsequential. His overriding concerns are to save his own skin at all cost. A mere whisper of social boycott is enough to send him grovelling before the clergy. He will prostrate and humiliate himself just to save his skin even if he has done no wrong. As the community is almost his only world, a Bohra has a paranoid fear of isolation. This fear the clergy exploits. Like outcast by other communities Bohra boycotted persons are not considered as part of the society, rather they will be loathed and denied their share of respect and dignity. In the eyes of Bohra community members they become untouchable. No Bohra will say '*Salam*' nor will reply '*WalaikumSalam*'.

In such a situation of wet blanket, the reformists find it very hard to engage the orthodox Bohras face to face and fail to convey their mission of reform to them, that they are not 'anti Syedna', nor 'anti religion' but they only wanted to make a separation between religious and secular matters and are demanding to restore the civil liberties and human rights of Bohra person being citizens of India. The iron curtain is due to wide spread myths, superstitions, falsehood, religious ignorance and fear of *Kothar* among orthodox Shababs. Most orthodox Bohras who shuns reformists in public are happy to interact with them secretly. *ChhupiTehreek* and reach out among Bohra masses to increase awareness, understanding of Quran and true religion is likely to bring down the iron curtain. Merely holding conferences or celebrating Golden Jubilee will not achieve much. It is very important to seek the answers to the question, "Why the numbers of reformists is steadily decreasing from about 1980 onwards?"

D. Slow Pace of Social change

The liberal reformists accept the reality of the present status with its criticism as well. They propose a set of immediate and mid-range reforms that will work to modify the unacceptable features of the present and move society towards a more satisfactory set of institutions and practices in the future. Gradual transformation is the model of change for them.

Bohra social reform movement's infusion into the existing social structure of the Bohra way of life and thought; the society would be preserved, while its members would be transformed. Since the Bohra reform movement proclaimed the supremacy of reason over blind faith, of individual conscience over outside authority and brought in its train new concept of human rights and social justice.

The reformists reject the very idea of blind, unquestioning or absolute obedience to any religious or worldly authority in the absence of Imam who is supposedly in seclusion. The reformists draw their inspiration and guidance from the authentic sources which are available in the form of various books written or compiled during and under the supervision of Imams, the teaching of religion as found in these sources and books. *Dai* has no authority from Imam to claim total obedience to him. The real difference between the orthodox Bohras and reformists is not on the question of *Da'i* but on the total submission and absolute obedience of Da'i. The orthodox have been misled by Syedna in believing that unquestioning and absolute obedience to *Da'i* is part of Bohra faith. Syedna has been elevated to the position of divinity through clever manoeuvrings of the *Kothar*. Orthodox Shababs are required to kiss Syedna's photos and it is compulsory to keep Syedna's photos in their homes and shops for his blessings. The reformists oppose this and consider it as deviation from the basic *Isma'ili* doctrines. Here the doctrine of *ismah* (infallibility) is very central. The orthodox are forced to believe that along with the Imam, a *Da'i* also enjoy the status of infallibility. According to authentic Ismaili literature the *ismah* is only for *nabi, wasi* and Imam and not for the *Da'i*. The reformists have very sound spiritual basis for this position. The *Kothar* now has made the orthodox believe that infallibility applies to secular or worldly matters too. Thus the orthodox and the reformists differ on this issue. Firstly, the reformists do not accept the doctrine of *ismah* for the *Da'i*. Secondly they believe that *ismah* is restricted to only religious matters and does not apply to worldly affairs.

Bohra social reform movement aims at making gradual change, maintaining peaceful crusading and use of non-violent means based on Gandhian philosophy. Hence in the last 48 years, though they get success in social transformation in terms of *misaq*, *raza* and *baraat*. The reformists perform rituals and all religious activities without *Raza* (prior permission) of Syedna. Seeking Syedna's *Raza* before carrying out every religious activities, even before going to Haj is akin to *Shirk* (associating partners with Allah). Syedna's blind followers are ignorant about *Shirk*. *Shirk* is the greatest sin which Allah will never forgive. Reformist give original *misaq* (oath of allegiance) for Imam as it existed before. The 51st *Dai* Syedna Taher Saifuddin Saheb modified it to total submission to himself. Reformists never declare *baraat* (social boycott) against any voice of dissent. Instead they respect the voice of dissent and try to satisfy it by reasoning. The reformists do not believe in inflicting their point of view on any one, not even on the orthodox Bohras. They accept the right of orthodox also to believe and practice what they want. Similarly, they do not want others to inflict their viewpoint on them or to coerce as the *Kothar* does, forcing Bohras to submit to its authority on pain of social boycott. The reformists resent when the orthodox treat them as outcast. The reformists are true Dawoodi Bohras and adhere to the doctrine of their faith very sincerely. No one else can decide on their behalf whether they ceased to be Dawoodi Bohras or not.

It is futile to think that modern education by itself will bring about desired change. Social behaviour, as pointed out, is much more complex and determined by several factors. Human behaviour is not finally determined by modern education alone. Moreover the modern education, at least in India, is not designed to develop critical consciousness among its recipients. It is designed more to conform to authorities than to critically evaluate its worth. It is hardly intellectually stimulating. Our educational institutions are more centres of acknowledgement rather than centres of knowledge. Add to this the fact that Bohras hardly send their children to university for higher education. Also, they are hardly interested in humanities or subjects like philosophy. They are more interested in subjects who would boost their knowledge and efficiency for their trading activities. Such education lays least emphasis on developing critical consciousness.

It is true in pursuing this; the reformists have neglected other important reforms of social change. Particularly what about the women? And why is there no improvement in women's status? Why the practice of women *khatna* (FGC/FGM) is still continuing? Why are women continued to be confined in a secluded room during *iddah* period after husband's death contrary to the requirement and spirit of the Quran and *Daim-ul-Islam*? Why are women continued to be deprived of inheritance? Why there is no reform in divorce and maintenance etc.? Why Nikah form has not yet been revised to give equal rights to women? Why has any improvement not occurred in the women's status, honour and dignity? The main objective of present study is to find out the new status of Bohra women in the context of Bohra social reform movement. It is something more than Bohra women empowerment.

When we dwell on this theme of empowerment of Bohra women, basically we are concerned with gender relations. Does empowerment put Bohra women on an equal footing with men in the society? Theoretically reformist women have equal rights to vote, to contest, to elect and to participate in decision making bodies as per the Constitution of Dawoodi Bohra *Jamaat* and CBDBC. But practically, they are not articulate enough to express their opinion; they have a culture of silence. They have legs but they are not motivated enough to walk towards the key positions of decision making bodies.

The customary laws based on *shariat* have yet another stigma attached to Bohra women. For illustration a woman chose to not follow the restrictions of *iddah* after her husband's death in 2012. She came out of her home to *Jamaat Khana*. But, instead of encouraging and supporting her, the then *Jamaat* Secretary issued a harsh letter which stated that "Being a member of Dawoodi Bohra Community where you belong to, you should know that *Jamaat* operates within the limits of *Shariat* and your decision to step out of your home is a violation of *Shariat* laws. Hence, we condemn this and instruct/advise you to obey the rules of iddah. Your reply is expected at the earliest." Receiving the letter of condemnation, the woman of 60 years of age, with broken heart, adopted *iddah* as per the prevailing rigid Dawoodi Bohra norms (we have discussed it earlier). In this case, the supporting fact was that she was already separated from her husband and had applied for divorce in the *Jamaat* office. As we know, the logic behind *iddah* is to identify and establish whether the widow is pregnant or not from her deceased husband. In this case, firstly, she was an old lady who had achieved menopause and could not conceive. Secondly, it was not possible in the scenario of long time separation. Thirdly, she did not do *nikah* during *iddah* period which might be a valid reason of the violation of Islamic law.

As according to Qur'an the widow cannot marry to a certain period (4 months and 10 days). Her fault was that she just came out from the house, which is a permissible act according to Bohra's most revered book *Daim-ul-Islam*, authenticated by 14th Imam Al-Mu'iz Li-Din Allah. Still, the patriarchal society compelled the poor woman to mourn over her separated husband. It proves the patriarchal mind set of reformists' *Jamaat*. Reformists' *Jamaat* seems to believe that reform is complete with the election of Jamat members, and nothing else is required to be done. That is why reformists do exactly whatever the orthodox Shababs do.

The Bohra Youth Association (BYA) and its Girls' Wing is the pioneer of the modern mass reform movement in Udaipur. It was a powerful organisation in 1970s. All the influential charismatic senior leaders from BYA took up various positions of responsibility in the Dawoodi Bohra *Jamaat* when it was formed. In due course Dawoodi Bohra Jamat became more powerful than the parent organisation BYA. On the other hand, the new leaders in BYA and its Girls' Wing were not mentored by experienced senior leaders about the basic principles, aim and objectives of reform movement. It is the responsibility of the young leaders of BYA and it's Girls' Wing to give new life to reform movement by taking up reform issues pending since last 50 years. Presently BYA looks to *Jamaat* for directions and funds; it should be the other way round. If *Jamaat* is the government then BYA and its Girls' Wing is a ruling party. They must form a "Think Tank" to give direction and momentum to the reform movement. BYA must be more powerful than the Jamat for any meaningful reforms to occur.

Suggestion for the Achievement of Bohra Women Empowerment:-

Dismantling Patriarchy

Patriarchy established hegemony of male over female. It is due to unequal power relations. It is a social system in which males hold primary power and predominate in roles of leadership, moral authority, social privilege and control of property. Society imposes gender biases the minute a child leaves their mother's womb and enters this world. We are taught that girls need to be quiet and reserved while boys must be assertive and outspoken. Women apologize even when they are right. Women shrink themselves so that their partners can feel bigger etc.

In the traditional Bohra community, decision making was the monopoly of the males. Women were not allowed to attend such bodies of *Jamaat*. But with the beginning of reform movement, the elected *Jamaat* body came into existence and women were granted equal rights on the basis of gender equality.

A Bohra woman might be an elected member of local *Jamaat* executive member of CBDBC but her status at the family and community level remains the same. They are required to perform dual role in the society. Their primary role consists of caring activities. They are required to look after children, aged and sick people. They have to cook food and manage the house hold chores. In the present situation of unemployment when petty business ceased to be an economic enterprise, an increasing number of men go abroad; which makes the female head of the family. It is she who takes care of family members and takes decisions for maintaining the family etc. However the responsibilities of women have increased in the present era and the inequality has also increased. This is a tragic situation.

In Bohra community, women are not allowed to attend a funeral at the graveyard; they are also not allowed to lead in congregation prayer (*Namaz-e-Imamat & Namaz-e-Janaza*). They are not allowed to recite *Azan* from the mosque. They are not allowed to perform *nikah, misaq, talaq* etc. It is all a social and cultural construct. There is nothing in fact in the sex which disqualifies a woman to do particular things in a society. Hence gender discrimination persists almost in all societies. The dreams of women may differ, their struggle even more so but their need for air to breathe is the same? When one moves across cultures, similar problems can be seen surfacing everywhere. And the only solution lies in deconstruction of patriarchy.

Vibrant and Strong Women Organisation

A vibrant and powerful Bohra Women's Organisation is needed for the empowerment of women. Such an organization that can act for the welfare of women must have complete administrative and financial freedom to work, without any interference of community and religious leaders. It should be functional in nature and enhance women welfare irrespective of their community, religion, caste and class. It should adopt human rights in general and emphasize on women's plight and adversities particularly as it is one of the main objective and should also be connected to mainstream organizations.

'Bohra Youth Girls'Wing' is functional in Udaipur among the reformists' group with the slogan –

'There is no limit on what you can achieve.
There is no barrier that stops you to reach for the stars.'

Girls' Wing was successful in bringing out Bohra women from their houses to roads and empowers them for street agitations against ban on the Galiakot *ziyarat* in 1970s. It motivates women to make their presence felt in All World Conferences and other such public meetings. Members of BYA Girls' Wing encouraged women to narrate their stories of harassment and sufferings resulting from social boycott to the 'Nathwani' and 'Tawatia' enquiry commission.

Girls' Wing also enlightened and educated women about their Islamic rights, human rights. But it could not play an instrumental role in the eradication of practices like *Khatna*, inhuman rules during *iddah*, woman inheritance, divorce and maintenance etc. Because the amount of ignorance about the true religion in reformists is not less than the orthodox Shababs. After all the reformists were very blind followers of Syedna before 1970s and their knowledge of religion is limited to what Syedna gave them in their sermons.

Present status of BYA Girls' Wing

Its activities are generally limited to the Bohra Youth women of Udaipur.

It is not an independent body to make decisions in favour of women's interests.

It works like an extension of local Bohra *Jamaat* and Bohra Youth Association.

Jamaat has powers to revoke its decisions in the name of *Shariat* and religion. And it often does so, ignoring the guidance given in the authentic books from Imams and previous spiritual Dai's. *Jamaat is* controlled by statusquoists, except the formation of *Jamaat* through elections; there is practically no difference between the blind followers of Syedna and the reformists!

It is officially not associated with other national women organisations.

No representation of Girls' Wing is in other bodies of Dawoodi Bohra *Jamaat* such as Masjid Committee, *JamaatKhana committee*, *Talaq* Committee etc.

Though, it was in contact with other women's organizations and celebrated Women's Day with them. A 'Women Commission' was also formed in the 14th All World Conference in 2011, but the irony is that women's status has not changed in the society. For any improvement to happen, Girls' Wing has to reassert itself, be more proactive and take initiatives without looking to the *Jamaat* for direction or support. In fact *Jamaat* is BYA's and its Girls' Wing's offspring.

'Sahiyo', 'WeSpeakOut' are newly emerging Bohra women organisations which are surprisingly doing fantastic efforts against FGC/ FGM without the support of CBDBC. Now the matter of FGC is in public domain. It became an issue of human rights' violation on one hand and Girl Child Abuse on the other hand. A Public Interest Litigation (PIL) is filed in the Supreme Court to ban it. After one hearing, the pro-FGM party demanded that the case be transferred to five members Constitutional Bench. The Supreme Court accepted it and new Bench has yet to be formed to hear it again.

Sahiyo is an organisation that seeks a collective solution towards ending the practice of female genital cutting (FGC) because it is child abuse. Sahiyo used social media to reach out to Bohras. They had also done the first ever online survey on *Khatna* which involved Bohra people from 17 countries around the world. To spread the word even further, they conducted workshop and peer support program because there are so many people who are not even aware of what had happened to them. They also connect with NGOs who further connect them with Bohra women.

Co-founder of Sahiyo, Filmmaker Insiya told to Mansi Khandelwal during interview to Indianwomenblog.org, said, "However we had our share of difficulties in this process. Social Media backlash, people telling us that it is wrong on our part to stop a religious practice, (it is not religious). But our motive is to actually educate people about the hazards of this practice. We came from a very peaceful space, and we have no intention to antagonize anybody. So if a 7 year-old has undergone a cut, her mother or grandmother might have done it with the best of their intention, but what has happened to that young girl is something that is never discussed and the child then have to grow up with the memories of that pain."

WeSpeakOut is the largest survivor-led-movement to end Female Genital Mutilation/Cutting (FGM/C) amongst Bohras. Since its formation in 2015, it has been actively involved in campaigning within the community about the physical, emotional and psycho-sexual trauma caused by FGM.

It has been instrumental in spreading a public conversation on the practice of FGM/C, which is secretive and done without consent of minor girls. This conversation has made the Bohra community confront how this practice, which is intertwined with notions of customs, traditions and religion, subjects its women and children to violence and violates their human rights. WeSpeakOut has also attempted to engage with the clergy, to push them to work towards putting an end to this century old regressive practice.

We Speak Out has petitioned to the Government, Women and Child Development Ministry, National Commission for Women and several other governments and non-government bodies. It has also petitioned to the United Nations Human Rights Council and highlighted the prevalence of FGM in India urging for action against the practice.

In response to the affidavit submitted by the Ministry of Women and Child Development to the Supreme Court of India on Dec., 2017, during the hearing of PIL filed by a Delhi based woman advocate, stating "At present there is no official data or study (by National Crime Records Bureau, etc.) which supports the existence of FGM in India", WeSpeakOut in collaboration with 'NariSamtaManch' sponsored a project and published the report entitled *The Clitoral Hood A Contested Site* (*Khafz* or female Genital Mutilation/Cutting (FGM/C) in India. it is a timely study as it helps build much needed evidence before Supreme court when the petition will heard again.

Social media has played a crucial role in bringing to both the organisation in lime light. The young and middle aged English educated women who are suffering due to cut but did not speak out get chance to speak and share views how to overcome this inhuman practice. Previously it was presumed that in India, the problem is prevalent in Dawoodi, Alvi and Sulaimani Bohras only but when this story reached to South India by media, Keralian Muslim girls too came out and joined the campaign.

The young English medium educated women of Udaipur reformists group should take inspiration from Sahiyo and WeSpeakOut and start campaign against the stern practice of iddah, and other anti-women traditions. Women activism must be visible. We hope the young English speaking generation of reformists would take interest in the women related problems of Bohra society. They would use social media as their medium of publicity and soon get rid of it. They need affirmative organisational support within and outside community-which may pull them towards national mainstream.

Knowledge about Religion and Scriptures

Knowledge is power. Those people who have a better knowledge can control all situations and circumstances in their life. It creates self-confidence and patience which enables one to overcome the adversities in life. It is the vital tool to get positive changes in the society and country.

Reformists must have knowledge about the objectives of reform and the means by which they wanted to achieve their goals. If we do not have proper knowledge then we cannot teach to other people. For example a teacher cannot teach well without thorough knowledge of his subject. A doctor without knowledge in surgery cannot be a successful doctor. An advocate without proper knowledge of law cannot plead well for his client. Hence when religious rituals and religious sanctions become hurdles in the way of reform, the only weapon for overcoming these hurdles is the knowledge about scriptures of religion and religious literature.

As a reformer has to argue against established beliefs, he/she must have thorough knowledge of these beliefs on one hand, and of what he/she wants to establish against those beliefs on the other hand. No reformer can ever succeed in persuading his/her people without thorough knowledge of the scripture of his religion. Knowledge of the modern social and natural sciences is highly necessary along with the religious scriptures. Be it Ram Mohan Roy among Hindus or Sir Syed among Muslims, they had thorough knowledge of their respective scriptures. Ram Mohan Roy quoted Vedas to prove there is no mention of *Sati* in them. Sir Syed had thorough knowledge of the Holy Qur'an to advocate reform among Muslims. Sir Syed faced stiff opposition from orthodox 'Ulama' because he was first among the Muslims in India to advocate the cause of natural sciences which were being rejected. Sir Syed came out with an ingenious approach for reconciliation of religion and natural sciences. He said the Qur'an is revealed work of God and nature is work of God, so how can there be contradiction between the Word of God and Work of God.

One can imagine that when reformers with such thorough knowledge of their own religious tradition had to face such stiff opposition what of those who lack any or have half backed knowledge of their religious traditions. Bohra reform movement succeeded in challenging Syedna's hegemony in non-religious and secular matters, because there were so many stalwarts who had thorough knowledge of *Isma'ilis* and Dawoodi Bohra scriptures. Now most of them have passed away. So the young generation should think in this direction and should establish an Islamic Centre of Study or revive the Indian Institute of Islamic Studies which is defunct after Asghar Ali Engineer's death.

It is the main task of reformer to recognise the core teachings of a religion and the accretions of various social traditions, which lead to distortion of core teaching of religion. Of course, the people find it extremely difficult to distinguish between the core teachings and the social accretions. For them both are inseparable. Not only has that, these social accretions become much more important than the core teachings of religion. And over a period of time these social accretions even replace the core teachings. It is Allah who decides to send His messenger or create a reformer amongst the people. As per the Qur'anic teaching Mohammed (PBUH) being the last prophet we can now expect reformers only.

The traditional intellectuals oppose reform not only because their position is threatened, they oppose it also because their world view is based on old teachings. Since they remain ignorant, by and large; of the scientific changes or technological changes taking place around them, they denounce these changes as 'satanic' as they challenge the traditional teachings. They think these changes are totally against teaching of religion.

Young women should come out with the zeal to study religious scriptures like Qur'an, *Daim-ul-Islam, Tuhafat-al-Qulub, Risalas* of Syedna Hamiduddin Kirmani, Syedna Qadi-al- Nauman, SyednaMoyyed-al-Shrirazee, etc. Like the former reformists they should draw their inspiration and guidance from these authentic sources of Bohra religion. Especially when they have to argue against women related established belief like *khafz, iddah, miras* (inheritance) *talaq* (divorce) and maintenance.

Some reformists already have knowledge of the above religious books which they should share with others. Relevant excerpts from the above books, which could make people, think critically about *Kothar*'s false claims of divine powers and misguidance should be widely publicised and circulated among orthodox Shababas in print and soft copies.

Women Reservation: Quotas

Reservation or quotas are used as measure to increase the representation of historically excluded or underrepresented groups in politics.

Till today the reformists are not interested in any reservation for women in the various decision making bodies. Consequently women members are by and large invisible in the actual decision making bodies (local *Jamaat* or CEC of CBDBC) and rarely influence the more significant reform policies and debates which indicates the complete lack of support to women members. Hence women related issues are not addressed properly.

Therefore, strong commitment and will to promote women's leadership in Bohra reform movement is highly needed. Looking to the importance and need I introduced a resolution for one third women reservation in last AGM (Annual General meeting) of local Dawoodi Bohra *Jamaat* Udaipur in May 2018. It was included in the agenda but due to lack of time, it was postponed for next meeting. Let us hope the Udaipur local *Jamaat* would do justice to women by granting1/3 reservation in *Jamaat* membership and would establish the doctrine of gender justice and bring Bohra women at par with national policy for women.

Patience

A reformist leader has to have almost inexhaustible fund of patience. One who is short on this can never succeed. Also it is important to note that success of reform movement cannot always be gauged in terms of numbers who follow the reformer. A reform movement generally does not appeal to the masses. Normally it has greater appeal to the intellectuals who have capacity to critically examine things. Masses just follow. A reformer has to work against well entrenched beliefs hence she needs to argue persuasively and hence need for great deal of patience. She needs to acquire good communication skill, express oneself in a reasoned persuasive and convincing manner, without getting impatience. She must be supportive while they share their story. Let them share their stories as much as they are comfortable without any interruptions or contradictions. Everyone has their own journey. No two stories are the same. It is advisable to end the meeting with some light conversations.

To Bring Different Reformist Groups Under a Single Umbrella

During field study I came across a number of reformists groups who are working in different regions with the same objective of social awareness among Dawoodi Bohras against *Kothar's* malpractices. The voices are many but they are scattered. They are afraid to contact or liaise with CBDBC and Bohra Youth because they are afraid of social boycott. Central Board of Dawoodi Bohra Community (CBDBC) must take the initiative and contact them covertly and extend all possible help to them to spread the reform movement among the reluctant orthodox Shababs. The task may be little bit difficult but not impossible. There are a few old reformists' centres. One "Roshan Khayal Jamaat of Malegaon" (about 25 families) who has kept distances from CBDBC and do not come to its conferences and functions. Udaipur Bohra Youth group who act and react according to its local demands and situations. The other pockets of resistance and reason are - Mumbai (about 50 families), Hyderabad (about 40 families), Aurangabad (about 30 families).The reformists outside India are non-resident Indian (NRIs) Dawoodi Bohra group such as BYANA (Bohra Youth Association- North America), UK, European countries and African countries etc.

Following are the some newly emerging reformist group:

1. Bohra Tehreek
2. 'Bohra for Change', Pune, Maharashtra
3. 'Maalummat', Ahmadabad, Gujarat
4. 'Awaaz' Indore, Ujjain, Madhya Pradesh
5. 'Sahiyo' International body of women against FGM
6. We SpeakOut- Pune, Maharashtra, Delhi, Rajasthan.

We have some suggestions to bring them under a single umbrella:

1. With the passing away of stalwarts, younger leaders have taken their place. The seniors should express faith and trust in them and give them freehand to work. The seniors must also look for talented potential leaders in the next generation, mentor them and prepare them for future challenges, for continuity and for growth of reform movement.
2. Set a co-ordinating committee of all the centres who may meet and decide a minimum common programme like the coalition government in India.
3. Today we are living in a Cyber World ,hence efforts must made to reach out the orthodox Bohras by social media like-website, Twitter, Blog-writing, Facebook, Instagram Messenger, WhatsApp, etc.
4. 21st century is of youngsters. In reformists group the dominating age group is of (20 to 40). The reformist should encourage them to spare some time for community affairs. A large group of Engineers and Doctors in 1970s in Bombay and Udaipur were very active in the reform movement in spite of meagre salaries of those times and all kind of hardships. The younger generation now is better placed to take up leadership of reform movement with various resources at their command.
5. Efforts must be made for the integration of different groups of reformist under a single umbrella, to avoid duplication of work and bring synergy with their coordinated actions.

Self-Discipline

Self-discipline means self-control, which is a sign of inner strength and control of action and reactions of oneself. Self-discipline gives power to stick to decisions and follow them thorough, without changing one's mind. Bohra reformists are continuously struggling against the hegemony of Syedna who possess all the power to crush the opposition with heavy hands. The reformists support the individual freedom and respect the voices of dissent. Having lived under Syedna's slavery, the reformists are not used to newly win complete freedom of expression. Sometimes this freedom of expression results in chaos where everyone wants to have his say without listening to other's views .In the absence of a charismatic leader, anyone with some ideas thinks he is a leader. In such a situation all are leaders without any followers.

Communication experts should be invited in Youth camps, where they can train and orient people to observe self-discipline in order to effectively and responsibly use their freedom of expression for the cause of reforms and smooth functioning of various institutions and committees.

Constitutional Rights

The reformists should demand forcefully to the government of India to enforce rights of minority within the minority community so that the minority community is not deprived of all the rights guaranteed in the Indian Constitution. The severe persecution of the reformists Bohras and their continued sufferings makes it very urgent. The reformists Bohras are crying for justice. The benefits of the constitutional rights must reach every member of the minority community and not only to the powerful coteries. The government of India turns a blind eye towards suffering of minorities within minorities for political reasons. The vote bank politics has its own compulsions as the top priority of the ruling party is to win elections rather than enforce constitutional provisions.

It is important to note that Article 25 is preceded by the qualification 'subject to public order, morality and health'. What the Bohra priesthood is doing is the very negation of this important condition. He is disturbing public order, morality and health of society. The very community he heads is going through great turmoil because of the Syedna's authoritarian ways. It is for the Law Courts, the Minority Commission, The National Human Rights Commission and human rights organisation and activists to safeguard the rights of minorities within minorities by insisting on proper enforcement of the rights of reformists Bohras in general their women in particular.

To sum up, fighting for social reforms and changes is an extremely challenging task. When we want social change the status quo is disturbed and those who benefit from it will use all means, fair or foul to prevent change. False propaganda and violence are the usual tools used by them.

For about half century the Bohra reformists have been struggling hard for their democratic and human rights while upholding their religious beliefs. There is a great deal of discontent in the Bohra community today. In fact, a section of the community is seething with anger but finds itself helpless in front of the priests. Many have resorted to legal action but soon realise that they cannot get the better of the priests who have immense resources in their favour.

The CBDBC has established its identity as a representative body of reformists all over the world. *Kothar* does not recognize CBDBC, it wants to destroy it. It approaches individuals to win them over and isolate the leaders. Obviously it does not want to negotiate principles. It refuses to acknowledge the values and rights the reformists are fighting for. Dictatorial *Kothar* will never like to lose its complete control over the lives of Bohras by accepting reformists' demand of elections for autonomous local *Jamaats* and accountability.

What is to be done then? Should one give up in despair? Certainly, one must never give up. A struggle draws strength from the nobility of the cause, not just from physical success. Even Mahatma Phule and Dr Ambedkar have not succeeded in that sense and yet their ideals continue to inspire millions of people to continue their struggle.

Reformists' success will depend on how fast and how much they can spread awareness about futility of worshipping Syedna, about true religion and falsehood of *Kothar* among the orthodox blind followers of Syedna.

Women's Role

Empowered women cause healthy changes in a society by discharging different responsibilities in different roles. No society can achieve sustainable progress with a minimal or negligible role of women. In a true sense, a society is considered to be developed when both the gender contribute in accordance with their potentials.

Though one cannot expect drastic change in the status of Bohra women in India in near future but one can certainly hope for incremental changes. The number of Bohra women activists is on the increase as pointed out earlier. This will further increase with the passage of time.

There is also great need for internal critique and at least educated young volunteers attempt an honest criticism of position and status of women in the community and consolidate efforts for change and reform. They also tend to be defensive and reactive. Time has certainly come to be proactive for improving Bohra women's status in India.

They have to continue their struggle till they over-throw the repressive, undemocratic and authoritative *Kothar* and re-establish the humanistic, enlightened and progressive *FatimiNizam* which will be free of unjust and oppressive practices and will have freedom and uniform democratic setup for judicious management of community's socio-economic and gender affairs.

Syedna and his administration must understand that the times have changed. If they want to be relevant now and in the next generation, they have to reinvent themselves. The brain washing cannot go on forever. And people too must come out of their slumber. They have to religiously educate themselves. It is said 'God helps those who help themselves.'

Hope that the reformists cause will prevail. The 21st century is of reformists and really of women empowerment.

Bibliography

Reports

1. Annual Report of State Commission for Women, Rajasthan, 2002.
2. Census Report of India, 2011.
3. Lakshmi Anantnarayan, Shabana Diler, Natasha Menon, *The Clitoral hood A Contested Site, Khafz* or female genital mutilation / cutting (FGM/C) in India (A Project Report in collaboration with we speak out Nari Samta Manch, 2018).
4. NHRC Report, 2002-2008.
5. Rajasthan Development Report. Academic Foundation, Government of India, 2006.
6. Report of justice Nathwani Commission (Dawoodi Bohra Commission) 1979.
7. Report of Violation of Human Rights of Dawoodi Bohras by D.S. Tewatia (Retd.) Chief Justice of Calcutta High Court and Kuldeep Nayar, President of the Citizens for Demcoracy, Aug. 1998.
8. Sachar Committee Report, 'Social Economic and Educational Status of Muslim Community of India, Prime Ministers' High Level Committee, Government of India, 2006, p. 11.

Books

1. Aga Khan, *The Memories of Aga Khan,* Simon and Schuster, New York, 1954.
2. Ameer Ali, *Spirit of Islam,* Editions in 1891, 1922, 1953, ISBN: 9780-391-003415.
3. Asghar Ali Engineer, 'the reformists and their religious beliefs (booklet by BDBC) p. 1.
4. Asghar Ali Engineer, *Islam challenges in 21st century,* Gyan Publishing House, New Delhi, 2004, p. 108.

5. Asghar Ali Engineer, *Problems of Muslim Women in India,* Orient Longman, Bombay, 1995.
6. Asghar Ali Engineer, *The Bohras,* Vikas Publishing House, Gaziabad (U..P.), 1980.
7. Azad, *Tarjumanul Quran,* Sheikh Gulam Ali & Sons, Lahore , 1947.
8. Aziz Ahmed, *Islamic Modernism in India and Pakistan* (1857-1964), Oxford University Press, 1967.
9. B.N. Pande (Ed.), *National Integration,* Secular Democratic Forum, Allahabad, 1970.
10. Begum Naz, *Sir Syed Ahmad Khan,* National Book Foundation, 1922.
11. Charles Tilly, *Social Movements,* 1768-2004, Paradigm Publishers, Boulder, 2014.
12. D'Arcus, *Boundaries of Dissent: Protest and State Power in the Middle Age,* New York, Rutledge, 2006.
13. Dobson, C., *Social movements: A summary of what works.The Citizen's Handbook: A Guide to Building Community in Vancouver,* 2001, Retrieved Dec 2, 2006, from http://www.ven.bc.ca/citizens-hanbdook/movements.pdf.
14. Fayzee, A.A.A., *The Religion of the Ismailis in India and ..... Contemporary Islam,* I.I.A.S., Calcutta, 1970.
15. Fowarekar, J. *Theorizing Social Movements.* London: Pluto Press, 1995.
16. Frantz Fanon, *The Wretched of the Earth,* Grover Press, New York, 2004 (New edition).
17. Ghanshyam Shah. *Protest Movements in Two Indian States. Study of Gujarat and Bihar Movements,* Ajanta Books International, Delhi, 1977.
18. Ghanshyam Shah. *Social Movements in India, Review of Literature,* Sage Publication, New Delhi, 2004.
19. Heimsath, C., *Indian Nationalism and Hindu Social Reform,* Princeton University Press, Princeton, 1964.
20. Irobel Coleman, *Paradise Beneath Her Feet: How Women Are Transforming and Middle East,* Random House, 2010 (Paper Book, 2013).
21. Jean Dreze and Amartya Sen, *India: Economic Development and Social Opportunity* (Kindle Edition), Clarendon Press, 1999.
22. Jeff Goodwin and James Jasper, *The Social Movement Reader - Cases and Concepts,* (2nd Ed.), Wiley Blackwell, Oxford, 2004.
23. John Idriss Lahai, Khanyisela Moyo (Eds), *Gender in Human Rights and Transitional Justice,* Springer, 1978.

24. Lewis M. Killian, *Social Movement,* University of Delwara, Press, New York, 1994.
25. Mahadeo Desai, *Maulana Azad* (Gujarati), 1946, Digital Library, India Texts.
26. Marcogivgni, Dong, McAdam and Charles Tilly (Eds.), *How Social Movement Matters,* University of Minnesota Press, Minneapolis, 1999.
27. Maulana Abul Kalam Azad, *India Wins Freedom (An Autobiographical Narrative),* Orient Longman, India, 1959.
28. Maulana Muhammad Ali, *Holy Qu'ran,* Lahore, 1973.
29. Melucci Alberto. *Nomads of the Present: Social Movements and Individual Needs in Contemporary Society,* Philadelphia, Temple University Press, 1989.
30. Mian Bhai Mullah Abdul Hussain, 'A Short Note on Dawoodi Bohras', *Gulzare-Dawoodi,* Progressive Publications, Surat, 1920, p. 2.
31. Moin Shakir, *Khilafat to Partition,* Kalamkar Prakashan, New Delhi, 1970.
32. Qamruddin Khan, *Status of Women in India,* Sterling Publishers, Delhi, 1992.
33. Radha Kumar, *The History of Doing: An Illustrated Account of Movements for Women's Rights and Feminism in India 1800-1900,* Zubban, 1993.
34. Raja Ram Mohan Roy, *The Serpent and the Rope,* Orient paper back, Delhi, 1986, p. 35.
35. Raka Ray and Mary Fainsod Katzenstein (Eds.), *Social Movements in India: Poverty Power and Politics,* Row man Little Field, USA, 2005.
36. S.C. Mishra, *Muslim Communities in Gujarat,* Asia Pub. House, Bombay, 1964.
37. Sayeeda Saiyidain Hameed, *Voice of the voiceless: Status of Muslim women in India,* National Commission for Women, 2000.
38. Sbran Lambert – Hurtey, *Muslim Women Reforms and Princely Patronage,* Nawab Sultan Jhan Begum of Bhopal, Routledge, 2007.
39. Shah Waliullah, *Hujjat-ullah-il-Baligha* (The Profound Evidence of Allah), Vol. 1, Sheikh Gulam Ali & Sons, Lahore.
40. Shibani Roy, *The Dawoodi Bohras – An Anthropological Perspective,* B.R. Publishing Corporation, Delhi, 1984.
41. Shireen Hunter (Ed.), *Reformist Voices of Islam: Mediating Islam and Modernity,* Routledge, Dec. 2014.

42. Sinichi Shigetomi and Kumibo Mabino (Eds.), *Protest and Social Movements in Developing World,* Edward Elgar Publication, Japan, 2009.
43. Sir Syed, *Muqalaate-e-Sir Syed,* Vol.1, edited by Sheikh Mohammed Ismile, pp. 75-81.
44. Smelser, N.J. *Theory of Collective Behaviour,* New York: Free Press, 1965.
45. Snow Nancy, *Handbook of Public Diplomacy,* Rutledge, 2008, p. 338.
46. Starr, A. *Naming the enemy: Anti-corporate movement confront globalization.* London: Zed Books, 2000.
47. Sundra Grey and Marian Sawer, *Women's Movements: Flourishing or in'Abeyance?,* Rutledge, Flipper, 2008.
48. Sydney Tarrow, (3rd Ed.), *Power in Movement: Social Movements and Contentious Politics,* Cambridge University Press, Cambridge, 2011.
49. W.C. Smith, *Modern Islam in India,* Lahore, 1943.
50. Woods mall, R. *Muslim women Enter a New World*, George, Allen and Unwin, London (1983).
51. Zald and McCarthy. *Social Movements in an Organizational Society: Collected Essays.* Transaction Books, 1987, pp. 188-190.
52. Zenab Banu, *Deprivation of Women's Human Rights and the Strategies for Resolution*, Kanishka, New Delhi, 2014.
53. Zenab Banu- *'Galiakot se Galiakot tak'* (Hindi booklet) published by Khan Mohammedji Sugra Bai Trust, Udaipur, 1979.
54. Zenab Banu, *Muslim Women in Political Process in India,* New Delhi, 2016.
55. Zenab Banu, *Politics of Communalism,* Popular Parkashan, Bombay 1989.

Research Articles

1. Alok Deshpande, "President's note for bill against social boycott", *The Hindu,* 30th July, 2017.
2. Ambika Pandit and Mohua Das, "Activist hopeful after Supreme Court calls FGM unacceptable", *The Times of India,,* 10th July, 2018.
3. Anumeha Yadav, "The Iron Grasp of the High Priest", *Tehelka Magazine,* Vol. 8, Issue 26, Dated 02 July, 2011.
4. Asghar Ali Engineer, "The Bohra reformists and the Bohra priesthood", *Islam and Modern Age,* Vol. 3, No. 6, June 2000.
5. Asghar Ali Engineer, Reform movements in Indian Islam – A dissenting perspective, *Bohra Chronicle,* June 2017.

6. C. Offe, 'New Social Movements: Challenging the Boundaries of Institutional Politics', *Social Research,* 1985: Winter, 52(4), 817.
7. Diani, Mario 'The Concept of Social Movement'. *The Sociologica Review,* 40:1, (1992), pp. 1-25.
8. E. Gruenbaum, "Socio-cultural Dynamics of Female Genital Cutting: Research Findings Gaps and Directions", *Culture, Health and Sexuality,*7(5), 429-411.
9. Ghanshyam Shah. "Revolution Reform, or Protest: A Study of Bihar Movement", *Economic and Political Weekly,* Vol. XII, No. 17, April 23, 1997 (Special article).
10. H.K. Sanchawala, "Expulsion of His Holiness Dr. Mohammed Burhanuddin Saheb from Tanzania (Pamphlet), Surat.
11. Hilal Ahmed, "Asghar Ali Engineer (1939-2013) emancipatory intellectual politics", *Economic and Political Weekly,* June 2013.
12. Irfan Engineer, "The Bohra Pontiff, Muharram and the Prime Minister", *The Bohra Chronicle,* Oct. 2018.
13. Kalpana Sharma, "The Dawoodi Bohra", *PUCL Bulletin,* Aug. 1982.
14. Kiran Mehta, "Reformists are not anti-religious", *Clarity,* February 24, 1991, p. 5.
15. Kumkum Chaddha, 'Divinity under dispute', *Hindustan Times*, Sunday Magazine, Oct 3, 1993, p. 9.
16. Kumkum Chaddha, 'Divinity under dispute', *Hindustan Times*, Sunday Magazine, Oct 3, 1993, p. 9.
17. Lawyer's Collective and Speakout on FGM, "Female Genital Mutilation: A Guide to Eliminating Practice of FGM in India", *Lawyer's Collective,* New Delhi, 2017.
18. Manoj R. Nair, 'Bohraejumaat cards raise privacy concerns', *Hindustan Times (Mumbai)*, 9 Oct, 2015.
19. Mansoor Ali Commander, "Coming of an age: Dawoodi Bohra Jamaat (Reformist), Udaipur", *The Bohra Chronicle,* Feb. 2019.
20. Melvyn Thomas, 'Bohra reformists come together to fight fundamentalism', *The Indian Express News Line,* Saturday, Feb 5, 2005.
21. Melvyn Thomas, "Bohra reformists come together to fight fundamentalism", *Indian Express, Express News line,* Saturday, Feb. 5, 2005.
22. Oomen, K.T., 'Sociological issues in the analysis of social movements in independent India', *Sociological Bullets,* Vol. 26 (March 1977), pp. 14-37.

23. Payal Gwalani, "Another dictates of Bohras: Only select caterers to provide food as special events", *Mumbai Mirror,* 21st January, 2019.
24. Qudsiya Contractor, "Muslim Women and the Challenge of Religion in Contemporary Mumbai", *Economic and Political Weekly,* Oct. 28, 2017, Vol. Nos. 42-43.
25. Ram Paniyani, "Sabrimala Shrine and Women's Entry", *Secular Perspective,* 10.6.2018.
26. Rehana Ghadially, 'All for Izzat: the practice of female circumcision among Bohra Muslims', *Manushi*, No. 66, 1991.
27. Sabula Meena Gopal, "Body Gender Sexuality: Politics of Being and Belonging", *Economic and Political Weekly,* April 24, 2010, Vol. XLV, No. 17, p. 44.
28. Saifuddin Insaf, '*Kothar*'s miserable defeat in crushing the reformist movement in Udaipur', *The Bohra Chronicle*, 1-4-1998, p. 5.
29. Shabbir Hussain Madraswala, 'Bohras: The Scourge of Social Boycott', *Souvenir,* to commemorate the 10th All World Dawoodi Bohra Conference, Udaipur, 1999.
30. Shabbir Hussain Madraswala, "Bohras: The Scouge of Social Boycott', *Souvenir,* to commemorate the 10th All World Dawoodi Bohra Conference, Udaipur, 1999.
31. Shabbir Hussain Madraswala, "Bohras: Waiting for Gorbacho", *The Times of India,* Patna, Wednesday, March 11, 1992.
32. Staff Report, "Maharashtra Nod for Bill Against Social Boycott", *The Hindu,* April 4, 2016.
33. Teesta Sitalwad, "Syedna's Slaves", *Communalism Combat,* March 1999.
34. Vartika Neeraj 'Genital mutilation plagnesthousands of Bohra women in India, https://*thewire.*in/worn, 27 July2018.
35. Yogender Sikand, "A Lone Woman's Battle Against Priestly Tyranny", *Rediff.com,* March 23, 2011.
36. Zarina Bhatty, "Feminists or Reformists", *The Hindu,* March 16, 2003.
37. Zenab Banu, 'Riht to Inheritance of Muslim women', in Asghar Ali Engineer (ed), *Problems of Muslim Women's in India,* Gyan Publishers, New Delhi.
38. http://www.vagabomb.com/In-Historic-Protest-Women-Fight-against-Female-Genital-Mutilation-in-India/
39. http://theladiesfinger.com/lets-talk-female-genital-mutilation/
40. http://www.idiva.com/news-work-life/the-most-inspiring-indian-women-of-2015/15121824

41. http://www.bbc.com/news/world-asia-india-35129466
42. http://www.muimbaimirror.com/mumbai/others/Chucking-the-anonymity-veil-17-women-call-for-ban-on-genital-mutilation/articleshow/50036285.cms.
43. http://www.dnaindia.com/mumbai/report-bohra-women-campagin-for-outlawing-female-genital-muitilation-2153937
44. http://www.thequint.com/women/2015/12/30/silence-nomore-dowoodi-bohra-women-crusade-against-fgm
45. http://www.thequint.com/india/2015/12/05/i-suffered-genital-mutilation-support-me-to-stop-it
46. http://cj.ibnlive.in,.com/stop-female-genital-mutilation/45584/
47. http://www.msn.com/en-in/news/watch/stop-female-genital-mutilation/vp-AAgo9cO
48. http://www.elespectador.com/noticias/elmundo/blkoguera-puso-pie-una-minoria-tumbar-ablacion/india-articulo-606104
49. http://www.huffingtonpost.com/entry/indian-women-ban-fgm us 56993990 e4b0b4eb759e3 efd?section=india
50. http://news.trust.org//item/20160112150723-xkmft? source = lead Carousel
51. http://www.themalaysianinsider.com/world/article/indian-women-speak-out-againt-female-genital-mutilation
52. http://news.yahoo.com/india-urged-ban-fgm-women-break-silence-secret-153700977.html
53. http://www.allgov.com/india/news/top-stories/womens-group-calls-for-ban-on-genital-mutilation-in-india-so-can-you-1191974.html
54. http://www.asianetnews.tv/web-story/opffbeat/India-urged-to-ban-FGM-as-women-break-silence-on-secret-rutual-42650
55. http://nofgm.oprg/2016/01/10/petition-to-end-female-genital-mutilation-in-india/
56. http://www.ndtv.com/health/month-long-campaign-on-female-genital-mutilation-launched-1274532
57. http://www.business-standard.com/article/pti-stories/online-petition-against-female-genital-mutilation-lauynched-116020401300 1. html.
58. http://www.thenewsminute.com/article/female-genital-mutilation-survivors-launch-month-long-campaign-38640.
59. http://indiatoday.intoday.in/story/mnonth-long-campaign-on-female-genitasl-mutilation-lalunched/1/589361.html.

60. http://indiatoday.intoday.in/story/rptng-after-change-in-para-5/1/588025.html.

61. http://www.deccanherald.com./content/527358/month-long-campaign-female-genital.html.

62. http://www.mid-day.com/articles/online-petition/against-female-genital-mutilation-launched/16929172

63. http://punjabstarnews.com/online-petition-against-female-genital-mutilation-launched/

64. http://www.thehindu.com/news/cities/mumbai/news/online-petition-against-female-genital-mutilation-article8196598.ece?css=print

65. http://www.freepressjournal.in/online-plea-against=-fecmale-genital-mutilation-launched/ 773068

66. http://www.business-standard.kcom/article/pti-stolries/month-long-campaign-onfemale-genital-mutilation-launched-1160206007641.html.

67. http://www.thequint.com/videos/2016/02/05/female-genital-mutilation-must-be-stopped-and-thisd-could-be-a-start.

68. http://indiatoday.intoday.in/video/women-ruise=against-female-genital-mutilation/1/587469. html.

69. http://weww.firstpost.com/livingh/many-stay-silent-to-avoid-backlash-this-female-genital-mutilation-victim-is-speaking-out-and-you-should-listen-2615284.html.

70. http://timesofindia.indiatimes.com/city/mangaluru/Bohra-women-strenghten-campaign-to-end-FGM-in-India/articleshow/50868268.cms.

71. http://www.dnaindia.com/health/report-international-day-for-zero-tolerance-of-fgm-ngo-sahiyo-s-petition-to-end-female-genital-mutilation-in-india-2174354

72. http://www.thecitizen.in/index.php/OldNewsPage/?Id=6502&Against/Cutting/Up/Women

73. http://netzfrauen.org/2016/02/056/38112/

74. http://www.scoopwhoop.com/Barbaric-Female-Genital-Mutilation-Is-Very-Much-A-Reality-In-India-But-These-Women-Want-To-Eng-It/

75. http://www.thehealthsite.com/news/shocking-80-of-bohra-women-have-been-subjected-to-female-genital-mutilation-survey-v0216/

76. http://www.catchnes.com/social-sector/30-female-genital-mutilation-survivors-push-to-end-barbaric-practice-1454655949.html

77. http://www.catchnews.com/life-society-news/the-horror-of-fgm-bohra-community-shames-women-by-kcutting-genitals-1454749683.html

78. http://m.dailyhunt.in/news/india/english/catch-news-epaper-catchnew/the-horror-of-fgm-bohra-community-shames-women-by-cutting-genitals-newsid-49366231.

79. hjhtp://www.governancenow./com/news/regular-story/dawoodi-bohra-women-practice-female-genital-mutilation

Journals

1. Economic and Political Weekly.
2. Gender Studies.
3. Indian Journal of Political. Science Association.
4. Indian Journal of Politics.
5. Indian Journal of Secularism.
6. Islamic Voice (Bangalore).
7. Middle East Journal Washington D.C.

Newspapers

1. All World Bohra Journal
2. Bombay Mirror
3. Bombay Samachar (Gujarati)
4. DainikBhaskar (Hindi)
5. DNA
6. Jurrat (Urdu)
7. Milli Gazette
8. Muslim Mirror
9. Rajasthan Patrika (Hindi)
10. Seerat (Urdu)
11. The Bohra Chronicle (English & Gujarati)
12. The Business Standard
13. The Economic Times
14. The Hindu
15. The Hindustan Times.
16. The Mint
17. Times of India

Web Sites

1. anjumesaifee.tripod.com
2. dawoodi bohras.org.uk

3. http://groups google.com/forum/m/topic/secularperspective
4. http://www.facebook.com/dawoodibohra/
5. www.dawoodi.bohras.com
6. www.dbwrf.org
7. www.fatimidawat.com.
8. www.malumaat.comdawoodibohra.
9. www.mumineen.org.
10. www.narisamtamanch.org.
11. www.sahio.com.
12. www.thebohras.com.
13. www.thehindu.com/nws/national/other.states.
14. www.wespeakout.org.

Index

E

J

K

T